YOUR SICK CAT

This book is dedicated to my parents, Nicholas
and Elero, who taught me the joy of learning and
the value of knowledge

YOUR SICK CAT

The Cat Owner's Guide to Understanding and
Managing Illness and Injury

Nico Maritz BVSc MRCVS

Editions Wild Berry & Friends
Edenbridge, Kent, UK

DISCLAIMER

Whilst every effort is made by the publishers and the author so see that no inaccurate or misleading data, opinion or statement appear in this book, they wish to make it clear that the application of the data and opinions in this book are beyond their responsibility. Accordingly the publishers and the author and their employees, officers and agents accept no responsibility or liability whatsoever for the consequences of any such inaccurate or misleading data, opinion or statement.

The author has made every effort to ensure the accuracy of the information herein. However, appropriate information sources should be consulted, especially for new or unfamiliar drugs, procedures or current clinical opinions. It is the responsibility of the reader to evaluate the appropriateness of a particular opinion in the context of actual clinical situations, and with due consideration to new developments.

Cover photograph: Wild Berry & Friends
Cover design: Wild Berry & Friends
Illustrations by Blanche M A Ellis

Copyright © 2006 by Nico Maritz.
Illustrations copyright @ 2006 Blanche M A Ellis

First published in the UK in 2008
by Wild Berry & Friends Ltd.

British Library – Cataloguing in Publication CIP Data: a catalogue record for this book is available from the British Library.

ISBN   0-9550803-2-0 / 978-0-9550803-2-6

The information in this book is true and complete to the best of our knowledge. All recommendations are made without any guarantee on the part of the publisher, who also disclaims any liability incurred in connection with the use of this data or specific details.

Manufactured in the United Kingdom by CPI Antony Rowe.

Editions Wild Berry & Friends
P. O. Box 134 – Edenbridge, Kent TN8 5BW
E-mail: wildberrystudio@aol.com
Website : www.sirnorman.com

Contents

Foreword

The cat is very much a part of many modern families. As cat owners we expect and demand the same level of medical care for our cats as for ourselves. This book was written to help cat owners understand how vets diagnose and treat the common illnesses and injuries that beset our pet cats.

I have found that most people who take their cats to the vet want to be part of the decision making process. They want to understand why the vet does what they do during the consultation, how they arrive at a diagnosis and ultimately how they select the most appropriate treatment.

I have always felt that most medical reference books for pet owners approach the subject from the wrong perspective. Reference books usually offer an alphabetized list of conditions and are only useful to pet owners if they already know what the diagnosis is. This book deals with illness and injury from the perspective of the cat owner. Most cats are taken to their vet for one of the reasons listed in the table of contents. The title of each chapter describes the most common symptoms noticed by cat owners and the chapter then explains how the vet translates that symptom into a specific diagnosis. Each chapter in this book has been written in the form of a consultation with your vet. The chapter will explain what questions the vet is likely to ask and how they interpret the answers you give them. The next part of the chapter explains how the vet will examine your cat and how they interpret what they find. Once the diagnosis has been made, the chapter will discuss most appropriate treatment options for that specific condition.

Many diseases and illnesses will have symptoms that overlap considerably with other conditions. Thus many conditions will appear in two or more chapters. The most difficult part of writing a book like this is to avoid too much repetition but at the same time I do not want the reader to have to flip backwards and forwards through the text to gather all the information they need. I want each chapter to be read and understood as a single entity and thus I inevitably repeat information in different chapters. To keep the volume of this book to a reasonable size there are, however, occasions where I have had to advise referring to other chapters for further amplification or explanation of conditions listed in the chapter being read.

This book is not intended to replace the consultation with your vet. It is intended to empower you with information so that you will have a more pro-active role in the process of caring for your cat. By consulting the appropriate chapter before visiting your vet you should have a good idea of what the diagnosis is likely to be and how to best assist the vet in arriving at a definitive diagnosis and selecting the best treatment. Similarly, once you and your cat have returned home from the vet, you can consult this book to reaffirm what was said and done during the consultation.

This book describes how I treat cats presented to my clinic in accordance with mainstream medical knowledge. Most vets will do exactly as I do as we are all trained in much the same way. However, the processes of diagnosis and treatment are constantly evolving and changing as our level of knowledge expands, so your vet may have a different opinion regarding the best treatment option for your cat. There are many ways of treating any single medical condition or injury and every vet will have their own preferences, but the broad principles and concepts tend to stay the same.

I hope that this book will be useful to everyone who takes the time and the interest to consult it.

MY CAT IS STRAINING TO PASS URINE (PEE) OR FAECES (POO) BUT NOTHING OR VERY LITTLE IS COMING OUT

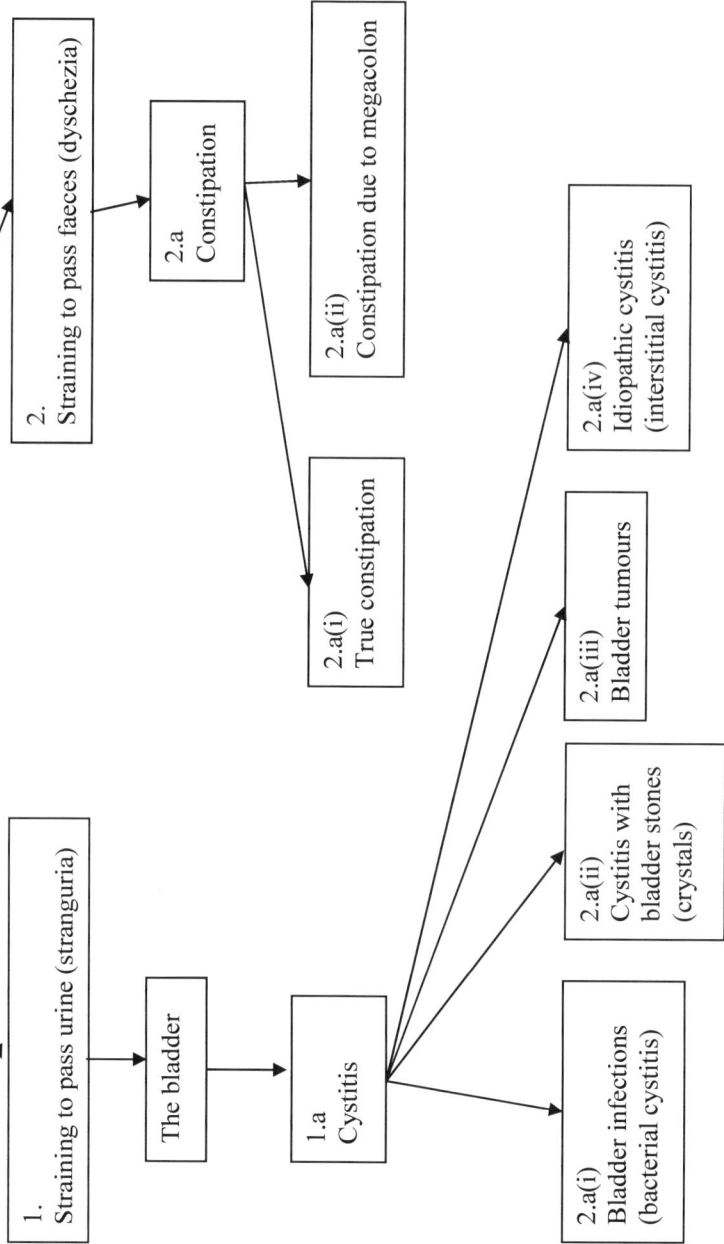

```
                    1.                                    2.
          Straining to pass urine (stranguria)    Straining to pass faeces (dyschezia)
                    │                                      │
                    ▼                                      ▼
              The bladder                              2.a
                    │                              Constipation
                    ▼                              ┌─────┴─────┐
                  1.a                              ▼           ▼
                Cystitis                        2.a(i)      2.a(ii)
                    │                       True constipation   Constipation due to megacolon
     ┌──────┬───────┼───────┬────────┐
     ▼      ▼       ▼        ▼
  2.a(i)  2.a(ii) 2.a(iii) 2.a(iv)
  Bladder Cystitis Bladder  Idiopathic cystitis
  infections with  tumours  (interstitial cystitis)
  (bacterial bladder
  cystitis)  stones
            (crystals)
```

1

My Cat Is Straining To Pass Urine (Wee) Or Faeces (Poo) But Nothing Or Very Little Is Coming Out

Cats are often presented to me with the comment that they are crouching or squatting more frequently in their litter tray or in the garden without producing urine or faeces. This is often the only symptom that something is wrong and the cat seems otherwise well. Sometimes people also notice that their cat seems to frequently lick and clean their genitals in between attempts in the litter tray. Most people will suggest to me that they think their cat is constipated. There are two possible explanations for the cat's behaviour, i.e. the cat is either experiencing difficulties passing urine or they are struggling to pass faeces. If the problem is difficulty urinating (weeing) the technical term is stranguria. If the problem is difficulty passing faeces (poo) the technical term is dyschezia. I will discuss each problem and the possible causes separately later in the chapter.

The vet's initial questions will guide their thoughts to the problem area and their questions will go something like this:

- Is the cat male or female?
- Have these symptoms occurred previously at any time in the cat's life?
- How long has the cat been showing these symptoms?
- Does the cat pass any urine or faeces at all when attempting to go in the litter tray or outside?
- Does the cat lick and clean their genitals more often than normal?
- Does the cat seem otherwise well or do they seem ill?
- Have you seen the cat pass urine or faeces and if so how much did they pass and what did it look like?

You, the cat owner may not actually know the answer to some or all of these questions and it is important to say that you do not know rather that guess at an answer. This is because these questions are intended to help the vet determine where the problem lies and how serious it may be.

Careful observation of both urination behaviour (peeing) and defecation behaviour (pooing) should tell us which activity is occurring normally and thus we will know whether the straining is due to difficulties in passing urine or faeces. If the cat is straining frequently but seems to be urinating normally then we know that the problem is in the intestines, the rectum or the anus. If the cat is straining frequently but is passing normal faeces then we know the problem is in the lower urinary system, i.e. the bladder, urethra, prostate, vagina or penis.

If the symptoms have been present for more than 48 hours it is unlikely to resolve itself. If the cat is licking and cleaning their genitals more often than normal then the problem is more likely to be in the urinary system than in the intestines or rectum. The vet will probably be thinking that if the cat is female the most likely diagnosis might be cystitis, whereas if the cat is male the diagnosis may be an obstructed or blocked penis. If a male cat has had an obstructed penis for more than two days they are likely to be very ill or becoming very ill. If the male cat is passing very small amounts of urine at each attempt then he is likely to be in a less severe condition than the male cat who is passing no urine at all. If a female cat does seem to pass very small amounts of urine at each straining attempt then it is very likely that she has cystitis. If the cat seems ill in addition to the symptoms of straining then their case would be potentially more serious and more urgent than a cat who seemed otherwise well.

Once the vet has considered the answers to their questions they will examine your cat. The most important part of the examination of a cat with these symptoms is examination of their belly. The vet will gently feel the cat's belly with their hands. The vet is actually feeling the organs inside the belly and is checking the bladder and the intestines and rectum. If the bladder feels very large and painful then the possibility of an obstruction in the penis is quite likely. If the bladder is completely empty and painful when the vet touches it then cystitis is quite likely. If the bladder feels normal then the vet will move on to feel the intestines and especially the rectum. The rectum is the last portion of the intestine which leads to the anus. Faeces are stored in the rectum until the cat is ready to pass them. If the vet finds that there is a large amount of larger than normal faeces in the rectum then constipation is quite likely. Once the vet has determined whether the problem relates to urine or faeces they may recommend further tests to identify the exact site and nature of the problem in that organ system.

1 Straining to pass urine (stranguria)

The signs of stranguria are that the cat repeatedly attempts to pass urine. When these cats try to pee one will notice that they are straining much harder than normal to pee and that they produce very little or no pee when they are straining. They will also try to pee much more often than normal. The amount of urine that is passed at each attempt varies from nothing at all to small spots of urine. These small spots of urine are very often tinged with blood or may even look like blobs of "raspberry jam".

Stranguria is the result of a problem in the lower urinary tract. The urinary tract consists of a number of distinct components. The kidneys are the first part of the urinary tract. Every cat has two kidneys, a left and a right kidney. The kidneys are roughly situated just below the backbone under the last rib on either side of the body. The right kidney is slightly further forward than the left kidney. The kidneys have many functions including the production of urine. The urine produced by each kidney drains into a tube called a ureter which transports the urine to the bladder. Thus the left and right ureters lead from the left and the right kidney respectively to the bladder. The bladder is simply a bag for collecting urine, consisting of a thin layer of muscle, its function being to collect and store the urine produced by the kidneys. When it is full the muscle layer in the bladder wall contracts to push the urine out of the bladder through a single tube called the urethra. In males, the urethra passes through the inside of the penis and, in females, the urethra opens into the vagina. Thus male animals have a longer and narrower urethra than female animals whose urethra is shorter and wider. The urinary tract can be divided into two components. The upper urinary tract consists of the kidneys and ureters. The lower urinary tract consists of the bladder and urethra and the vagina or penis.

The symptom of stranguria tells us that the cat is experiencing problems in the lower urinary tract and thus the problem is most likely situated in the bladder or the urethra. There are a variety of different conditions which may cause problems in the bladder and urethra and often more than one problem may be present at the same time. All the various conditions are collectively referred to as Feline Lower Urinary Tract Disease, or FLUTD.

When I am presented with a FLUTD cat who is showing signs of a problem in the lower urinary tract (stranguria), I will often ask people to bring me a sample of the cat's urine. The easiest way to collect urine from the cat is to use non-absorbent pieces of polystyrene as cat litter. The polystyrene pieces may be gleaned from polystyrene chips used as packaging material in boxes and parcels to protect the contents or you can buy commercially prepared non-absorbent cat litter. If this method is impossible or impractical, such as in households where many cats use the same litter tray, the vet may obtain a urine sample by cystocentesis. Cystocentesis means using a needle and syringe to drain urine directly from the bladder, by passing the needle through the cat's belly into the bladder. It sounds like an unpleasant experience for the cat but I find that most cats do not even seem to notice the procedure and certainly don't seem to mind.

This information is important for several reasons. The reason for checking for the presence of blood is to confirm that there is inflammation in the bladder. The reason for checking the acidity (pH) is that if the cat's urine is not acidic enough they will be more prone to repeated infections or recurring bladder stones because they have less protection against bacteria and bladder stone formation. If the urine is not acidic enough the simple solution is to feed the cat a special diet to produce a more acidic urine which is more likely to kill invading bacteria and impair bladder stone formation.

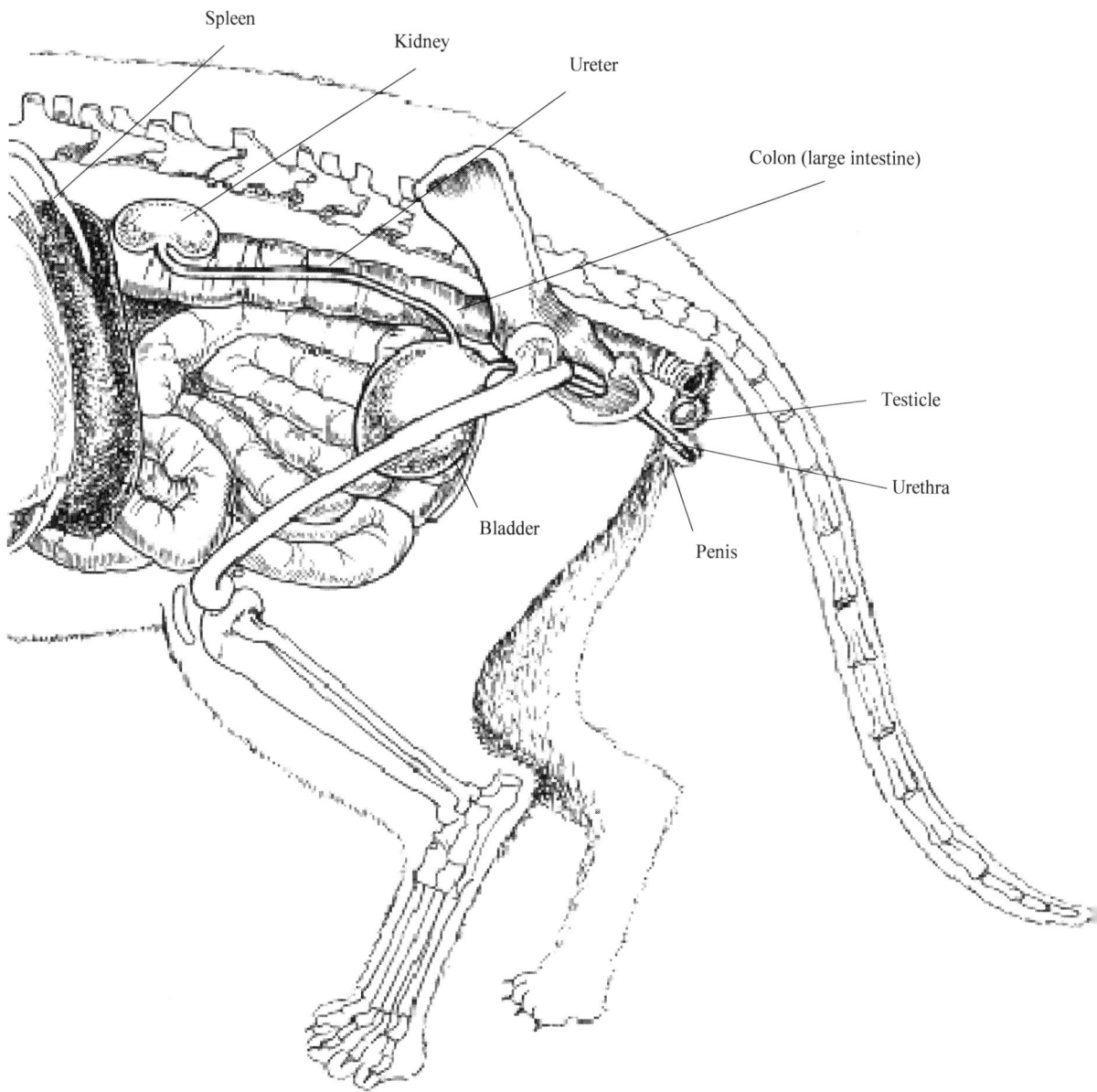

Fig 1. - Side view of a cat's abdomen to show the
normal size and position of the urinary tract.

This is similar to the wide range of special acidifying drinks available to ladies who suffer from repeated bouts of cystitis for the same reason, which is that, if the urine is not acidic enough it is easier for invading bacteria to survive and infect the bladder lining or for bladder stones to develop. The reason for checking for the presence of glucose is that if the cat is even mildly diabetic then the glucose in the urine will feed the bacteria, which makes it easier for them to survive in the bladder. This is why diabetic cats and people are especially prone to bouts of bladder infections. So if glucose is found in the urine it is not sufficient to treat only the cystitis; the vet should also determine why there is glucose in the urine and treat the cause to reduce the number of future episodes of cystitis.

Testing urine with a urine dipstick may be followed by more advanced tests which may include testing for the presence of microscopic bladder stones (crystals), testing for the presence of abnormal cells (tumour cells) and identifying the specific bacteria causing the infection and the most appropriate antibiotic to use. If crystals or abnormal cells are identified then appropriate treatment for bladder tumours or bladder stones must be implemented in addition to treating any infection in the bladder. This will be discussed in more detail in the next section. Additional tests for investigating bladder problems may also include ultrasound scanning of the bladder, X-rays of the bladder and occasionally taking biopsies from the bladder.

The bladder

The most common problems affecting the bladder are bacterial cystitis (bladder infection), bladder stones, growths (tumours) in the bladder and idiopathic (interstitial) cystitis.

1a Cystitis

The word cystitis is a very vague term which simply means inflammation of the bladder. This inflammation may be caused by infections, tumours, bladder stones or idiopathic (interstitial) cystitis.

1a(i) Bladder infections (bacterial cystitis)

A possible cause of cystitis is a bacterial infection in the bladder. Many cats and human beings, at some stage in their lives, will suffer from a bladder infection. This is called bacterial cystitis. Bacterial cystitis in all species is much more common in females than in males. This is because the bacteria which cause the infection must move up the urethra into the bladder to cause the infection. The female urethra is a much shorter and wider tube than in males and thus it is a shorter and easier journey for bacteria to move into the female bladder. This journey is much more difficult in male cats because the urethra is a longer and thinner tube. The most common source of origin of the bacteria is the anus. In females the anus is situated close to the vagina. Thus it is once again a shorter journey for bacteria to move from the anus into the opening of the urethra in females than it is in males where the opening is in the tip of the penis (inside the penis sheath), which is slightly further away from the anus.

Once bacteria have moved into the bladder they need to move into the bladder wall to cause an infection. The natural defence systems of the bladder are the infection-fighting cells in the bladder wall and the acid pH of the urine. Urine in cats is usually slightly acidic and this acidity tends to kill invading bacteria. Some cats produce urine which is not acidic enough and these individuals are more prone to infection because bacteria entering the bladder are more likely to survive. If the bacteria are able to penetrate into the bladder wall the bacteria will start to multiply and thus cause an infection and inflammation. This process produces an uncomfortable burning sensation in the bladder which makes the muscle layer in the bladder wall contract. The bladder is therefore in a constant state of spasm, which makes the cat feel like they need to urinate even though there is little or no urine in the bladder. This sensation of burning and contraction of the bladder makes cats feel like they need to urinate all the time so they will make frequent and prolonged attempts to urinate. However, because the bladder is constantly contracted, little or no urine collects in the bladder so little or no urine is passed at each attempt to pee. The inflammation in the lining of the bladder may cause microscopic blood vessels in the bladder lining to rupture so the urine may contain blood. This blood is sometimes visible to the naked eye giving the urine a pink or red appearance although, in mild cases, the amount of blood in the urine may be so small that it can only be detected by testing the urine. In more severe cases, portions of the bladder lining may be passed out with small amounts of urine and these bits of the bladder lining look like blobs of "raspberry jam".

Once the vet has determined that the cat has a bladder infection (bacterial cystitis) and no additional bladder problems are present, then the treatment will consist of appropriate antibiotics and sometimes also anti-inflammatory treatments to ease the discomfort. If any additional bladder problems are identified, e.g. abnormal urine acidity, glucose in the urine, bladder tumours or bladder stones, then these must also be corrected to ensure a good recovery and to reduce or eliminate the risk of recurrent infections.

1a(ii) Cystitis with bladder stones (crystals)

The technical name for a bladder stone or bladder crystal is a urolith. Cats can produce different types of bladder stones. Certain types of bladder stones develop in urine which is too acidic (low pH), other types develop in urine which is not acidic enough (high pH) and other types may develop in any level of acidity (any pH). The urine produced by cats is usually slightly acidic with a pH of 5–6.5. If an individual cat produces urine with a different acidity then that individual may be prone to developing bladder stones. The most common bladders stones are called struvite stones and these develop in urine which is not acidic enough, i.e. the pH is too high.

Many of us grew crystals in jars when we were children. The easiest way to do this is by dissolving the maximum amount of table salt possible in water and then placing a small twig in the water. After a few days you will see small crystals forming on the twig. The twig is necessary to provide a structure for the crystals to form on. Bladder stones (bladder crystals) develop in much the same way. The various types of bladder stones develop from various normal chemicals found in normal urine. The requirement for the formation of crystals from these chemicals is that the acidity of the urine must be correct for the formation of a particular type of crystal and there must usually be something for the crystal to grow on. In the case of bladder stones the crystals grow on blood cells or bladder lining cells that have become detached and that float around in the urine. The most common reason that red blood cells may be found floating in urine is that the cat may have a bladder infection as discussed earlier or idiopathic (interstitial) cystitis. The clumps of blood cells in the urine act like the twig mentioned above and the bladder stone forms around this clump of cells. In this way, bladder infections may develop into bladder infections with bladder stones. The cells that line the bladder are like skin cells in that new cells are constantly being formed and old cells are constantly shed. When the old bladder lining cells are shed into the bladder then bladder stones may form around these clumps of shed cells. The bladder stones have sharp edges which scratch the lining of the bladder and this causes inflammation and cystitis symptoms appear. If bacteria enter the bladder then it is much easier for them to invade the bladder wall through these scratches and thus bladder stones may lead to bladder infections. This explains why bladder infections and bladder stones often occur at the same time in an individual.

The bladder stone starts off as a microscopic crystal which usually forms on detached bladder lining cells or blood cells in the urine. These crystals usually remain so small that they can only be seen when urine is examined under a microscope. In some cases, however, the crystals may continue to grow until they are as large as grains of sand and in extreme cases the crystals grow as large as a golf ball. The microscopic crystals can be imagined as being similar in appearance to grains of sugar so that even the smallest crystals have sharp edges which cause irritation and microscopic cuts to the lining of the bladder. The larger the crystal becomes, the more irritation it produces, inflaming the bladder wall and causing cystitis, which may become even more uncomfortable if a secondary bladder infection develops.

The symptoms seen in cases of bladder stones/crystals of any size are the same symptoms that can be seen with a bladder infection. The bladder stones/crystals produce an uncomfortable burning sensation in the bladder, which makes the muscle layer in the bladder wall contract. The bladder is therefore in a constant state of spasm which makes the cat feel like they need to urinate even though there is little or no urine in the bladder. This sensation of burning and contraction of the bladder makes cats feel like they need to urinate all the time so they will make frequent and prolonged attempts to urinate. The bladder, however, is constantly contracted so little or no urine collects in the bladder and little or no urine is passed at each attempt to pee. The inflammation in the lining of the bladder may cause microscopic blood vessels in the bladder lining to rupture, so the urine may contain blood. This blood is sometimes visible to the naked eye, giving the urine a pink or red appearance although, in mild cases, the amount of blood in the urine may be so small that it can only be detected by testing the urine. In severe cases, portions of the bladder lining may be forced out with the urine and look like blobs of "raspberry jam".

Once the vet has determined that bladder stones/crystals are present they will need to identify the type of stone or crystal. The level of acidity (pH) of the urine may give the vet a good idea of what kind of bladder stone/crystal is present as certain stones can only develop at specific pH levels. I feel that direct analysis of the stones/crystals is always necessary because some types of stones/crystals may develop in urine of any pH and in some cases two different types of stones may be present. Microscopic crystals and crystals the size of grains of sand are identified by examining them under a microscope. Larger bladder stones will have to be removed from the bladder by performing an operation to open the bladder and remove the stones. These large stones will then be sent to a specialist laboratory for analysis and identification.

In male cats small bladder stones may pass out of the bladder and become stuck in the urethra in the penis. If male cats have one or more bladder stones lodged in the urethra they will be very uncomfortable because the bladder is continually filling with urine which the cat cannot pee out. This leads to severe distension and discomfort of the bladder and the stones must be removed immediately to prevent the bladder from bursting. The second reason that these stones must be removed immediately is that as the urine accumulates in the bladder, the waste chemicals in the urine may produce a toxic effect in the body which will prove fatal if the urine is not removed from the bladder.

The first step in these cases may thus be to remove the urine from the bladder using a needle and syringe. The needle is pushed through the abdominal wall and into the bladder and the urine is sucked out with the syringe. If the cat is very ill the vet may have to stabilise the cat using intravenous fluids administered through a drip line into the cat's veins for one or more days. It is very important that the cat is stabilised before being sedated or anaesthetised to remove the obstruction. Cats have to be sedated or anaesthetised to be catheterised because they will not allow us to do it while they are awake. Once the cat is stable and strong enough to cope with sedation or full anaesthesia, the vet will then try to flush the stone or stones out of the urethra by squirting sterile water into the urethra through a catheter.

There may be one or many stones causing the obstruction and the size of the stones may vary from the size of a grain of sand to the size of a pinhead. Usually the obstruction is caused by an accumulation of many sand-grain-sized crystals clumped together in a blood clot. The obstruction may however be caused by one or more much larger crystals. Occasionally the obstruction is simply caused by a plug of blood cells.

Once the obstruction has lodged in the urethra it causes pain which then causes the muscles in the urethra go into spasm. This causes the urethra to clamp down on the obstruction so that the cat has even less chance of passing the blockage naturally. Once the vet has flushed the stones back into the bladder, they will usually rinse the bladder several times (via the urinary catheter placed into the bladder) with sterile water to try to remove all the small stones and crystals. Once the bladder has been thoroughly rinsed the vet may either leave the catheter inserted into the bladder for a day or two or they will remove the catheter immediately. There are two reasons for leaving the catheter in position for a day or two.

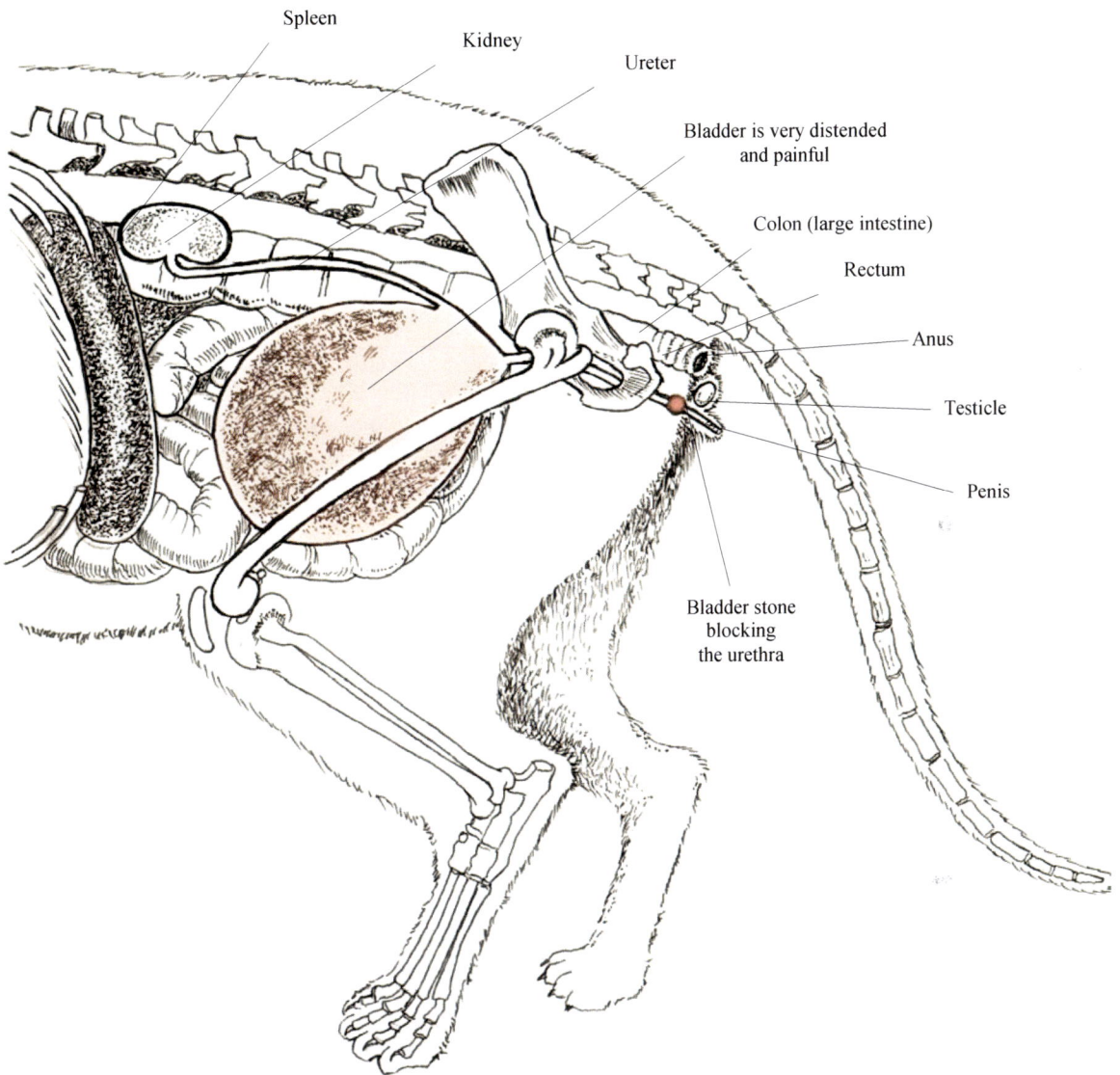

Fig 2. – Bladder stones may become lodged in the urethra. The stone completely blocks the urethra and the cat will be unable to urinate (pee). The bladder is greatly distended and painful as urine accumulates. If the stone is not removed the cat will die.

The first reason is to allow the vet to flush the bladder repeatedly for one or more days. The second reason is that the catheter stops the painful urethra muscle spasm from clamping down so that any remaining crystals can be naturally urinated out via the catheter. Either way I would usually also treat the cat with anti-inflammatories or painkillers and antibiotics while I am waiting for the laboratory results. I would use anti-inflammatories to remove the pain from the urethra so that the cat is able to urinate more easily and pass any remaining crystals/stones from the bladder. I would also use a short course of treatment with prazosin to stop the muscles in the urethra from going into spasm. Effectively this medication is a smooth muscle relaxant and the intention is to avoid spasm of the urethra so that any crystals/stones remaining in the bladder can be passed naturally with the urine.

The biggest risk is that the urethra may be damaged by the stones or crystal and the scar tissue that forms may cause narrowing of the urethra. In the male cat the urethra is a very thin tube to begin with and if the scar tissue causes further narrowing the cat may experience permanent difficulty urinating. If the scar tissue does cause significant narrowing of the urethra the vet may have to remove the penis and create an artificial opening similar to a vagina. The catch-22 is that this operation may lead to more complications during the healing process and further problems in the future. Female cats do not tend to get bladder stones stuck in the urethra because the female urethra is much shorter and wider than in the male.

Once the bladder stones/crystals have been identified and removed the vet will be able to plan a strategy to try to avoid the formation of new stones/crystals. This is usually achieved by feeding a special type of food to ensure that the cat will produce urine with the correct level of acidity. This will prevent stones/crystals that can only develop under very high or low acidity levels from developing again. The vet will also treat the cat with antibiotics if they find that there is a bladder infection at the same time as the bladder stones/crystals being present as these two problems often go hand in hand for the reasons discussed earlier.

1a(iii) Bladder tumours

Cats may develop tumours in the wall of the bladder at any stage in their lives. These tumours may be benign growths or malignant (cancerous) growths. The difference between a benign growth and a cancerous growth is that a benign growth is not potentially life-threatening. A benign growth is not likely to spread to other parts of the body and does not cause a great deal of harm to the tissue it is growing from. An example of a benign growth is the human wart – it is not life-threatening and does not cause major harm to the skin that it grows from. A cancer is completely different in that it may spread to different parts of the body causing harm at those sites and/or it may cause massive harm to the tissue it is growing in. An example of a cancer is human breast cancer.

Bladder tumours are very rare in cats. The most common bladder tumours in cats are called transitional cell carcinomas and squamous cell carcinomas. These are both highly malignant cancers. Less common tumours are polyps in the bladder wall and these are benign growths. The symptoms of a bladder tumour are very similar to symptoms of cystitis in that affected cats are seen to strain to urinate and very often only manage to pass small amounts of urine which may be blood-tinged. The presence of a bladder tumour is confirmed by finding tumour cells in the urine or more commonly by ultrasound scanning or X-raying the bladder. Once these tests have confirmed that a tumour is present then a biopsy must be taken to identify what type of tumour it is. Once the tumour has been identified the vet will advise you on the most appropriate course of action.

If the tumour is a polyp then it can usually be removed. The biggest problem encountered when removing a polyp is where the polyp is positioned within the bladder. If the polyp has grown from the bladder neck then removal may be very difficult. The bladder neck is the point where the bladder leads into the urethra, the tube taking urine out of the body via the penis or vagina. If the polyp has grown from the bladder neck then the success of the surgery will depend on whether the surgeon can save most of the bladder neck or successfully reconstruct it when the polyp has been removed. Even if the surgeon can do this the next possible complication may be that the cat will be incontinent either temporarily or permanently after the surgery.

If the tumour is cancerous then the chest and the abdomen (belly) should be X-rayed and the belly should be scanned to see if the cancer has spread. I feel that if there is no sign of any spread elsewhere then surgery to remove the mass could be considered. The surgery involves entering the abdomen and the bladder and removing the mass. If the cancer has grown from the bladder neck then removal may be very difficult or even impossible. Two important points to consider when removing the mass are that not just the mass should be removed but also a margin of normal healthy tissue in every direction to try to ensure that no cancer cells are left behind. The second issue is that the mass can only be removed if vital blood vessels and nerves supplying the bladder and other tissues and organs in the area can be left intact. A very frustrating situation arises when the surgeon finds that the mass cannot be removed in its entirety. In these cases the only remaining option is to try to eliminate the mass by radiation therapy and/or chemotherapy. Many surgeons would want to at least attempt to debulk the mass prior to proceeding with the radiation or chemotherapy. This would involve removing as much tumour tissue as possible without damaging any vital structures trapped in the mass. In many cases, even if the surgeon is able to remove the mass, it might be advisable to follow up on the surgery with radiation and/or chemotherapy to ensure that no tumour cells, which may have spread on a microscopic level to other tissues, are able to grow into a new tumour. There are many different types and ways of using radiation and chemotherapy and the most appropriate protocol will often only be decided after a specialist histopathologist has examined the tumour. For this reason some vets would want to perform surgery in cases where there is more than one tumour mass present or where there is clear evidence of tumour spread to other parts of the body. The object of the surgery in these cases would be to obtain a biopsy of the tumour for analysis by a histopathologist so that the best radiation and/or chemotherapy strategy can be formulated. Bladder cancers are, however, highly malignant and often respond poorly to any form of treatment. Many of my clients may not want to go through all the above steps for any variety of reasons and ask if we could just "cut to the chase" in terms of trying to help the cat cope with the problem for as long as possible.

This would often imply one of two strategies. The first would be to treat the symptoms of pain or discomfort for as long as possible and when the treatment fails to alleviate the cat's suffering then humanely put him or her to sleep. The most effective way of trying to achieve this is with anti-inflammatory and pain-killing treatments. The treatment would involve tablets or injections for the remainder of the cat's life. The treatment is intended only to alleviate the cat's pain and suffering and give them as much good-quality, pain-free, happy life as possible. I accept that this is not a scientific approach to the problem but many people do not have the financial resources to do more than this or they may not want to subject the cat to any more than this. The overriding consideration must always be the welfare of the cat and if this unscientific approach delivers results in terms of alleviating symptoms then I have no moral problem with it.

Many people feel strongly about cancer in respect of the "futility" of any treatment, or feel that they would want the option of humane euthanasia for themselves in the event of a diagnosis of terminal cancer. Many people feel that it is not humane to ask their pets to accept the discomfort, pain or suffering that may be caused by some types of cancer. Others want to treat only the symptoms of the cancer; most importantly any pain or discomfort. Many will request euthanasia when the treatment is no longer able to eliminate pain and discomfort or when they feel that the quality of life has deteriorated despite symptomatic treatment. People have often watched friends or family members lose the battle against cancer. These people will often request humane euthanasia for their pets with cancer and I feel that this is a reasonable request in the face of a diagnosis with a terminal prognosis. I personally would not deny the request for euthanasia of a cancer patient because we are not all able to cope with the emotional strain of caring for a pet with a terminal condition. Many people, living with this "sword of Damocles" over their heads, succumb to stress and anxiety and this will often adversely affect the pets living with them. There is never a good time to say goodbye to a pet but sometimes, if they are on a downhill slide, it is better to let them go before they hit rock bottom.

1a(iv) Idiopathic cystitis (interstitial cystitis)

The word "idiopathic" means "of unknown cause". Thus the term idiopathic cystitis means that the cat has cystitis but we don't know why. These cats have severely inflamed and painful bladders and the pain causes the bladder to be constantly in a state of contracted spasm. So the symptoms one will notice are the same as for all the other types of cystitis, i.e. the cat makes frequent and prolonged attempts at urination (weeing) producing little or no urine at each attempt (stranguria). The urine that they do manage to pass may be blood-tinged or may look like blobs of strawberry jam if small pieces of the bladder lining are being passed out with the urine. The vet can only make a diagnosis of idiopathic cystitis if all of the above possible types of cystitis have been eliminated. Thus the vet must prove that there is no infection in the bladder, that there are no crystals in the bladder and that there are no growths in the bladder. The vet will achieve this by analysing the urine and taking X-rays of the bladder and doing an ultrasound scan of the bladder. Usually the only thing that the vet will find after performing all of these tests is that there is blood in the urine and that the bladder wall is inflamed and thickened. Once the vet has proved that there is no explanation for the cystitis they will make a diagnosis of idiopathic cystitis. This type of cystitis is the cat equivalent of interstitial cystitis which many human beings suffer from.

Idiopathic cystitis is unfortunately the most common type of cystitis that cats suffer from and because we do not know what causes it, we do not know exactly how to treat it. Human beings with this type of cystitis are equally frustrated by this condition as it is very uncomfortable and there is often no effective treatment for it. The condition seems to flare up for a few days to a few weeks and then will resolve without any treatment for a while only to flare up again in the future. The effect of this long-term recurrent pain is that many cats who suffer from this condition may become very grumpy or withdrawn.

We know very little about idiopathic/interstitial cystitis but I will explain what we do know. The bladder wall, like all other parts of the body is built out of cells. Think of these cells as if they were bricks forming a wall. The bricks in the wall are held together by cement. In the case of living tissue this cement is called "interstitium". Individuals who suffer from idiopathic/interstitial cystitis have poor quality interstitium (cement) holding their cells together. In these individuals the interstitium is leaky, i.e. urine can soak into the cracks between the cells. The urine thus leaks in-between the cells, causing pain and inflammation because the urine irritates the nerve endings in between the cells. The irritated nerve endings send pain messages to the brain and the pain causes the muscles in the bladder wall to contract, making the cat feel like they constantly need to urinate (wee). When they do try to urinate it often makes the pain worse and the affected cat may growl or cry when they attempt to urinate. Thus idiopathic cystitis is sometimes called "interstitial" cystitis because the cause of the problem is leaky "interstitium". We also know from human research that individuals who suffer from interstitial cystitis are often "highly strung", i.e. individuals who tend to worry or are prone to stress. We do not know why this psychological state influences the bladder but there does seem to be a connection.

Treatment for idiopathic/interstitial cystitis is based on trying to treat the possible underlying cause, i.e. stress and leaky interstitium. One of the treatments involves adding glucosamine and chondroitin sulphate to the diet. These are chemicals that the body uses to make the interstitium (cement) that hold the cells together, making a good seal between the cells. The rationale is that by providing more material to make interstitium, the cat will be able to make more, and higher quality, interstitium that will be better able to hold the bladder cells together, reducing the number of leaks. Avoiding leaks in the interstitium means that the nerve endings in the bladder wall are not irritated so there will be no pain or inflammation. There are currently two products containing glucosamine and chondroitin sulphate licensed for this use and they are appropriately called "Cystaid" and "Cystease". These products do not seem to help all affected cats but certainly do seem to help some individuals. The tablets need to be given to the cat for the rest of their life. The tablets may cause vomiting in some individuals initially but by reducing the dose for a while they usually get used to the tablets and can take them without side effects for the rest of their lives.

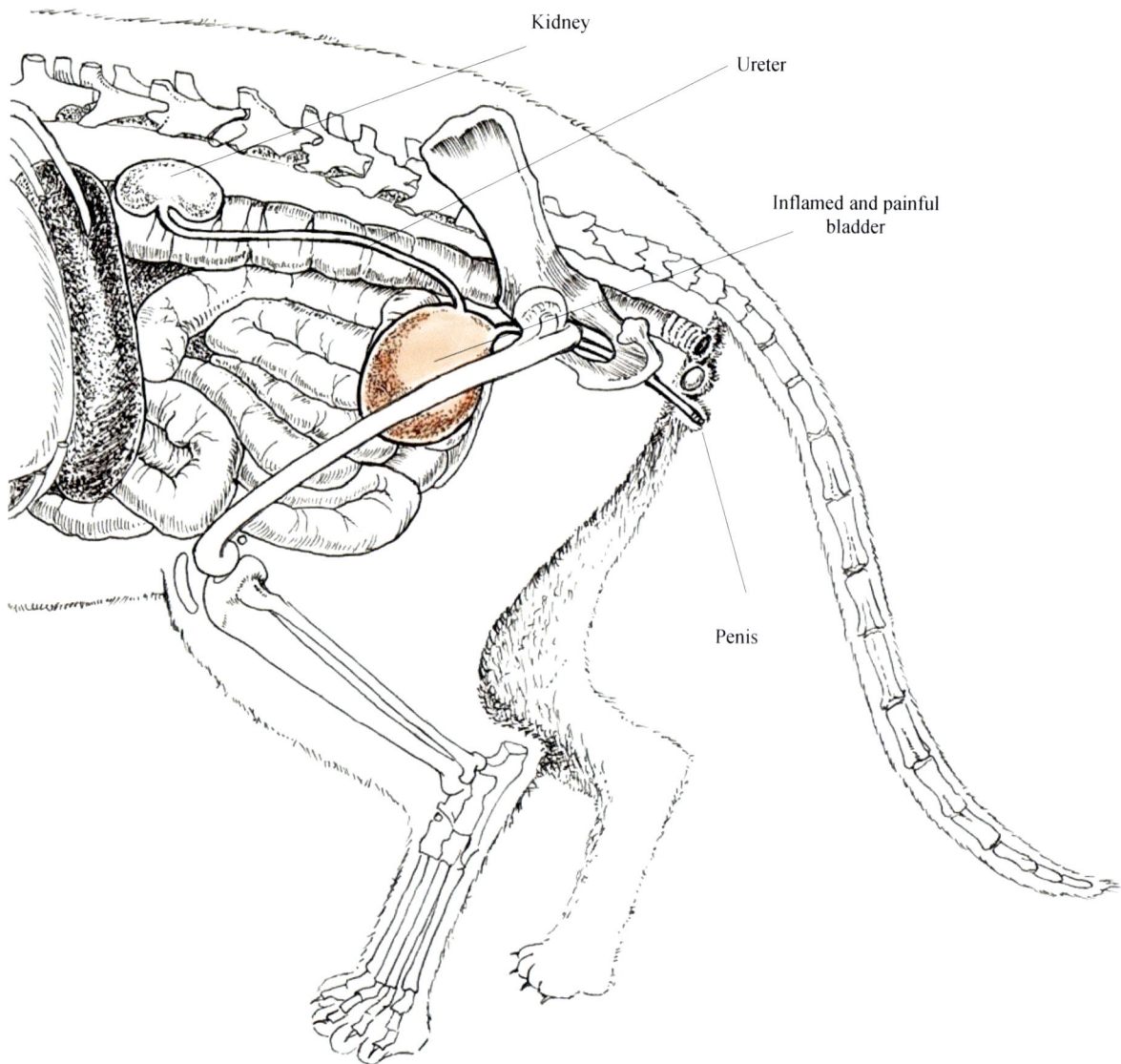

Fig. 3 – Idiopathic cystitis causes severe pain and
inflammation in the bladder

Another treatment protocol is aimed at reducing stress in the cat's life. Stress may not be immediately obvious and most people respond to the suggestion that their cat may be stressed by stating that there is no cause of stress for the cat and that the cat definitely does not seem stressed at home. This may often seem to be the case to us as cat owners but the life of a cat is often fraught with stress. Simple things like a new cat in the area or subliminal bullying between cats in a household are common causes of stress in a cat. There is often no outward sign of conflict or stress but behavioural studies have shown that pet cats often experience high levels of stress in modern living. This is because cats are naturally solitary creatures and modern living means that they often live with other cats under the same roof or are exposed to your neighbour's cats. This increased contact with other cats is often enough to cause stress in what nature intended to be a solitary creature. Most cats are not significantly affected by this modern lifestyle because they, like most human beings, have adapted to this way of life. Treating cats for stress may be achieved by using pheromones and/or by using human medications for stress, such as amitryptyline.

I feel that it is important to trial stress treatment for cats suffering from repeated bouts of interstitial cystitis even if you feel that your cat is not stressed. The preferred way of doing this is with cat pheromones which are introduced into the air in your home by using a plug-in diffuser similar to many air fresheners available on the market. Human beings are unable to smell the pheromones but cats do. Pheromones are simply chemicals that all living beings secrete from their bodies as scent. The function of this scent is sometimes obvious, e.g. flocks of birds use this scent to recognise and identify each other, as do mothers and their offspring in large herds of animals. Human beings also secrete pheromones and it is often this chemical that draws people together on a romantic level. Even though we do not consciously smell the other person's pheromones our subconscious identifies the scent they are giving off and it is often this scent that attracts us to someone else.

The pheromones in the diffuser in your home are synthetically produced cat pheromones which mix with your cat's pheromones, making your house smell very strongly of your cat. You and I will not be able to smell anything different but to your cat the house will smell very strongly of its own pheromones so their "den" or "lair" will feel like a very safe and secure place to them. By creating a safe "den" which smells only of your cat, the message the cat receives is that this is a safe place and free of any intruders and dangers. The effect of this is that the cat does not feel threatened or stressed at home. One should trial this approach for at least three months before assessing its effectiveness at treating interstitial cystitis.

In addition to the above measures to alleviate stress one should also strive to make the cat's urine as dilute as possible. This is the single most important thing to do for cats who suffer from interstitial cystitis. Cat's urine is usually very concentrated and this will often aggravate the interstitial cystitis because the concentrated urine leaks between the bladder lining cells and causes a type of "stinging" pain which makes the cystitis worse. This is the same effect as spilling something like lemon juice onto a cut or a graze on your lips or skin. The lemon juice stings in the cut but if the juice was diluted with water it would sting less and if it was diluted with a lot of water it would probably not sting at all. So if we can ensure that the cat produces very dilute urine, then there will be less pain in the bladder and less aggravation to an already inflamed bladder lining. The obvious way to produce more dilute urine is to drink more water. This may be difficult to achieve in cats as they cannot be forced to drink water. The easiest way to increase their water intake is to add water to their food and try adding a small amount of a chicken stock cube to their drinking water to encourage them to drink more. Another effective trick is to buy a small purpose-made drinking water fountain made especially for cats, available from most pet shops. Most cats are intrigued by moving water and will tend to drink more water from a fountain than from a water bowl

If all of the above approaches fail, one may trial specific stress-relieving medications as used by human beings. The most common medication used for this purpose in cats is amitryptyline and if this medicine is trialled we should use it for at least three months to assess its effects on the recurring bouts of cystitis.

If the above treatments fail then one may be reduced to treating the symptoms of the interstitial cystitis as and when it flares up. I feel that we should use anti-inflammatories and pain relief when the symptoms appear because they help the condition to be more bearable even though they do not fix the problem. This is the same rationale as taking medication for yourself when you have a cold or a bout of flu, i.e. the medicine does not heal you but it makes you feel better while you heal naturally. An important point to make is NEVER to use human medicine on you cat without asking your vet first as some medicines like paracetamol are very poisonous to cats. Another medication which is also often used to treat the symptoms of the cystitis is prazosin. This medicine relieves the muscle spasm in the bladder and urethra and this helps both to alleviate pain and to reduce the risk of the spasm acting like a blockage in the urethra of the male cat. If spasm in the urethra of the male cat means that the cat cannot urinate, then they suffer the same risks as discussed in the section on bladder stone blockages in male cats.

Most bouts of interstitial cystitis will only last for two days and the cat usually starts urinating normally once the inflammation subsides. I would always suggest seeking your vet's advice when the symptoms do flare up because it is always sensible to treat the pain and spasm and because sometimes the symptoms may be caused by another cause of cystitis which requires a different type of treatment.

2 Straining to pass faeces (dyschezia)

Straining to pass faeces may look exactly like the straining associated with the urinary tract problems discussed earlier. Careful observation of both urination behaviour (peeing) and defecation behaviour (pooing) should tell us which activity is occurring normally so that we can then know whether the straining is due to difficulties in passing urine or faeces. If the cat is straining frequently but seems to be urinating normally then we know that the problem is in the intestines, the rectum or the anus. Even if you are unsure as to which area is causing the straining the vet should be able to determine whether the difficulty lies with urinating or defecating by careful examination of your cat by feeling the bladder and intestines and rectum. Once the vet has determined that the problem relates to passing faeces they may recommend further tests to identify the exact site and nature of the problem in that organ system.

Straining to pass faeces may be the result of problems in the lower intestine, the rectum or the anus. The most important point to make at this stage is that straining to pass faeces does not necessarily mean simply that the cat is constipated. The straining efforts (dyschezia) may be the result of constipation or may be the result of inflammation in the rectum (colitis).

2a Constipation as a cause of dyschezia

2a(i) True constipation

Cats may become constipated just as human beings do. Constipation means that faeces (poo) accumulate in the rectum but the individual is unable to pass them out of their body. The cat will continue eating food and thus more faeces will accumulate in the rectum. Once faeces have been in the rectum for more than a day or two, the faeces will start to dry out and become very hard. Once the faeces have become hard they will start to scratch the lining of the rectum, causing pain which will make the cat reluctant to try to pass these hard faeces. The process continues until there is a large amount of faeces in the rectum and the lumps of faeces are too big to pass through the pelvis. The vet will usually be able to make a diagnosis of constipation simply by feeling the large volume of hard faeces in the rectum. Once they have identified that constipation is the problem they will advise that the cat have an enema.

Most vets will give the enema simply by flushing warm soapy water into the rectum through soft plastic tubing. The idea behind an enema is initially to soften and dissolve the faeces, converting them from hard painful lumps into a liquid slurry. As more water is flushed into the rectum this slurry will drain out of the rectum. The enema may take quite some time to dissolve the hard lumps of faeces and often the vet will repeatedly have to squirt more water into the rectum while massaging the rectum to make the faeces break down into smaller pieces as the water softens them. Once the faeces have been removed the vet will examine what was in them. One may sometimes find a large amount of the cat's fur in the faeces and the strands of hair have the effect of tying all the faecal balls together. If the vet finds a lot of fur in the faeces then the next question to answer is why so much fur should be in the intestines. The most common reason is that the cat has an itchy skin condition which makes them lick and groom themselves more than normal. This means that more fur is swallowed than normal and the fur strands may tie large faecal balls together. If the vet finds that a large volume of fur in the intestine is the cause of the problem, they will need to investigate the cat's skin to identify and treat the skin problem otherwise the cat will simply become constipated again.

2a(ii) Constipation due to megacolon

The second most common cause of constipation is a condition called megacolon. The name of this condition describes the problem, i.e. "mega" means larger than normal and colon refers to the large intestine. Megacolon happens when the colon loses its ability to move faeces from the small intestine towards the anus (bum). As more faeces accumulate in the colon from the small intestine, the colon starts to stretch and enlarge. With time the colon may become very large due to a sizeable accumulation of faeces, hence the descriptive term "megacolon". This problem may arise because of a problem with the nerve supply to the colon in cases of spinal trauma. The most common example of this problem is a cat who has suffered damage to the lower portion of the spine after having been hit by a car. The spinal damage may also mean that the cat will have additional symptoms like hind leg paralysis, tail paralysis or bladder paralysis. Thus a cat who has been in a motor vehicle accident should be checked for damage to the spine. This can be done by simply observing the ability to move all their body parts and to pass urine and faeces. If any of these functions is impaired or lost the cat will require tests to evaluate the extent of the damage. The vet will usually advise X-rays to check the spine and the bones of the lower back. In some cases the vet may need to recommend specialised X-rays called myelograms. Sometimes even an MRI scan will be required to evaluate the extent of the damage. If the megacolon is the result of spinal trauma then the treatment will require an enema and treatment for the spinal trauma. Treatment for a spinal injury will sometimes involve only medication like anti-inflammatories and time while the damage heals but some cases will require spinal surgery.

Damage to the spine is not always due to trauma. Tumours growing in or near the spine may compress and damage the spinal cord. This problem will also require X-rays and possibly an MRI scan to find the tumour, and surgery will usually be the only option to try to help the cat. The surgery will endeavour to remove the tumour and the tumour will then be analysed by a histopathologist to identify it. Some tumour types will then require chemotherapy or radiation therapy after surgery. Spinal tumours are fortunately rare in cats but when they do occur most cats will not do very well despite surgery and/or chemotherapy and radiation therapy.

Once the vet has excluded damage to the spinal cord as a possible cause of megacolon, they will often suggest testing the cat's thyroid hormone levels and their blood potassium levels. Low thyroid levels and low potassium levels are very rare causes of megacolon but if they are found to be abnormally low on blood tests then the cat will need to be supplemented to correct the problem. The supplementation will be in the form of tablets which the cat will probably need to take for the rest of their life and the dosage will need to be adjusted occasionally based on follow-up blood tests.

In most cases of megacolon the cause of the problem is never identified. The colon simply loses its ability to function normally. These cases are treated by feeding types of food and food supplements that will keep the faeces very soft in the intestines. The intention is that if the faeces are very soft, i.e. virtually the consistency of wet cement, they are more likely to slide from the small intestine, through the dysfunctional colon, to the anus and out of the cat. There are many ways to keep the faeces soft and sloppy. One may add fats and oils to the cat's diet, e.g. butter/margarine or olive oil. One may also try adding natural laxatives like raw liver to the cat's diet. Lactulose is a very useful liquid supplement to soften faeces. Once you have identified what works for the individual cat then you will need to experiment with the dosage required to keep the faeces very sloppy but without causing diarrhoea. Most cats will need these supplements forever to prevent future constipation but by using them they will be able to live normal, active and comfortable lives.

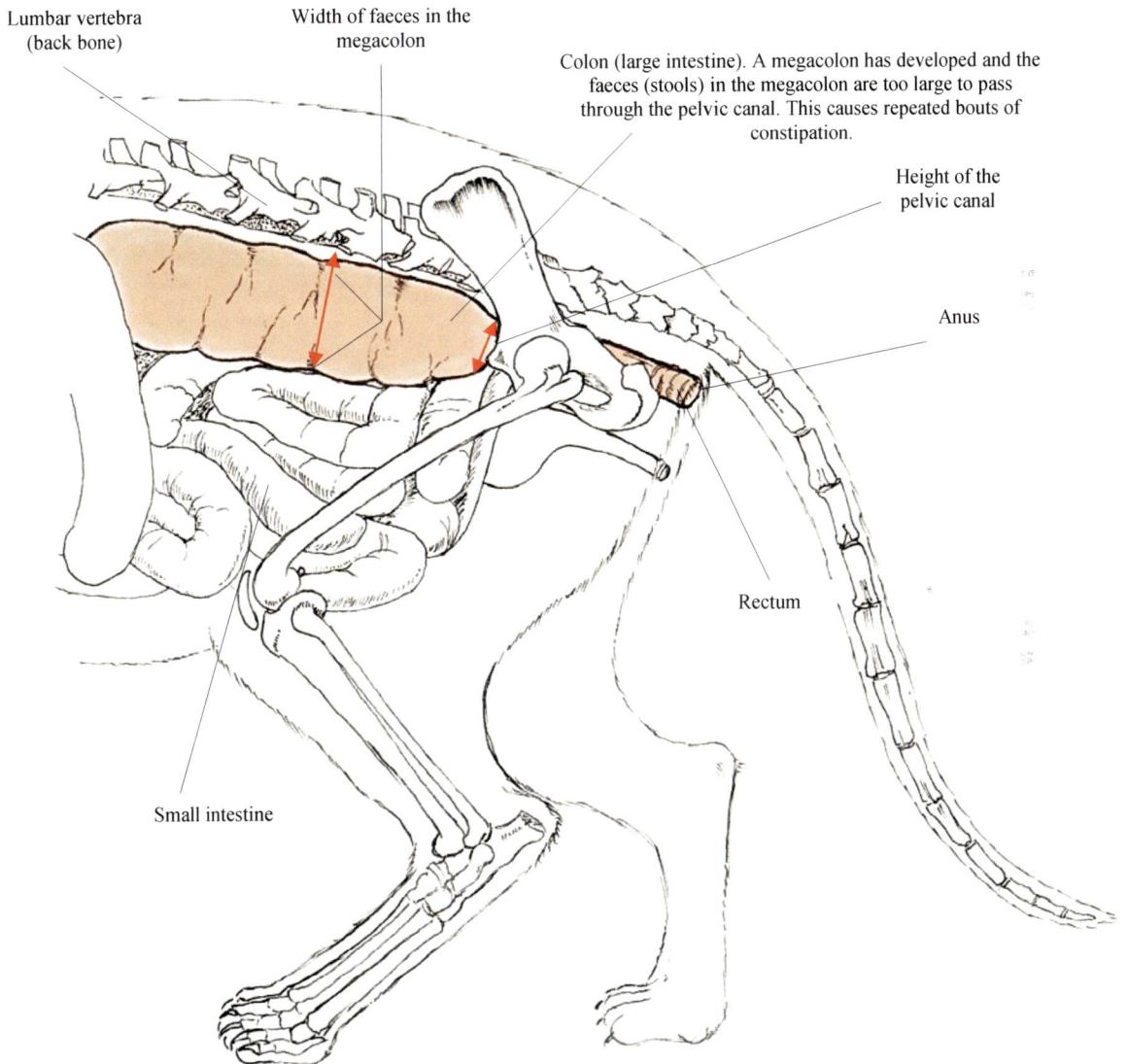

Lumbar vertebra
(back bone)

Width of faeces in the
megacolon

Colon (large intestine). A megacolon has developed and the faeces (stools) in the megacolon are too large to pass through the pelvic canal. This causes repeated bouts of constipation.

Height of the
pelvic canal

Anus

Rectum

Small intestine

Fig 4. – Megacolon in a male cat.

```
                                    ┌──────────────────────────────────┐
                                    │  MY CAT IS PEEING IN THE HOUSE   │
                                    └──────────────────────────────────┘

┌─────────────────────┐   ┌─────────────────────┐   ┌─────────────────────┐   ┌─────────────────────┐
│ 1.                  │   │ 2.                  │   │ 3.                  │   │ 4.                  │
│ Peeing in the house │   │ Peeing in the house │   │ Remove or reduce the│   │ Make the cat feel   │
│ as a result of      │   │ because of          │   │ cause of the stress │   │ safe in the house   │
│ bladder problems    │   │ territorial marking │   │                     │   │                     │
│                     │   │ (stress)            │   │                     │   │                     │
└─────────────────────┘   └─────────────────────┘   └─────────────────────┘   └─────────────────────┘
```

2

MY CAT IS PEEING IN THE HOUSE

Acommon problem encountered with cats is that they may start peeing in the house, on the carpets or on the furniture, for no apparent reason. Although the reason for this behaviour may not be obvious there is always an underlying reason and it must be identified in order for us to solve the problem. Simply washing and cleaning the soiled area every time the cat pees there will not solve the problem. Cats urinate in the house and on the furniture for one of two reasons, i.e. either they have a bladder problem and or they are deliberately doing it to mark their territory.

1 Peeing in the house as a result of bladder problems

The first reason possible reason for peeing in the house and on the furniture is that the cat has something wrong with their bladder like cystitis. Cystitis and all its various causes are discussed in detail in the chapter on straining to pee. Cystitis simply means that the bladder is inflamed, which makes the bladder contract and this in turn makes the cat feel that it needs to pee all the time. This is exactly the same sensation human beings experience when they have cystitis, i.e. we constantly feel the urge to pee because of a burning sensation in the bladder. Thus we try to pee more often than normal and when we try to pee, very little urine is produced and it hurts. If the inflammation in the bladder is severe enough the pee may be tinged with blood or there may even be what appear to be small blobs of "raspberry jam" in it. These blobs of "raspberry jam" are in fact pieces of the lining of the bladder. Repeated efforts at straining to pee in male cats may also suggest that there is a blockage in the urethra (the tube leading from the bladder to the penis). If there is a blockage the cat will repeatedly strain to pee but very little or no urine will be passed.

Both cystitis and urethral blockages will cause the cat to frequently crouch down and spend one or two minutes straining to try to pee. These conditions are painful and some cats may cry out in pain when they strain to pee and often sit down afterwards and start vigorously licking the penis or vagina. Thus medical problems may cause the cat to pee or try to pee more often than normal and it is so uncomfortable that they simply do not have time to go outside or go to the litter tray to pee. In these cases the cats are peeing in the house because they feel they have to go immediately and cannot wait. The result is that although the cat appears to be deliberately peeing in the house with this problem, they actually can't help it.

This problem is characterised by frequent attempts to pee, pain when peeing, only small amounts of urine being passed, genital-licking, and the cat will be physically distressed by the experience.

Once we have determined that the cat is peeing in the house because they have cystitis we must determine why they have cystitis so that we can choose the most appropriate treatment for them. The various types of cystitis and the most appropriate treatment for each type is discussed in the chapter on straining to pee. Once the cystitis has been treated the cat will stop peeing in the house and/or on the furniture.

2 Peeing in the house because of territorial marking (stress)

The second reason that cats may suddenly start peeing in the house is that they are marking their territory. The big difference between marking territory with pee and peeing because of bladder problems is that territorial marking is not painful. In the case of territorial marking the problem is psychological rather than physical. Thus if the cat is peeing in the house to deliberately mark the house as their territory, you will not notice any of the physical symptoms that you would see if they were peeing in the house because of medical bladder problems. So with this problem, although it is abnormal that the cat is peeing in the house, there are no other abnormal symptoms like straining to pee, crying out when peeing, or licking the genitals, and they pass large puddles of pee rather than the very small amounts of pee that we see in cases of cystitis.

So if your cat has started peeing in the house, the first thing to determine is whether the cause of the problem is medical or psychological. If the peeing is due to a medical problem we must identify and treat the problem. Please refer to the chapter on straining to pee for a full discussion of the diagnosis and treatment of the various medical problems which may cause this symptom. If we were sure that the cat has no medical problems then we would regard this as a psychological problem. Vets refer to this as a behavioural problem or inappropriate elimination behaviour. When I use the term psychological problem this most commonly means that the cat is stressed and they pee in the house to mark their territory as a response to the stress. Most people would immediately respond to the suggestion that their cat is stressed by disputing this. This is because most cats seem to be very content and relaxed at home and it is difficult to imagine that the relaxed cat you see sleeping on your sofa is stressed. When vets use the word stress in relation to cats, the causes and symptoms are much more subtle than they are in human beings.

Let's talk about what may cause cats to feel stressed. The first point to make is that cats are actually solitary creatures. Wild cats like tigers, leopards and pumas live alone in large territories which they "own" and patrol to keep other cats out. The only wild cats that live in social groups are lions; all other cats live alone and avoid contact with each other. Wild cats will establish a large territory for themselves where they live and hunt. If another cat invades their territory they will fight the invader and drive it off. The only time they seek out the company of other cats is to mate with them and once the female is pregnant the male and female will again separate and return to their solitary lifestyle. The presence of another cat is thus seen as a threat (except at breeding time) and this threat causes stress because it means that the cat will have to fight to defend its territory.

Now consider the life of your pet cat. Their instinct is to establish a home territory to live in. Modern living means that you and many of your neighbours each own one or more cats. Each of these cats must establish their own territory and because there are so many cats living in a relatively small area they will frequently bump into each other. The natural system would be that each cat would "own" a large enough territory to avoid much contact with neighbouring cats but modern housing means that they only have a very small territory and frequently come into contact with other cats. This is further compounded by the fact that your cat does not have automatic ownership of your garden just because you own it. Cats have no regard for our fences and boundaries and each cat will try to establish as large a territory as they can and ignore our garden fences. The result is that your cat is under a lot of pressure to claim your garden as their territory and they will often encounter your neighbour's cat and both cats will feel under threat and feel they have to fight to defend their territory. Cats are just like human beings in that some individuals are more aggressive and assertive than others and thus a natural hierarchy will develop in the cats living in your neighbourhood. There will always be one "top cat" and all the other cats will live in fear of them. Then there will be a second most dominant cat and a third most dominant cat and so on until one cat is at the bottom of the hierarchy, living in fear of all the other cats. The amount of threat and fear your cat lives with every day depends on where they fit into the social hierarchy of all the cats in your area.

If your cat is the "top cat" in the area they will have relatively little stress but if they are nearer the bottom of the social ladder they may live with a lot of stress every time they venture out of the house. Thus the only territory where your cat feels relatively safe is usually inside your house. When they go outside they will be aware that there will very likely be conflict with another cat in dispute over who owns your garden. Consider living this type of life yourself. If, every time you went out of the house, there was a high probability that you would have a physical fight with your neighbours you would very soon be concerned about leaving the house. As this situation drags on over the months and years you would most likely become stressed to the point of having anxiety attacks even when you just see your neighbour when looking out of your windows. The situation is exactly the same for your cat and cats with a timid personality may become so stressed by it all that they elect to become house cats and virtually never go outside. This works well for them if they have a litter tray indoors but, if they don't, every time they need to go outside to pee or poo it will feel like running the gauntlet of danger because they know another cat is likely to feel that they are invading their territory and will attack them to drive them off. Thus the constant struggle to defend their territory is a cause of stress despite the fact that your cat may look very relaxed and content when you see them sleeping or playing in your house.

The stress caused by conflict with other cats may be compounded by having two or more pet cats at home. As discussed earlier, cats are solitary creatures so if you have two or more pet cats you are forcing two solitary creatures to live together in one territory inside your house. Cats have adapted to a great extent to this urbanisation in the same way that human beings have adapted to living in much greater proximity to each other in the modern world. The result is that two cats may adapt to sharing your house and although it is not entirely natural, they may become quite content to live this way with only occasional conflicts. This is similar to asking two or more people to get married and live together in a house. If the individuals get on well they may be happy to live together despite occasional arguments and disagreements. But if they don't like each other there will inevitably be more stress and conflict between them. This stress and conflict may not be obvious in the sense that the people don't physically attack each other but, psychologically, there may be outright war between them. This psychological struggle may not be apparent to their friends and family when they visit but there is nonetheless significant stress and anxiety affecting both individuals.

Thus when we ask two cats to share our house as our pets they may get on very well or they may dislike each other and suffer from stress and anxiety just as some people do. A lot of this stress and anxiety, in cats and human beings, comes from the subtle hostility that we feel and from the "mind games" that individuals in conflict play with each other. For example, if you and your husband are on the brink of divorce, he may start deliberately leaving the toilet seat up because he knows this infuriates you. People who visit you will not be aware of this point of conflict but it causes you stress and frustration nonetheless. Your cats are just the same; they may do subtle little things to antagonise each other without you realising it. A common example of this is if you have two cats who don't get along and you feed them in the same room. If one cat feels hungry and wants to go into the room for some food the other cat may deliberately sit in the doorway to that room. This creates a dilemma for the hungry cat who wants to eat but does not want the conflict which will arise when they try to walk past the other cat to get to the food. You may not be aware that this conflict is going on but it will be very real to your cats.

Thus if your own cats do not get on with each other, or they do not get on with other cats in the area, their life may be very stressful without you being aware of it. Cat politics may be very violent or very subtle. When your cat feels threatened and stressed by another cat, their instinct is to retreat to their own "territory" where they feel safe. They can only feel safe and secure in what they are sure is their own territory. The easiest way for them to create this safe haven is to have a place which smells like their own natural smell without any other cat's smell. This is the same process that street gangs of youths in big cities use to define their own territory or "turf". Gangs in cities will each have their own territory and often they will mark out this territory with visual markers like graffiti. When the gang member is in his own territory he will feel safe and if he sees his gang's graffiti around him this will reinforce the sense of security in that environment. Cats do not use visual markers like graffiti, they use odour markers by rubbing their scent onto the furniture and peeing at strategic places. Once the environment smells very strongly of themselves, this will demarcate a safe territory for them. When they feel under threat they will feel the need to place more scent markers (graffiti) or reinforce old scent markers with their facial scent or their urine.

Cats use two types of scent markers. The obvious one is their urine but they also have scent glands on their cheeks which they rub onto objects. This is why you often see your cat rubbing their face onto you and objects in the house. What they are doing is marking you, and the objects in the house, with their graffiti. Nature is very economical and the cat will mark an object with either urine or facial sent. There is no need to mark an object with urine and facial scent because this is a waste of resources. Because we cannot smell the facial scent left by rubbing their faces on objects, we don't mind if cats do this but we do mind when they mark things by peeing on them because we can smell the pee. Thus one form of cat graffiti is acceptable to us but the other is not.

The way cats mark things with scent from their faces is that there are glands on the surface of their cheeks which produce pheromones. Pheromones are simply chemicals that all living beings secrete from their bodies as scent. The function of this scent is sometimes obvious, e.g. flocks of birds use this scent to recognise and identify each other, as do mothers and their offspring in large herds of animals. Human beings also secrete pheromones and it is often this chemical that draws people together on a romantic level. Even though we do not consciously smell the other person's pheromones our subconscious identifies the scent they are giving off and it is often this scent that attracts us to someone else. Although you and I will not be able to smell anything, a cat's pheromones infuse your house with its scent, making it feel like a safe and secure place to them, free from intruders and dangers.

A third type of cat graffiti is scratch marks on objects. Most people think that cats scratch trees and furniture to sharpen their nails but in fact what they are doing is marking heir territory with these scratch marks. This is also unacceptable to us if the cat is leaving scratch marks on our furniture. Once again the cat will not mark an object with scratches *and* scent as this is uneconomical so they will do one or the other.

If your cat suddenly starts peeing in the house you need to observe them closely and examine the spot they have urinated on. If there are no signs to suggest a physical problem then it is most likely that your cat is stressed and is marking their territory. Another way of trying to differentiate between territory marking and increased peeing because of cystitis is to consider whether the cat is peeing on horizontal (flat) surfaces or vertical (upright) surfaces. Conventional wisdom is that cats pee on vertical surfaces to mark their territory so if you find pee on horizontal surfaces then they are probably not marking territory, suggesting that the cause of the problem is cystitis. This rule is correct most of the time but not always. I would advise people to differentiate between the physical and psychological explanations for the problem by looking for symptoms of physical discomfort and straining, and how often the cat needs to pee and how much urine is produced at each attempt, as discussed earlier in the chapter. The vet will usually be able to determine whether the problem is physical or psychological by feeling the cat's bladder during examination. If the bladder feels normal then the peeing is territorial marking due to stress.

Once we have concluded that stress is the cause of the problem we have to consider how to solve it. This is done in two ways; by removing the cause of the stress if at all possible, and by making the cat feel safe in the house so they don't feel the need to mark the house with urine.

3 Remove or reduce the cause of the stress

It is not usually possible to completely remove the cause of the stress. If your cat is stressed by one or more of your neighbour's cats, you can't to ask your neighbour to rehome their cat. Usually you will not even know which cat or cats are threatening your cat. Cats living in the area will usually eventually have a state of truce after a period of conflict. Once each cat has established their territory your cat may live peacefully within the established hierarchy and boundaries for months or years. When a new cat moves into the area and starts challenging other cats to establish a new territory, the ripple effect often runs through the whole local cat population as cats use the opportunity to try to promote their standing in the hierarchy and enlarge their personal territories. This leads to renewed fighting amongst all the cats and your cat may become involved. This upset in the cat community may trigger stress in your cat and lead them to pee in the house to reinforce their feeling of safety at home.

Although we don't usually know which cat is the cause of our cat's stress, sometimes it is very obvious. Sometimes you will actually see one particular cat frequently prowling your garden and beating your cat up. This bully may even enter your house to pick a fight with your cat inside your home. If you suspect or know that your cat is being threatened by one or more cats outside then you can take several measures to try to remove the cause of the stress. If your cat sits at a particular window and watches the threatening cat then keep the curtain drawn over those curtains. If your cat does not see the enemy all the time they will be less stressed. If the problem cat enters your house to threaten your cat then get a cat flap from the pet shop which comes with a transponder you can put on your cat's collar which lets only your cat in and out of the cat flap.

If one or more of your other cats are causing the stress then feed your cats in separate rooms. This means that if the dominant cat is in the room with the food, the stressed cat has the option of eating in a different room to avoid contact with the dominant cat. This also applies to water bowls and litter trays, i.e. place water bowls in more than one room and if you provide litter trays then put them in two or more rooms.

4 Make the cat feel safe in the house

When your cat is being stressed by your other cats or by your neighbours' cats they will want to mark your house with their own scent as a form of graffiti to reassure themselves that they are safe at home, as discussed earlier. They do this by peeing in the house at strategic spots and rubbing their faces on objects. As also mentioned before, they don't pee and rub their faces in the same spot – each spot will be marked with either pee or pheromones (facial scent). Since we can't smell the pheromones and so don't mind if the cat marks their territory with those, but do mind if they use pee, the obvious solution is to convince the cat to do all the marking with pheromones and not use pee at all.

The preferred way of doing this is with cat pheromones which are introduced into the air in your home by using a plug-in diffuser similar to many air fresheners available on the market. The pheromones in the diffuser in your home are synthetically produced cat pheromones which mix with your cat's pheromones, making your house smell very strongly of your cat. You and I will not be able to smell anything different but to your cat the house will smell very strongly of its own pheromones so their "den" or "lair" will feel like a very safe and secure place to them. By creating a safe "den" which smells only of your cat, the message the cat receives is that this is a safe place and free of any intruders and dangers. The effect of this is that the cat does not feel threatened or stressed at home and so will not feel the need to mark the house with their urine if the smell of their pheromones is already doing the job.

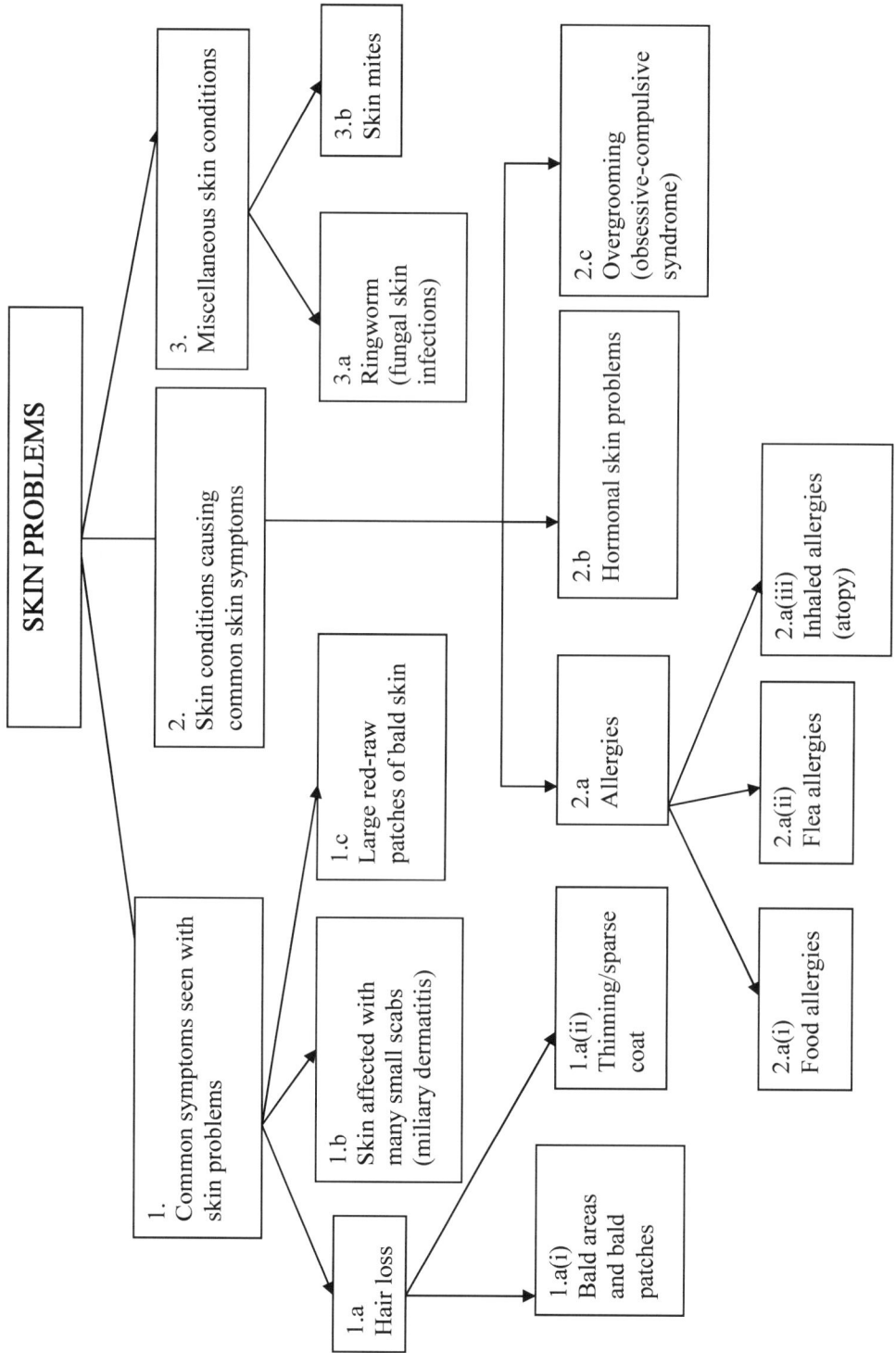

SKIN PROBLEMS

1.
Common symptoms seen with skin problems

2.
Skin conditions causing common skin symptoms

3.
Miscellaneous skin conditions

1.a
Hair loss

1.b
Skin affected with many small scabs (miliary dermatitis)

1.c
Large red-raw patches of bald skin

1.a(i)
Bald areas and bald patches

1.a(ii)
Thinning/sparse coat

2.a
Allergies

2.b
Hormonal skin problems

2.c
Overgrooming (obsessive-compulsive syndrome)

2.a(i)
Food allergies

2.a(ii)
Flea allergies

2.a(iii)
Inhaled allergies (atopy)

3.a
Ringworm (fungal skin infections)

3.b
Skin mites

3

SKIN PROBLEMS

Cats, like most mammals, have two types of hairs – primary hairs and secondary hairs. The primary hairs are the long thick hairs covering the body, forming the obvious fur that we see when looking at a cat. If you part the hairs of the fur to see the skin you will notice that there are softer, thinner and shorter hairs in between the primary hairs. These are called secondary hairs and many people refer to them as the "undercoat".

1 Common symptoms seen with skin problems

The three most common skin symptoms in cats are:

- Hair loss (bald patches or larger bald areas)
- Small scabs on the skin (miliary dermatitis)
- Large red-raw patches of completely bald skin which look like ulcers

The symptoms are usually very obvious but we may encounter several variations of each problem. The first condition is hair loss. This may consist of only one or two bald patches or multiple bald patches or large areas of baldness. Another type of hair loss is simply generalised thinning of the coat, where there are so few normal hairs that we can see the cat's skin through their fur. The skin in the bald areas or areas of thin fur may appear normal or may have many small scabs. In some cats the fur may appear normal but when the cat is touched we can feel many small scabs. These scabs may be found mainly on the head and neck or may be all over the cat's body. Cats with red-raw bald patches may have pus and blood oozing from deep holes in the skin or the area may simply look like a deep graze which is oozing clear fluid and sometimes forms a large scab. Whatever form the hair loss may take, it is usually the result of the cat licking and biting the hair and the skin. The cat appears to be grooming itself more than normal but is actually "scratching" its itchy skin using its tongue. This is simply the way a cat responds to itchy skin, and is commonly called "overgrooming". Human beings would respond to the same itchiness in their skin by scratching with their fingers.

I will discuss each of these symptoms individually but sometimes we may notice two of these symptoms present at once. The explanations which follow should help to clarify the cause of the symptoms or combination of symptoms. There is considerable overlap in terms of the same problem causing a variety or combination of skin symptoms so I will discuss the symptoms initially and the causes in the second half of the chapter.

1a Hair loss (baldness)

Hair loss may take one of two forms, either one or more areas of baldness or simply a very thin coat (too few hairs). The first point to make is that it is normal to have a very sparse covering of fur directly in front of each ear in most breeds of cat. The hair covering in this area may be very thin in oriental-type breeds such as Siamese cats and moggies descended from Siamese cats. If there are no scabs in this area then sparseness of the hair in this area is quite normal.

1a(i) Bald areas and bald patches

When you notice an area of "baldness" on your cat you will usually notice that it is not completely bald, i.e. the skin isn't fully exposed but rather it is covered by hairs much shorter than the hairs on the rest of the body. The first thing to do is gently touch the bald spot – the hair in this area will feel either very soft or very "spiky". It is important to determine this, as it is your first clue as to what the cause of the problem is. Consider your own hair on your head for a moment. If you shave the hair or cut it very short then it will feel spiky while it grows out but if you pull the hair out it will feel soft and downy when it re-grows. The same principle applies to your cat. If the hair in the bald spot feels spiky then we know that the hair has been "cut" by the cat biting the fur. If the hair in the bald spot feels soft and downy then we know that the hairs have been pulled out or have dropped out and new hair is regrowing.

Bald patches with spiky hairs thus tell us that the cat is biting the fur in that area. The most commonly affected areas are the top of the lower back, at the base of the tail and sometimes the bottom half of one or both front legs. However, any other part of the body may also be affected. The obvious assumption is that something is making the skin itchy enough to make the cat bite at the fur over the itchy part of the skin. So the conditions to consider are those things which cause such intense itching that they make the cat bite at their skin. The most common conditions which cause such intense itching are severe skin allergies and skin parasites like fleas. Both of these conditions will be discussed at the end of the chapter.

Bald patches with soft downy hair tell us that either the cat is pulling their fur out, or that the hair has fallen out and is re-growing. The most commonly affected areas are the underside of the cat's belly and the inside and back aspects of the hind legs. The affected area may involve the entire underside of the belly and inside thighs or only part of the area. The most common cause of the problem in these areas is usually that the cat is "overgrooming", i.e. the cat is licking and grooming their skin more than normal. This may not be obvious to us as pet owners and many people will comment that they haven't noticed the cat spending more time than normal grooming itself, but remember that we don't see what the cat is doing when it is out and about or when we are asleep at night. Overgrooming is the cat equivalent to human beings scratching their itchy skin. The three most common causes of patches of soft downy hair are: overgrooming due to low-grade skin allergies, overgrooming due to psychological problems (similar to obsessive-compulsive syndrome in human beings), and overgrooming due to hormonal disturbances (feline endocrine alopecia). All of these conditions will be discussed at the end of the chapter.

1a(ii) Thinning/sparse coat

As discussed at the beginning of this chapter cats have two types of hair which together form their fur (coat). When all or most of the softer and shorter hairs of the undercoat (secondary hairs) have been lost but the primary hairs are still in position, the overall appearance is a thin coat similar to the thinning hair in balding men. The most common cause of this problem is that at the cat is inadvertently pulling the undercoat out due to overgrooming. The most commonly affected part of the body is the upper parts and sides of the chest and abdomen (belly).

One should part the fur and look at the skin in these cases. The skin may appear normal or there may be many small scabs on the skin. Each scab is usually about the size of a pinhead but may be even smaller. If you are not sure whether scabs are present or not then run your fingertips over the skin against the direction of hair growth. If you feel a gritty or sandy effect on the skin then look again and try to identify what the grit is. This gritty effect may be caused by small scabs on the skin or flea dirt. Flea dirt is a polite name for flea faeces (flea poo). Flea dirt looks like black grains of sand caught in the hairs of the coat. If you are not sure what the grit is then place a few grains of it on a white piece of paper and place a drop of water on the grit. Smear the wet grit across the page with your fingernail. If the smear is red then it is flea dirt, if the smear is not red then it is a scab.

So a thinning coat caused by the loss of the undercoat is usually the result of overgrooming caused by moderate skin allergies or fleas. Both of these conditions will be discussed at the end of the chapter.

1b Skin affected with many small scabs (miliary dermatitis)

I like the old-fashioned term "miliary dermatitis" because it accurately describes the symptom. The affected cat will have many small scabs on the skin which give the surface of the skin a gritty or sandy feeling when you run your fingers against the skin against the direction of hair growth. The word "miliary" means "gritty" or "sandy" and the word "dermatitis" means that the skin is inflamed. The scabs may be present only over the face and neck or they may be present over the entire body, especially over the backbone and sides of the chest and abdomen. Each scab is usually smaller than a pinhead and they are often easier to feel than to see. You may see them by parting the fur down to the skin. The fur in the affected area may appear normal or it may be thinning similar to the hair of balding men. The skin is usually very itchy, sometimes to the point of being painful, and your cat may resent you touching their skin. This resentment may be so severe that your cat hisses or lashes out at you when you run your fingers over the skin against the direction of the hair growth. The underlying problem in these cats is that they have a very severe skin allergy which causes the skin to become inflamed. This inflammation becomes so severe that small blisters form on the skin. These blisters then burst and form the tiny scabs you can see or feel. The skin may not look very inflamed but the fact that these scabs have formed indicates that it is severely inflamed. I would describe the level of discomfort as similar to the worst sunburn you have ever had; this explains why the cat may resent you touching its skin. The inflammation and scabs in the skin make it feel very itchy, similar to the way your skin itches when it is sunburnt. When you have sunburn you will notice that the skin doesn't just feel very itchy, some jolts of intense itchiness feel like prickles of pain in the skin. Cats with miliary dermatitis experience exactly the same sensations, which is why they spend a lot of time licking or grooming themselves and why they occasionally seem to jump and start feverishly licking or biting an area of skin. This action of excessive licking and biting is the equivalent of you scratching at your sunburnt skin. The most common cause of this intense level of itching and scab formation is severe skin allergy which will be discussed in the second half of this chapter.

The hairs are sparse in the affected area and there are many scabs between the hairs. When the affected area is touched the cat may complain or attempt to bite you.

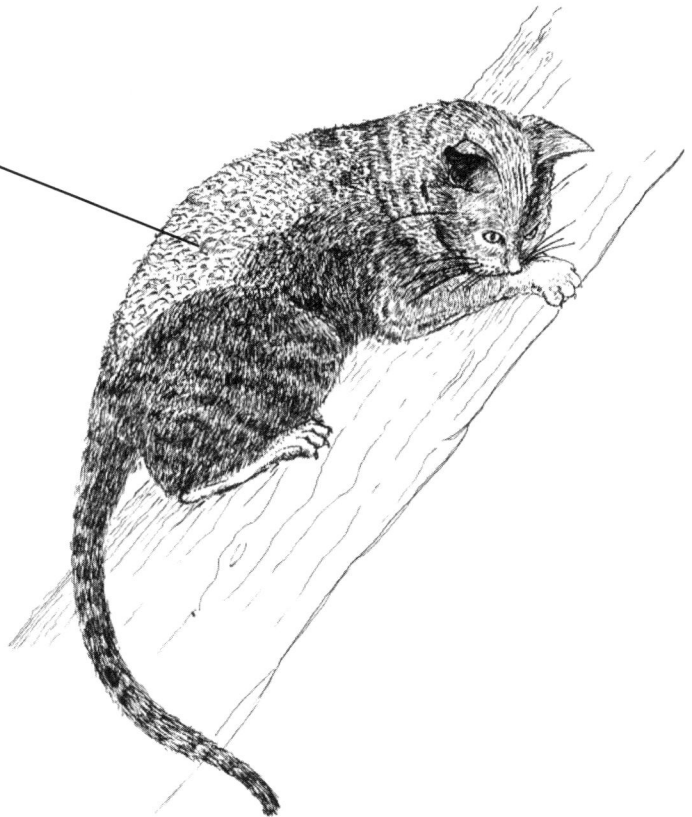

Fig 5. – Miliary dermatitis affecting a cat's back

Red scabs

Fig 6. – Miliary dermatitis affecting the face of a cat

1c Large red-raw patches of bald skin

One may sometimes find patches of completely bald skin on cats' necks or over the top of their shoulder blades (the withers). Not only are these areas usually completely bald, the skin is also red-raw and oozing clear fluid like a graze. These patches are usually the result of self-inflicted trauma, i.e. the cat is so itchy that they lick and scratch the skin until it bleeds. The surface of the skin may be completely removed to resemble a skin graze or the area may be covered in deep scratches inflicted by scratching with the hind paws. Similar but smaller areas may also be found on the head. These cats have severe skin allergies which are so itchy that the cat is driven to lick and scratch to the extent of self-harm, similar to the severe itchiness experienced by people with chicken pox. If these patches are found on the face or neck the underlying cause is usually severe skin allergy, whereas if the affected patch is over the withers it is usually caused by psychogenic problems like obsessive-compulsive syndrome triggered by an allergy.

If, however, you find a completely bald patch of skin with a large hole oozing blood and pus then the problem is usually a burst abscess. Cats often develop abscesses due to fighting with other cats. The design of a cat's teeth and claws is such that they do not tend to rip each other's skin during a fight like dogs do. Instead the teeth and claws inflict very small puncture wounds right through the skin. The bacteria and dirt on the tips of the teeth and nails are thus deposited under the skin, and the puncture wound is so small that the hole immediately closes and seals itself off. The result is that an infection will develop under the skin and as pus accumulates it has nowhere to go. Dogs, in contrast, tend to rip holes in each other's skin which are too large to seal off, so the wound is able to ooze and the blood and pus can drain out of it. In the case of cats the blood and pus will simply keep accumulating under the skin to form an abscess which is like a large boil. The abscess is initially very painful and the cat will not let you touch the area. Once a lot of pus has accumulated the abscess will mature like a boil and eventually it will burst. The way it bursts is that a soft spot of skin will develop over the abscess. This soft spot develops because the pus poisons the skin in the area and eventually a small area of skin will die off and fall out, making a hole through which the pus can drain. The cat will be aware of this process and will usually start to lick the part of the skin which is dying off. In the process of constant licking the cat will often pull the hair out of the skin because, as the skin dies, the hair becomes very loose.

The way to treat an abscess is to keep the hole open and give the cat antibiotics. The easiest way to keep the hole open is to use wet cotton wool to dab at the large scab which forms over the hole until the scab gets soggy and falls off. This must be done twice a day otherwise the scab will seal off the abscess and once again the pus will accumulate because it has nowhere to go. So it is necessary to keep the hole open to provide drainage, and administer antibiotics to remove the infection and painkillers to alleviate the pain. Antibiotics will usually be required for one or two weeks and the hole must be kept open twice a day for the same period of time.

2 Common causes of skin problems

The first part of this chapter explains that the most common skin problems in cats are skin allergies, fleas, obsessive-compulsive syndromes and hormone disturbances. These conditions vary in severity and this will usually determine the severity of the symptom. Many of the symptoms you notice are actually caused by the cat's response to the problem, i.e. licking and scratching. The extent of the licking and scratching will then determine the severity of the symptom. For example, mild itching will produce smaller areas of less severe damage to the skin and fur than more severe itching.

When you take your cat to the vet with a skin problem they will look for clues as to the cause of the problem. Their thoughts will go something like this:

Which part or parts of the body are affected? If the problem affects just the face and neck then food allergy or atopy are the most likely causes. (Atopy means that the allergy is caused by substances which are breathed in, such as pollens and house dust mites). If the problem affects the skin over the backbone and the side surfaces of the chest and abdomen (the belly) then food allergy, atopy or flea allergies are the most likely causes. If the problem affects only the underside of the belly and the insides of the thighs then hormonal problems or allergies which trigger overgrooming due to obsessive-compulsive syndrome are the most likely causes. If the problem affects the front legs then food allergy or atopy are the most likely causes.

What does the affected skin and hair look like? If the affected area is covered by short spiky hairs then allergies are the most likely explanation. If the affected area is covered by soft downy hair then overgrooming due to low-grade allergies, hormonal problems or obsessive-compulsive syndrome are the most likely causes. If the skin in the area has many small scabs then food allergies or flea allergies are the most likely causes. If the undercoat has been lost and the fur is very thin then overgrooming due to any type of allergy would be suspected. One or two red-raw patches of oozing skin which are present for more than two weeks would suggest a severe obsessive-compulsive syndrome which would normally have been triggered initially by an allergy reaction.

Is there any evidence of fleas on the cat? To look for fleas the vet will examine the whole cat but concentrate especially on the neck. They will part the fur and look for the actual fleas which are usually brown and only about one millimetre wide and two to three millimetres long. The fleas move very quickly so one will get only fleeting glimpses of them darting away from the area being examined. Even if no fleas are seen the skin should be examined closely. If there are small specks of what may look like black grains of sand, this is usually flea dirt – a polite term for flea poo. This tells us that there are fleas on the cat even if we have not seen any. To check whether the black granules are flea dirt, place one or two granules on a white piece of paper, apply a drop of water to the granule and smear it with your fingernail. If the smear appears red or reddish-brown then it is flea dirt. Even if you see no flea dirt it is a good idea to stand the cat on a white piece of paper and brush the coat so that hairs fall onto the paper. Then examine the paper for flea dirt scattered amongst the hairs. If you find fleas or flea dirt then it can be assumed that fleas play some part in the skin problem. However, to complicate the problem, some cats are so itchy that they groom themselves so often and so thoroughly that they remove all evidence of fleas and flea dirt. Thus the vet may still feel that fleas are the cause of the problem despite finding no evidence of fleas. This suspicion is usually based on where the skin and fur problems are situated and what they look like, as discussed in the preceding two paragraphs.

In the next part of the chapter I will discuss the various causes of the symptoms you have noticed in the fur and on the skin. Once again it is important to point out that it is often the individual cat's response to the problem that will determine the symptom in that particular cat. In other words, two cats with the same problem may appear to have very different symptoms.

2a Allergies

Cats develop allergies just as people do, often in response to the same things that cause allergies in us. The substance that causes the allergy is called the allergen and in cats the allergens tend to be certain types of food, insect bites (e.g. fleas), and occasionally inhaled matter (house dust and house dust mites, grasses and pollens).

The way that we, as human beings, manifest our allergies is to develop hay fever, asthma or skin eczema. Most cats with allergies will develop itchy skin or asthma or both. The route by which the allergen is taken into the body does not necessarily affect where in the body the allergic reaction will appear. Consider people with an allergy to nuts or bee stings; if they are exposed to nuts in their food or are stung by a bee, they will often develop severe swelling in their airways, which may cause suffocation. This demonstrates that the site of the allergic reaction does not necessarily have to be the same as the route of exposure to the allergen. The same concept applies to cats in that they generally manifest their allergies as inflammation and itching in the skin or inflammation in the lungs (asthma). The itching in the skin causes the cat to lick and bite their fur and skin more than normal. This is called overgrooming, i.e. the cat is grooming more than normal in an attempt to scratch the itching. This applies to food allergies, injected allergies like fleabites and inhaled allergies like pollens and house dust mites. Inhaled allergies are called atopy, and human beings and animals with atopy are called atopic individuals. Food allergy and allergy to fleabites are the types of allergy most commonly diagnosed in cats.

2a(i) Food allergies

Cats who are itchy and consequently overgrooming, either all over their body or only over the face and neck, will sometimes improve when they are fed a different kind of food, i.e. the degree of itchiness will reduce or disappear entirely. This raises the possibility of the individual being allergic to certain types of food or certain specific food ingredients. The same phenomenon occurs in human beings who are often able to alleviate their allergy symptoms, such as hay fever or asthma, by avoiding certain types of food. The most common types of food associated with allergies are wheat products, dairy products and beef. We have found that by eliminating one or more of these ingredients from a cat's diet, their itchiness will reduce or resolve.

The concept of individuals being truly allergic to certain types of food or food ingredients has raised a lot of speculation. The current thinking is that true allergy to certain types of food is in fact very rare and that most individuals thought to have a food allergy are actually only intolerant to certain types of food. This change in thinking has come about as a result of increased research into food allergy. It may sound pedantic but one should try to differentiate between a true food allergy and a food intolerance. In the case of a true food allergy it should be possible to fully resolve the cat's itching by feeding what are called novel foods. Novel foods are simply types of food made from ingredients that the cat has never eaten before. Because they have never eaten these ingredients before they cannot be allergic to them because allergies develop only after repeated exposure to a specific allergen. If the itching resolves when the cat is fed a novel food, then one should try feeding the original food again. If the itching immediately reappears it suggests that the cat is truly allergic to that type of food. Thus, if a cat is truly allergic to a certain type of food, we should be able to trigger the allergy (itching) every time we feed this food and the allergy should resolve every time we withhold this food. In research trials this is often not the case, i.e. the itching may resolve or reduce when a certain type of food is withheld, but when it is then fed to the cat at a later time the allergy is not triggered. These cats would then be regarded as being simply intolerant to that food rather than allergic to it. Food intolerance thus implies that feeding certain ingredients just makes the individual more susceptible to all their other allergies.

If it is suspected that an itchy cat is itchy because they are allergic or intolerant to a specific type of food, this would be investigated by elimination food trials. Simply put, this involves feeding the cat a novel food for eight weeks. If the symptoms resolve on the novel food but reappear when the original food is fed, then the cat has a true food allergy and the itching can be resolved by feeding the cat the novel food exclusively for the rest of their life. If the itching either doesn't resolve completely on the novel food, or doesn't recur when the original food is fed, then it can be concluded that the cat is simply intolerant to that type of food. In these cases it may be necessary to continue the search to identify what the cat is allergic to. In practice, it isn't always essential to continue the search, i.e. if the itching resolves when the cat is fed the novel food and their other allergies no longer cause any symptoms, then you can simply feed the novel food exclusively for the rest of their life.

The reality is that most itchy cats can be improved by feeding novel foods specifically prepared for cats with allergies. Even if these foods only reduce the level of itching without curing the problem entirely, they do make it easier to control the other allergies the cat may suffer from. Most of the well-known cat food manufacturers produce a novel food for cats with allergies and vets have different personal preferences as to which type of novel food they may recommend.

2a(ii) Flea allergies

This particular allergy is often called "flea bite allergy" and there are a number of relevant points to be made. The first point is that a flea bite allergy is not the same as a flea problem on the cat. Most cats will have a few fleas on them at various times of the year and they will lick and bite at the fleas for a few moments in response to the flea biting them. This response will usually only last for a few moments after the flea has bitten and then the cat will carry on doing what is was doing before. If there are hundreds of fleas on the cat and there is much more biting going on, then the cat spends more time licking, biting and scratching. I would describe this as a flea problem per se and simply treating the cat for fleas will correct the problem.

In the case of an individual with an allergy to flea bites, the problem is entirely different. Firstly, it takes only one flea bite to start the allergic reaction and even if the cat licks, bites and immediately kills the offending flea, the allergic reaction has already started. Consider a human being with an allergy to cats: It doesn't take hundreds of cats to set off their allergy. In fact it takes only one cat hair to set them off and even if they immediately removed that one cat hair it is too late because their allergy has already been set off, and they will then suffer full-blown hayfever for several hours or days. This complete overreaction by the body to an apparently minor irritation is what differentiates the allergy sufferer from everyone else. Contrast this to someone who is not allergic to cats; if a cat hair goes up their nose they will sneeze once or twice to dislodge that hair and then the sneezing stops. This same principle applies in cats; the cat who is not allergic to fleas will lick once or twice when a flea bites and will stop licking when the flea stops biting. If a flea bites a flea-allergic cat just once, even if that flea is killed immediately, the cat will be licking and biting itself for several hours to several days because the allergy has been set off.

The next point regarding flea bite allergy is that it is impossible to ensure that your cat is completely protected from fleas even if you are using the best products and the best treatment protocols. Statistically, sooner or later, one flea will slip through the defences and just one bite will trigger the allergy which, just like the example of the person allergic to cats, is completely out of proportion to the trigger that sets it off.
Thus one must accept that we must apply much tighter flea controls to allergic cats than to non-allergic cats and that despite our best efforts we can never achieve 100% flea control. We must, however, strive to achieve as close to 100% flea control as we can to reduce to a minimum the level of allergic reaction in the flea-allergic cat. This can only be achieved by treating all the pets in the household and the house with appropriate flea control products. This is further complicated by the fact that fleas are continuously developing resistance to these products, meaning that new products must be developed. The product which worked well last year may not be effective this year. The vet will advise on which products are currently efficient.

The symptoms of flea allergy are usually easy to identify. The cat is usually most severely itchy along the top surface of the lower back where the back joins onto the tail. This area over the top of the tail-base is often only covered with sparse hair because the cat is grooming much more than normal because it is itchy and is therefore pulling the undercoat out. The skin in the area is often covered with small scabs, possibly also small cuts and scratches caused by the cat biting, scratching and rubbing the area. You will often be able to see fleas in this area and if you scratch this area it may be so uncomfortable for the cat that they will hiss, spit or lash out at you. Flea allergies cause the skin to become very inflamed and this inflammation becomes so severe that small blisters form on the skin. These blisters burst and form the tiny scabs you can see or feel. This symptom is often called "miliary dermatitis", as mentioned earlier, because the many small scabs make the surface of the skin feel gritty or sandy. If flea dirt is present the "miliary" feel of the skin surface will be even more obvious.

Thus, to summarise, the most common skin parasite is the flea, which is easily visible to the naked eye. The fleas cause skin itching either just through biting the skin or because the bites cause an allergic reaction, as discussed earlier. All cats will suffer from fleas at some point in their lives. The flea has a four-stage life cycle consisting of the egg, the larva, the pupa and the adult stage. The stage we see on our pets is the adult stage. The adults live on blood which they suck from our pets and ourselves. The flea is black or brown in colour and is approximately two millimetres long. Fleas move very quickly and can jump large distances, moving along the cat's skin between the hairs over its entire body. The faeces of the fleas, euphemistically called "flea dirt", and composed primarily of undigested blood from their intestines, have the appearance of small black grains of sand lying on the cat's skin in the coat. Often we will be unable to see any live fleas on a cat but the presence of these black grains confirms their presence. If one is uncertain whether the black sand-like grains in the cat's coat are flea faeces a simple test is to place them on a white piece of paper, wet them with a small drop of water and then smear them across the paper. If the grains are flea dirt/faeces the smear will be red because the drop of water has softened the blood content of the grains. This confirms that fleas are present even if no live adult fleas can be seen. The best spot on the cat to check for flea dirt is at the base of the spine where it is attached to the tail, or on the neck.

Many flea remedies are available on the market but not all of them work equally well. This is because, over time, fleas develop resistance to the active chemicals in these products so new chemicals are being produced all the time. Fortunately, these new products are generally not only more efficient but are also more environmentally friendly, and safer for cats and their owners. To successfully control fleas one must treat all the cats and dogs in the household and treat the house itself. This is because the products available generally only work on one or two of the stages in the flea lifecycle. The products which we apply directly to dogs and cats work against the adult fleas and the products used to treat the house will work on one or more of the other stages.

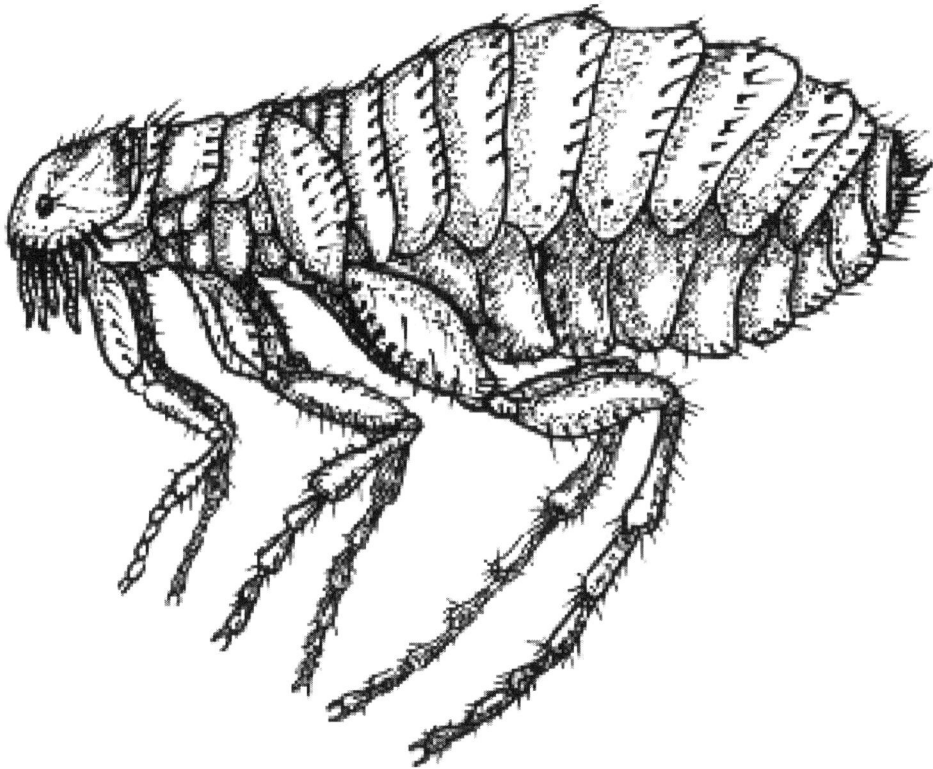

Fig 7. – The common cat flea

2a(iii) Inhaled allergies (atopy)

Inhaling certain substances may trigger allergic reactions in cats just as they do in humans. Pollens and house dust mites are the usual culprits. Human beings with an allergy to these substances usually respond by developing hay fever, asthma or eczema. Cats with allergies to these substances usually respond by developing asthma and/or skin allergies. The degree of the cat's allergic reaction will determine the extent of the symptoms we see, i.e. mild cases will usually cause such gentle itching that the cat responds by grooming only slightly more than normal. The result is that the damage to the fur is minimal so we may only notice small patches of soft downy fur on the front legs and underside of the belly where hair has been pulled out but is growing back. In more severely allergic cats the overgrooming may be so severe that they have very thin coats over their entire body, or the entire underside of the belly may be covered only with soft downy hair. The most severely affected cats will have miliary dermatitis, i.e. extensive hair loss with many small scabs over the body and/or the face and neck. The damaged hair may feel spiky because the cat is constantly biting the hairs off close to the skin.

How do we identify what is causing the allergy and how do we treat the problem?

The treatment of allergies in cats should be aimed at two levels. Firstly we should try to identify and avoid the substances that cause the allergy (the allergens) and secondly we need to relieve the itching.

The process of identifying the cause of the allergy may be expensive, time-consuming and, depending on the results, may not change the treatment options available to the affected individual. The way in which we try to identify the substances which cause the allergy (the allergen/s) is the same as in human beings. The traditional method is to inject very small amounts of all the substances the patient comes into contact with under the skin and measure the size of the wheal which forms. This sounds painful but people who have this testing done will describe it only as being uncomfortable. The test is done by injection a small amount of sterile water under the skin, producing a small swelling. This small swelling is called the control, which means that it is used to compare all the other reactions against. All the suspected allergens are then injected in the same quantity (diluted in water) into the adjacent skin and after about ten to thirty minutes the size of every swelling is measured and compared to the size of the control. The larger the swelling the more allergic that individual is to that specific substance. In this way a list can be compiled of all the substances that individual is allergic to. An alternative way of compiling this list is to have tests done on a blood sample to identify the allergens for that individual. Another option is to have the allergy testing done by a kinesiologist. There is at present no perfect method of testing for allergies and any system may produce errors for a variety of reasons but most allergens can generally be identified for each individual.

Once the list of allergens has been drawn up for that individual then, in some cases, a course of hyposensitisation can be trialled. This means that the substance that individual is allergic to is injected into it in slowly increasing concentrations over a period of several weeks to several months. The object of this exercise is to slowly build up the body's tolerance to that substance until it no longer produces an allergic reaction. This process produces little to no benefit in some patients and excellent results in others. Moreover, the benefits may be temporary or permanent so the medical community is divided on whether this is a justified mode of treatment or not. My feeling is that it offers the potential for, at the very least, a temporary reduction in medication for allergy in those cases where it works.

A further complication in identifying a list of allergens for an individual is that most individuals are allergic to several substances and most of these substances are factors beyond our control. What this means is that if the list of allergens includes a number of grasses and pollens commonly found in that environment, there is very little we can do to avoid them. Similarly if house dust and house dust mites appear on the list, we know from experience in managing human beings with these allergies that it is impossible to completely eradicate these allergens. Realistically, the only allergens we can act against are those in food and in skin parasites (fleas). If an individual is allergic to certain food types then we can avoid those foods, and we can significantly help an individual with flea-bite allergy by using good flea control measures.

Thus, even if a thorough list of allergens is obtained for an individual, we can only act against some of the substances on that list. Environmental allergens are beyond our control but by controlling those components we can, we will reduce the total number of things conspiring to trigger an allergic response in our pets and thereby reduce the total number of allergic reactions that will require treatment each year. This is the principle of maintaining the allergic individual below their "allergic threshold".

In those cases where our efforts at maintaining the individual below their allergic threshold fail, we should first find out why we have failed. It may be because the allergens are substances beyond our control, such as seasonal pollens, or it may be because we are still feeding the wrong food or using ineffective flea control products. If the allergens are environmental substances beyond our control then our efforts should be directed at controlling the symptoms of the allergy, i.e. inflammation and itching. This approach is called symptomatic treatment and the principle is to treat the symptoms when we cannot adequately treat the cause. In human beings we can achieve this very easily by using antihistamines which are freely available at pharmacists.

In the context of veterinary medicine, antihistamines very rarely have any effect at all. The only guaranteed way of controlling allergies in cats is by using cortisone in either tablet form or via injections. Most people object to the use of cortisone because they are concerned about reported side effects. I frequently encounter this objection to the use of cortisone or "steroids" and when I ask why, most people do not have a clear reason other than that they have heard that cortisone can "cause side effects". There are indeed possible side effects when using cortisone but this is true for any medication. Any chemical can produce side effects if not used correctly. Consider our use of aspirin or paracetamol to treat pain like headaches. If we take the recommended dose, then we get all the benefits without the side effects. If we exceed the dose or the duration of treatment, then we are very likely to suffer unpleasant side effects. The same applies to vitamin tablets – take the recommended number of tablets as often as advised and you will be healthy but if you take one hundred vitamin tablets at a time they may in fact kill you. So, yes, cortisone may produce side effects, but if used correctly is unlikely to cause any significant problems.

Cats are in fact very resistant to the side effects of steroids, i.e. they seem to derive all the benefits but very rarely develop any side effects. The most common side effect that can occur is that some cats on permanent steroid treatment may become overweight but this can usually be prevented or corrected by adjusting the dose of the treatment. A very rare side effect of steroid treatment in cats is it may cause diabetes mellitus (sugar diabetes). This is exceedingly rare but may be very serious and indeed even life-threatening if it is not treated. The indication that diabetes may have been induced is usually that the cat seems very unwell and eats and drinks very little or not at all within a few days of starting the steroid treatment. If you notice this happening in your cat, the vet will test their blood sugar levels. If they confirm that diabetes has been induced they will treat the cat for diabetes but this is usually only required until the steroid treatment wears off, when the cat will no longer be diabetic.

The cortisone (steroid) we use to control skin allergies in cats is the same thing that millions of human beings use all over the world to control their asthma without any side effects. The most commonly used cortisones are prednisone tablets or injectable steroids like dexamethasone or depo-medrone. This type of treatment is virtually identical to the natural steroid produced in all mammals' bodies by the adrenal glands, and when we take the synthetic form as tablets or injections, the effect is to temporarily increase the natural level of cortisone in the body. There are simple rules to be followed when using cortisone which, if followed, should prevent the development of any side effects. Should any side effects occur, they will usually resolve when the treatment is stopped. The rules are simple: where possible use very short courses of less than three consecutive days' treatment. If more than three days of treatment is required then do not stop the treatment abruptly when the symptoms have disappeared, instead reduce the dose gradually over one or two weeks until it is withdrawn. Use the lowest possible dose to control the symptoms in each individual. Every cat is unique and will require a different dose to control their itching.

The most common side effects that people report to me when their cats are on cortisone treatment are that they are slightly hungrier and sometimes drink more water and pee more. This side effect will go away when the treatment is stopped and will cause no permanent effect on the body. It is a transient side effect which is only seen in some individuals while on this treatment. The worst-case scenario is potentially a cat who needs to take cortisone (steroids) regularly throughout their life. In this situation the individual may start to get fat after a prolonged course of treatment, which may have to be adjusted to compensate. This side effect may have to be weighed up against the alternative problems encountered in the individual without treatment for their allergy. The benchmark is: which of these two options affects the overall quality of life of the individual the least? If the cat is not treated and the itching is so severe that the cat spends most of their time itching and thus licking, biting and scratching at the skin causing a succession of self-inflicted wounds that themselves require treatment, then I would personally rather treat the allergy in that individual and accept that they become slightly overweight. I feel that this side effect of long-term steroid treatment causes less of an impact on the individual's quality of life than enduring a lifetime of relentless itching. I imagine that the level of itching felt by the cat probably feels like the itching we experience with sunburn. The itching and discomfort caused by sunburn will never kill me but I certainly wouldn't want to spend my entire life suffering that level of discomfort. I would certainly choose to be slightly overweight rather than suffer lifelong sunburn.

A new product to control allergies is soon to be launched for cats. It is called cyclosporin and it has the same effect as steroids without the common side effects of steroids in most individuals. It is still a very new type of treatment and we as vets are still waiting to see what the long-term effects of this treatment might be. I have found that it seems to be an excellent treatment, not only because it has not produced side effects in the cases where I have used it, but also that it seems to work in cases where steroids do not.

The worst-case scenario of having to accept weight gain in individuals on long-term steroid treatment is rarely encountered in practice. My feeling at the outset of a severe case of skin allergy is to try all other treatment options before I accept that there is no alternative to a lifetime of intermittent treatment with cortisone. Some of the alternatives have been mentioned before, such as trialling different food to reduce the allergic threshold, eliminating fleas as best we can, and courses of hyposensitisation treatment. If none of these is appropriate or effective for an individual then other options can be explored. One alternative option is to explore the benefits of natural or homeopathic remedies. The most common natural remedies used are evening primrose oil, either in tablet form or in shampoo form, or homeopathic sulphur in tablet or powder form. These natural remedies are very variable in their effect, with some cats responding very well and others not responding at all. I feel that they are worth trying because even a partial response to this treatment would mean that cortisone would be required less often and at lower doses. The biggest problem with long-term evening primrose oil treatment is cost; the tablets are expensive and many people cannot afford to use them over extended periods of time. The option of using homeopathic sulphur is much more affordable but the response to treatment is equally unpredictable.

The objective of any of these treatments is to have the cat "comfortably itchy". What this means is to control the inflammation and itching caused by the skin allergy to the point were the impact on the individual's quality of life is negligible. This means that in the long term less medication is required, fewer possible side effects will occur, the expense to the cat's owner is less and the cat is comfortable enough to lead a full and happy life. The specific treatment and dose required to achieve this state of being "comfortably itchy" will differ from one individual to another. Finding the treatment and dose which will achieve this is often a matter of trial and error but is definitely worth it if one considers that without treatment the cat is living with the permanent sensation of sunburn.

2b Hormonal skin problems (feline endocrine alopecia)

Feline endocrine alopecia is a very poorly understood condition in cats and may not even be a genuine condition, i.e. it may not be a hormonal problem at all. This condition is called a hormonal (endocrine) problem simply because the only treatment that affected cats respond to is treatment with hormones. The hormone that is used is a progestagen called megestrol acetate, which is like a female hormone.

The usual symptom of feline endocrine alopecia is a cat with a very short, soft and downy fur growth over the underside of the belly and the insides of the thighs. In some of these cases the problem is obviously overgrooming, i.e. the cat is licking these areas much more than normal and thus pulling the hair out, but in some cases there is no evidence of overgrooming. More severe cases may present with miliary dermatitis as discussed earlier, or even red-raw weeping areas of self-inflicted damage to skin, usually over the face and neck. These cases are usually initially diagnosed as overgrooming or self-inflicted trauma due to the itching caused by skin allergies. They are therefore usually treated as skin allergies initially and in most cases the symptoms will go away after treatment. However, some of these cases do not improve when treated as allergy patients and it is then that your vet may suggest trying the hormonal treatment.

The usual protocol is to give the cat five milligrams of megestrol acetate twice a week for two weeks initially and then reduce the dose to five milligrams once weekly for another four weeks. The vet will then re-examine the cat and often find that the symptoms will have virtually disappeared, i.e. the fur has grown back normally.

Megestrol acetate is a potent progestagen which blocks the production of oestrogen. The confusion that arises is because we are not sure what effect the megestrol acetate is having, i.e. does it actually simply have an anti-allergy effect which works better than other allergy treatments, or does it in fact correct a hormonal disturbance, or does it simply soothe the cat's temperament psychologically? The psychological effect stems from the fact that overgrooming may not always be caused by an itchy skin. Overgrooming may be a symptom of stress and/or obsessive-compulsive syndrome in the same way that some people bite their nails, pick at their skin or tug at their eyebrows and hair. In cats and in human beings this sort of obsessive behaviour may simply reflect the personality of the individual or is may be induced by stress. The effects of treatment with megestrol acetate may be to alleviate psychological stress and so reduce obsessive-compulsive overgrooming behaviour. Thus we simply do not know why some cats will only respond to treatment with megestrol acetate but there are many cases which fall into this category.

Treatment with megestrol acetate is usually a last resort as it may cause several side effects, particularly damage to the bone marrow, which is responsible for producing red and white blood cells. Although this is a well-documented side effect in textbooks I have never encountered it in my patients so it may not be common. A second possible side effect is that it may cause tumours in mammary tissue (breast tissue). This is also a possible side effect but I have only encountered this once and it was in a cat which had been on progesterone treatment continuously for ten years. Megestrol acetate may also occasionally induce diabetes mellitus(sugar diabetes). In practice I only use the treatment when no other treatment has worked and when I do use it I only do so for six to eight weeks, as described earlier. I may have to apply a course once or twice a year but this type of use seems to be very safe and I have only very rarely encountered any significant side effects when the treatment is used in this way.

Over-grooming makes the fur on the belly and inside thighs short and soft. In severe cases these areas maybe completely bold. They may or may not be scabs in the affected areas.

Fig 8. – Symptoms of over-grooming

2c Overgrooming (obsessive-compulsive syndrome)

The concept of overgrooming as a manifestation of itchy skin and/or obsessive-compulsive syndrome has been touched on several times in this chapter. Overgrooming simply means that the cat is grooming, i.e. licking and nibbling their fur, more than normal. The effect of this is that the hairs may be bitten off short to give a spiky feel, or may be pulled out to give the skin a completely bald effect or simply a very thin covering of hair. Or, if the hair is regrowing at about the same rate as it is being pulled out, the affected area will have the soft downy feel of new hair growth. Overgrooming may be caused by itching in the skin or it may be an obsessive-compulsive behaviour caused by personality type or stress. The cause of the overgrooming is usually discovered when the underlying skin condition has been diagnosed, as discussed throughout this chapter. Thus there is usually an explanation for the increased level of grooming and treatment is aimed at the specific cause.

An additional type of obsessive-compulsive syndrome is severe self-inflicted trauma to the skin over the withers(between the shoulder blades) for no apparent reason. This is a rare condition but is distressing to the cat and to the people living with the cat. The symptom is usually a red-raw patch of bald skin that has deep gouges and scratches inflicted by the claws of the back paws. The cat will lick and scratch the area over the top of the shoulder blades to the extent that it is constantly bleeding, oozing and painful. There is usually no identifiable cause of the problem, i.e. the cat does not seem to be itchy anywhere else and there are no signs of fleas or other injury. The various treatments that vets may try include steroids, progesterone, tricyclic antidepressant drugs (similar to Prozac), antibiotics, and bandaging the back paws to prevent ongoing self-inflicted damage. The most effective treatment in my experience is megestrol acetate but the problem may take several months to resolve. There is currently no explanation for this condition but the good news is that it does ultimately resolve after extended treatment.

3 Miscellaneous skin conditions

3a Ringworm (fungal skin infections)

Fungi may infect the skin as primary skin infections. The most common fungal skin infection is the inappropriately named ringworm. Two types of fungi called Micosporum and Trichophyton cause ringworm infections. Ringworm infections are rare fungal skin infections but one must be on the lookout for these infections because they can spread to almost any animal including human beings. The classic appearance of the infection is a circular, reddish, scaly area of hair loss which may or may not itch. Sometimes only one such lesion is seen but more often many similar lesions appear at any site on the body. However, the infection often doesn't present with this classic circular lesion. It may produce almost any scaly, reddened area with or without hair loss or itching, affecting any area of skin at any position on the body. The lesions caused by this infection may appear similar to any of the skin symptoms discussed earlier in the chapter. It is a rare condition usually seen in longhaired cats, especially Persian cats, and is most common in cat breeding colonies or in households with many longhaired cats.

Sometimes the first suggestion that your cat has ringworm is that someone in the family, usually a child, develops the classic round, itchy and scabby skin lesion associated with this condition. In children the most commonly affected site is on the head and you, the parent, will notice the sudden appearance of a bald patch on your child's head. Once your doctor has diagnosed someone with ringworm they will usually ask if you have recently had contact with cattle or cats. The usual answer is that you have recently acquired a new kitten but the kitten has no signs of a skin condition. This is because cats may be asymptomatic carriers of ringworm, i.e. they have the fungus in their hair and skin but they do not develop any signs of the infection. This is often a shocking discovery for you as the cat owner but the condition is quite harmless.

The treatment for affected people and cats is very simple and effective. The diagnosis is made by testing hairs plucked painlessly from the skin. The treatment for the cat is simply a course of anti-fungal tablets for six to eight weeks. Most doctors will treat affected people with a topical cream applied to the affected area twice daily. I find that topical treatments are ineffective in cats and so use the tablet equivalent. Ringworm infections may, however, be difficult to eradicate in intensive Persian breeding colonies and in these instances I would advise treating all the cats in the colony for a minimum of 12 weeks and I would also advise regular bathing in anti-fungal shampoos. This extended and more intensive treatment protocol is usually only required in intensive breeding colonies. In my experience ringworm infections are uncommon but occasionally there will be outbreaks of the condition in local communities as it is quite contagious. These outbreaks are usually successfully eradicated within a few weeks.

3b Skin mites

Cats may very rarely be affected by skin mites like Notoederes cati or Sarcoptes scabei, also known as scabies, sarcoptic mange or fox mange. This is a highly contagious skin mite which can also affect human beings. The typical lesions associated with this mite are severely itchy, reddened areas of hair loss usually affecting the ears and face. This is probably the itchiest skin condition that cats can suffer from and affected individuals scratch and rub themselves incessantly. The lesions are not necessarily restricted to the areas mentioned above and many individuals will itch all over their bodies. The diagnosis is made by microscopic examination of skin scrapings taken from several sites over the body. There are often not many mites on the body so they may not be seen in the scrapings taken. The fact that no mites are seen doesn't necessarily confirm that there are none present. This is referred to as a false negative test result which means that although the test has shown that that individual has tested negative, the result may be false. This is because of the potential for "sampling error". Sampling error may occur because the sections of skin which are tested may not contain mites because there are often very few mites, spread sparsely over the body. So if I find no mites in a cat which I strongly suspect has sarcoptic mange, I will often treat them for the condition anyway just to eliminate the possibility. This is however a very rare condition.

4

VOMITING AND DIARRHOEA

There are many different causes of vomiting and diarrhoea in cats but there is an old saying in medicine which states "common things occur commonly". This is very true when trying to figure out why a cat is vomiting or has diarrhoea. When you take your cat to the vet with one or both of these symptoms they will initially ask you several questions to help them to make the diagnosis. It is very important to answer the questions as accurately as you can. If you do not know the answer to any or all of the questions then it is better to say so than to take a guess. These questions may include some of the following:

- How old is the cat?
- Have they had similar symptoms before?
- Is the cat vomiting, do they have diarrhoea or are they doing both?
- Have you recently changed the food you feed them?
- How many times has the cat vomited in the last 24 hours?
- What does the vomit and/or diarrhoea look like?
- Other than the vomiting and/or diarrhoea, does the cat seem well or do they seem unwell?
- Will the cat still eat food and drink water?
- How long have these symptoms been present?

These questions will help guide the vet's thinking which will go something like this:

The symptoms of vomiting and/or diarrhoea reveal that there is some sort of problem with the digestive system. The digestive system can be thought of as a long tube which digests food and eliminates waste products from the body. This tube is divided into four sections, each of which has a different function. The first section is the oesophagus, which is responsible for swallowing food i.e. transferring food from the mouth to the stomach. The second part of the tube is dilated to form a bag called the stomach which produces acid. Swallowed food is soaked in and mixes with this acid to produce a liquid slurry, called ingesta. The ingesta moves into the third part of the tube, the small intestine, where it is mixed with bile from the liver and digestive enzymes from the pancreas.

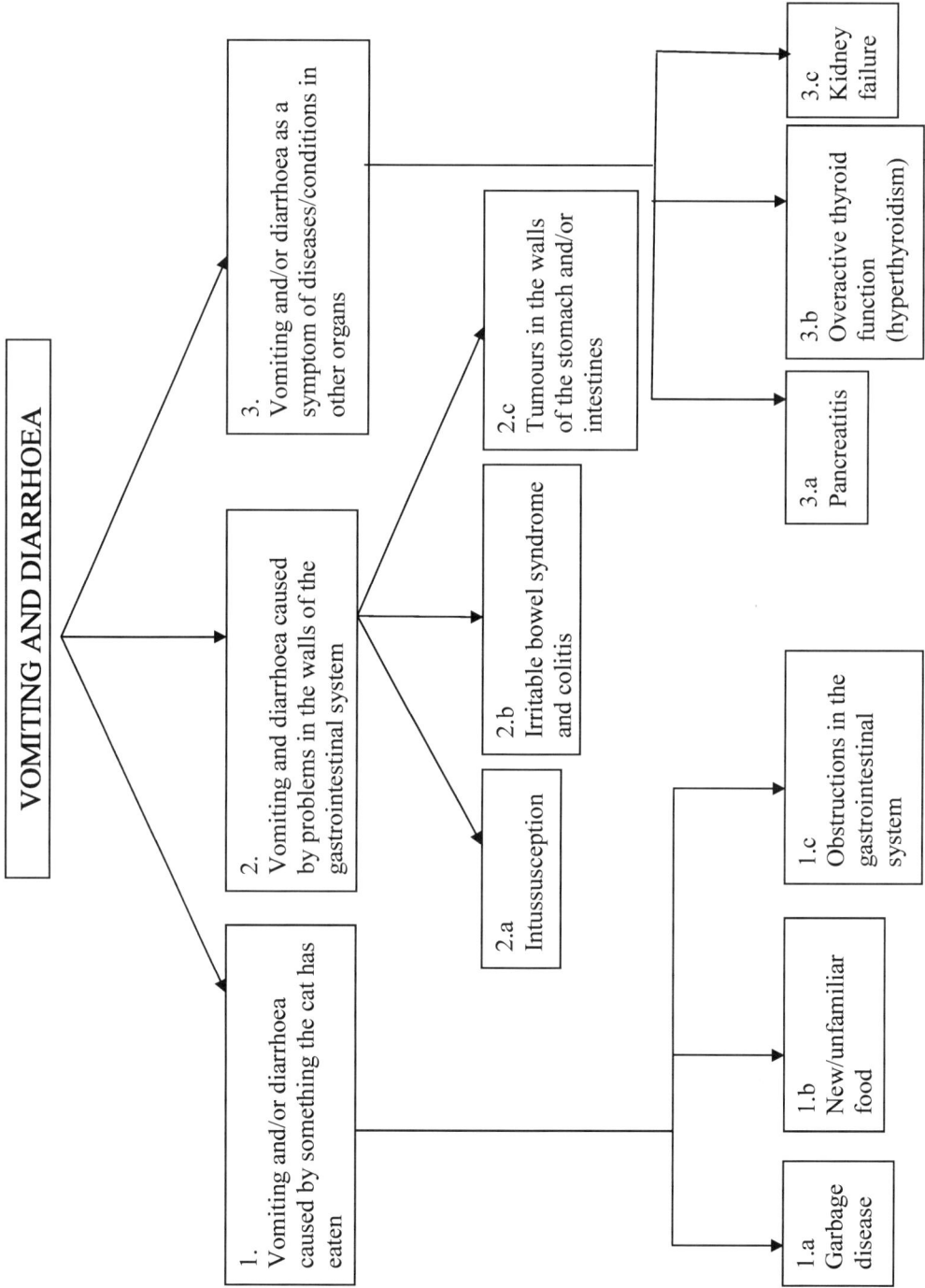

VOMITING AND DIARRHOEA

1. Vomiting and/or diarrhoea caused by something the cat has eaten

1.a Garbage disease

1.b New/unfamiliar food

1.c Obstructions in the gastrointestinal system

2. Vomiting and diarrhoea caused by problems in the walls of the gastrointestinal system

2.a Intussusception

2.b Irritable bowel syndrome and colitis

2.c Tumours in the walls of the stomach and/or intestines

3. Vomiting and/or diarrhoea as a symptom of diseases/conditions in other organs

3.a Pancreatitis

3.b Overactive thyroid function (hyperthyroidism)

3.c Kidney failure

As the ingesta moves along the small intestine it is digested and absorbed into the body via the bloodstream. The ingesta then passes through the ileocaecal valve into the large intestine. In human beings the appendix is a small pouch attached to the ileocaecal valve. Once the ingesta has passed into the large intestine, water is reabsorbed from the slurry into the body and the remaining solids are compacted into faeces (poo). When enough faeces have collected in the last part of the large intestine (the rectum), the cat will pass the faeces out of the body by defecation (pooing). The entire tube from beginning to end constitutes the gastrointestinal system. The walls of this tube have a number of layers. The inner layer is called the epithelium which is responsible for absorbing water and nutrients from the ingesta. The thickest layer is made up of muscle which contracts rhythmically in waves called peristalsis, moving the ingesta and ultimately the faeces along the tube.

Anything which interferes with the tube's ability to move food and wastes from the start of the tube (the mouth) to the end of the tube (the anus/bum), will activate its main defence system. This defence system operates by assuming that the tube contains something harmful and will attempt to reject this harmful material as quickly as possible through one end of the tube or the other. The primary defence mechanism of the digestive system is to eject harmful material either through the mouth via vomiting or through the anus via diarrhoea.

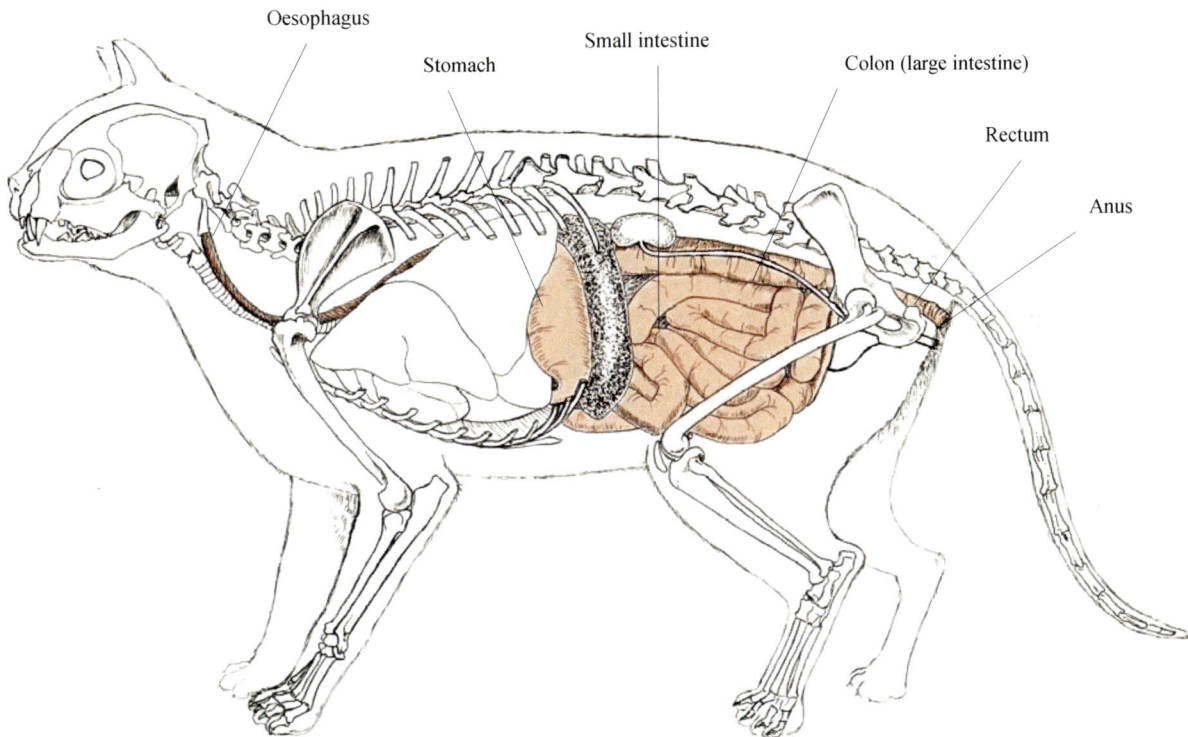

Fig 9. – Side view to show the normal size and position of the digestive system.

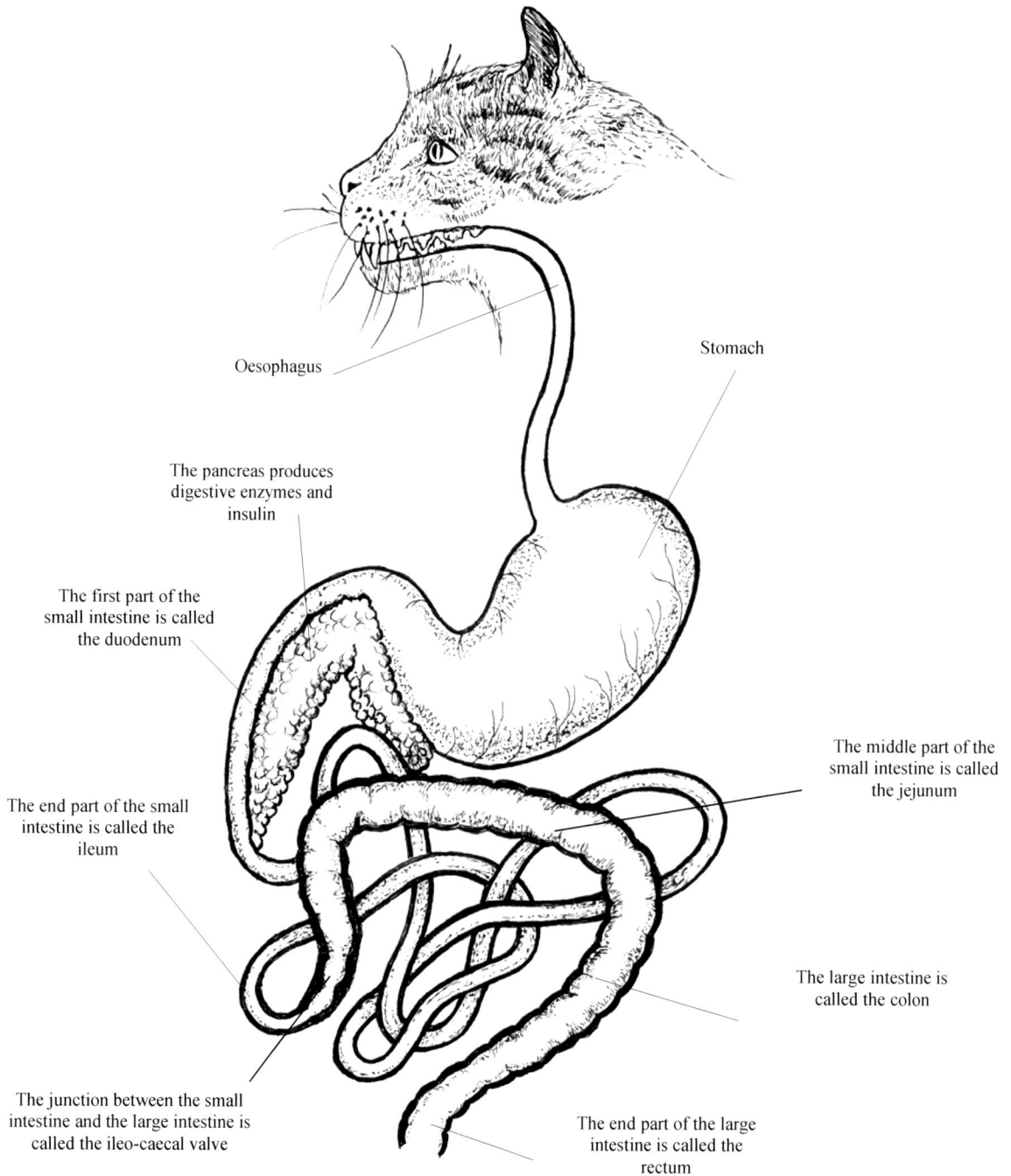

Oesophagus

Stomach

The pancreas produces
digestive enzymes and
insulin

The first part of the
small intestine is called
the duodenum

The middle part of the
small intestine is called
the jejunum

The end part of the small
intestine is called the
ileum

The large intestine is
called the colon

The junction between the small
intestine and the large intestine is
called the ileo-caecal valve

The end part of the large
intestine is called the
rectum

Fig 10. – Schematic representation of the digestive system.
The digestive system is simply a long tube for processing
food. Different parts of the tube are modified into various
shapes and sizes to perform different functions.

There are two broad categories of condition which may activate the vomiting and diarrhoea defence responses of the gastrointestinal tract. The first category includes all conditions located primarily in the gastrointestinal system, i.e. problems in the walls of the tube or problems in any of its chambers. The second category includes problems in any other part of the body which may irritate the gastrointestinal tract enough to activate its vomiting and/or diarrhoea defence responses.

Thus one of three things may cause vomiting and/or diarrhoea:

- Something that the cat has eaten
- Something that is happening in the walls of the gastrointestinal system
- Something wrong elsewhere in the body that affects the gastrointestinal system.

If the problem affects the stomach or upper and middle parts of the intestine (the small intestine), the symptom is usually vomiting. These cases often start as vomiting and may then later develop into diarrhoea as the problem moves from the stomach into the small intestine. If the small intestine is the site of the problem then the cat will often lose its appetite, seem lethargic and look very unwell.

If the problem affects the lower intestine (the large intestine), the symptom is usually diarrhoea only and no vomiting. These patients produce frequent small amounts of soft faeces, they defecate/poo much more often than normal, and seem to strain to pass these small amounts of faeces. People often mistake this straining for constipation. A cat with a large bowel diarrhoea will often have a lot of flatulence ("farting"), slimy or "jelly-like" faeces and bright red blood in the faeces. It will seem bright and alert and active and have a normal appetite. This is in stark contrast to cases of small intestinal diarrhoea where the cats look very sick and lethargic and lose their appetite.

The vet's next thoughts will progress as follows. If the only symptom is vomiting then the vet will suspect that the problem is situated in the oesophagus, stomach or upper intestine. The problem may be simply inflammation as caused by "garbage disease" and "unfamiliar" foodstuffs, or it may be due to obstructions in the oesophagus, stomach and upper intestines. Other possible causes of inflammation in the stomach and small intestine may include primary stomach problems such as excessive acid (heartburn), stomach and intestinal tumours, and non-specific inflammation (irritable bowel syndrome). The inflammation in the stomach and small intestine may, however, be due to problems elsewhere in the body, such as kidney problems, liver problems or pancreatic problems.

1 Vomiting and/or diarrhoea caused by something the cat has eaten

1a Garbage disease

The first common cause of vomiting and/or diarrhoea is that the cat has eaten something which has upset their digestive system. This may be something they have found and eaten in the house or garden or while out hunting. This is commonly called "garbage disease".

This is the same thing that we, as human beings, call food poisoning after eating food that has spoiled.

1b New/unfamiliar types of food

If the cat has recently eaten a different type of food that they may not have eaten before, like a different brand of cat food or table scraps, then this may also upset their tummy. The same thing happens to us when we go on holiday and eat foods that we do not normally eat. The common example is people who develop vomiting and diarrhoea while on holiday in exotic locations like India where it is described as "Delhi belly". The reason that we may develop vomiting and diarrhoea while on holiday is not necessarily that there is something wrong with the food but rather that our digestive symptoms are not accustomed to that type of food and so we develop an upset tummy. With time our digestive symptoms should usually become accustomed to this new food and the symptoms will disappear.

If the cause of the tummy upset in your cat is due to something that they have eaten the symptoms will usually start as vomiting and progress into diarrhoea but sometimes only vomiting or only diarrhoea is the symptom. The treatment for this category of problem is very simple. The principle of the treatment is to feed no food for 24 hours and provide only water for drinking. The rationale behind this is that the stomach and intestines are trying to empty themselves out by vomiting and diarrhoea and if we keep feeding more food the stomach and intestines will not reach a point where they are satisfied that they have emptied themselves. Once the digestive system has emptied itself it must be allowed 24 hours to rest which is why we withhold food for this period of time. After the 24-hour fasting period the cat should be fed a very bland food to start the digestive system working again.

This is the same approach that we apply to ourselves when we have a tummy upset, i.e. we lose our appetite and will eat nothing for a day. When we do start eating again, we tend to eat bland foods like toast and tea until the digestive system resumes normal activity and then we return to our usual foods. The same concept applies to cats; after a fasting period of 24 hours we should feed them only very bland food types. This would usually involve white meat like boiled or roasted chicken, turkey or white fish. The cat should be fed this bland food in small amounts offered three or four times a day, i.e. feed small amounts often. This will restart the digestive system without asking it to work too hard. The cat should be kept on this bland diet, feeding small amounts often, until the vomiting has stopped and two normal stools have been passed. The cat should then be gradually returned to their normal food by mixing their usual food with the white meat for a few days at about half meat and half cat food proportions. The amount of white meat mixed into the usual food is then gradually reduced until the cat is eating entirely their usual food without any further vomiting and diarrhoea. This simple process will solve most cases of vomiting and/or diarrhoea that have been caused by eating something that disagrees with the cat, and no further treatment should be required. If the problem does not resolve within 48 hours, or if the symptoms become worse then you should consult a vet for advice.

1c Obstructions in the gastrointestinal system

The causes of obstructions in the digestive system are most commonly something indigestible that the cat may have swallowed. These indigestible objects are called "foreign bodies". The most common foreign bodies found in the gastrointestinal system of cats are lengths of sewing thread or string or the ribbon from audiocassette tapes. This type of foreign body is called a linear foreign body. I don't know why cats try to swallow lengths of sewing thread but it is not uncommon. They often even swallow sewing thread which is still attached to a sewing needle. One end of the length of thread often loops around the base of the tongue and the rest of the thread extends down the oesophagus into the stomach. With time the loop around the base of the tongue will cut into the tongue like a snare, making the tongue very painful. A clue to this being the problem is that the cat will drool saliva and will want to eat but appear to be unable to take food into its mouth or swallow. This is because the snare around the base of the tongue interferes with the normal function of the tongue, i.e. lapping food, moving food around the mouth while chewing, and swallowing food and saliva. If you open the mouth and look under the tongue you will often see the snare effect around the base of the tongue. The vet will need to administer a general anaesthetic and will usually suggest an X-ray to see if there is a needle attached to the other end of the thread. Once they have taken the X-ray they will remove the thread and the needle if there is one. They may be able to do this simply by cutting the snare around the base of the tongue and pulling the thread out. If the needle does not come out with the thread the cat may need an operation to retrieve and remove the needle if the vet doesn't have an endoscope to retrieve it. So if a foreign body is lodged in the oesophagus (the swallowing tube leading from the mouth to the stomach) then the symptoms include repeated retching (the cat is trying to remove the problem by vomiting it out), drooling (the cat cannot swallow the normal production of saliva), and inability to swallow food.

If the vet doesn't see a snare around the base of the tongue and they suspect that there is a foreign body in the stomach or small intestine, they will probably suggest X-rays and/or abdominal scans. However, not all foreign bodies are dense enough to show up on X-rays. Bones show up on X-rays, for instance, because skin is thin enough to allow X-rays to pass straight through it, revealing the bones beneath. But some foreign bodies like pieces of string, thread, audiocassette tape ribbon, rubber, plastic and cork are also thin enough to allow X-rays to pass straight through them, so they don't show up on X-ray. However, they may interfere with the normal movement of gas in the intestine so a pocket of gas may prompt the vet to investigate further despite no visible foreign body showing up on X-ray. The vet may then suggest a barium study. This involves asking the cat to swallow barium liquid (which shows up on X-rays) and taking repeated X-rays of the abdomen to follow the movement of barium as it passes through the digestive system. The movement of the barium may then be seen to stop flowing at a certain point, or it may coat an invisible foreign body which will then show up on the repeated X-rays. Another way of looking for a foreign body is to use an endoscope. This is like passing a camera into the stomach to look around for a foreign body. Ultrasound is another tool which the vet may use to look for a foreign body, involving the same equipment and procedure that is used when scanning pregnant women.

If the cause of the problem is that the cat has a foreign body in the stomach or intestines then the symptoms may vary according to how the digestive system is able to deal with it. If it is a large foreign body like a knotted ball of string or a piece of rubber, it may remain in the stomach and cause random bouts of vomiting which may disappear for a few days only to return later. This happens because some large foreign bodies are too large to pass into the intestine and may float around in the stomach without affecting the cat. When these cats have eaten and the food is moved from the stomach into the small intestines, the foreign body moves with the food and may temporarily block its passage into the intestines, causing vomiting. When the foreign body then moves away from the valve connecting the stomach to the small intestine, the food is once again able to move into the intestine and the vomiting symptoms simply disappear. The foreign body in this instance acts like a ball valve in the stomach and only affects the cat when in the wrong position. These cases normally require a surgical operation to remove the foreign body.

If a linear foreign body, like a piece of thread or string, moves into the small intestine it may cause "plication" of the small intestine. This happens when the piece of string gets stuck in the intestine and the intestine continues creating peristaltic waves to move it along. The result is that the string acts like a curtain rail and a long length of intestine becomes pleated along the string like a length of curtain being bunched up on a curtain rail. Ultimately the intestine may become so tightly bunched along the thread that the thread cuts through the intestine like cheese wire. Once the intestine has been cut open it will leak ingesta into the cat's abdomen, causing peritonitis, which will be fatal if not treated quickly. The affected cat will become very ill once the plication (bunching) of the intestine starts because the plication becomes so tight that ingesta cannot move along the intestine. The initial effect is therefore the same as a blockage in the intestine and the cat will usually appear very sick, refuse to eat and will vomit in an attempt to clear the "blockage". Once the thread has sliced through the intestine, the cat will become profoundly ill to the extent that they collapse and are too sick to stand. The vet will suspect that plication has occurred simply by feeling the cat's intestines when they examine the cat's belly. They will then either advise further tests like X-rays and scans to confirm the diagnosis or may even advise immediate exploratory abdominal surgery. The solution is to remove the piece of string by surgery and, if the intestine has been cut open, the cat will need intensive care with drip lines and antibiotics to treat the peritonitis. Peritonitis is a very serious complication and cats may die from it despite all our efforts to help them. The best chance these cats have of surviving intestinal plication is rapid surgical treatment before the intestine is sliced open by the linear foreign body.

If a foreign body like a piece of rubber or plastic is small enough to move through the stomach valve into the small intestines, it may then get stuck in the small intestine. If it causes a complete blockage of the small intestine, then the symptoms will be severe, frequent, repeated, strenuous attempts at vomiting (the cat is trying to remove the object by vomiting it out) with no sign of diarrhoea. These cats generally feel very unwell and often refuse to eat or drink because the foreign body obstructs all movement of waste products through the intestines. Affected cats are at risk of dying from toxic shock if the waste products accumulate and have the effect of "poisoning" them. If the foreign body gets stuck in the small intestine but only causes a partial obstruction, then some food and waste products can squeeze past the obstruction and move normally through the rest of the intestine. In these cases the same symptoms appear as in a complete obstruction but the symptoms are less severe and the risk of death from toxic shock is less.

If the foreign body is stuck, whether it causes a total or partial obstruction, it will require a surgical operation to remove it. If the foreign body is small enough to pass through the entire digestive system them it will cause a range of symptoms as it passes from the stomach (vomiting), to the small intestine (vomiting and diarrhoea), to the large intestine (diarrhoea and straining movements as the cat tries to pass the object out of the body with the faeces). An example of a foreign body which is small enough to get stuck in the intestines of very young kittens is the eraser on the end of a pencil. I have seen two cases where kittens have bitten this eraser off the pencil and swallowed it. In both cases the piece of eraser caused a complete blockage of the small intestine. Another example is a young cat which swallowed a spongy type of human earplug – the type used to protect the ears of people shooting rifles and handguns. Once again this did not show up on the X-rays and was ultimately removed from the small intestine by surgery.

2 Vomiting and/or diarrhoea caused by problems in the walls of the gastrointestinal system

2a Intussusception

The intestines, as discussed earlier, can be thought of simply as a long tube for digesting food. In severe cases of vomiting and diarrhoea the forceful contractions of the intestines flow along the intestinal tube in the form of waves (peristalsis). If a powerful wave of contraction moves very rapidly towards a length of intestine that is stationary then the rapidly moving piece of intestine may slide inside the stationary intestine and get stuck in that position. This is the same effect we see when an extended telescope or telescopic car aerial is pushed shut. The effect of a piece of intestine slipping inside another piece of intestine is referred to as an intussusception. The intussusception effectively blocks the movement of food and wastes in the intestine and thus causes the same effect as an intestinal foreign body (blockage). If it causes a complete blockage of the small intestine then the symptoms are severe, frequent, repeated, strenuous attempts at vomiting (the cat is trying to remove the "object" by vomiting it out) and often also signs of repeated, strenuous attempts at diarrhoea (the cat is trying to remove the "object" by defecating). These cats generally feel very unwell and often refuse to eat or drink because the intussusception may obstruct all movement of waste products through the intestines. Affected cats are at risk of dying from toxic shock if the waste products accumulate and "poison" them. If the intussusception only causes a partial obstruction, then some food and waste products can squeeze past the "obstruction" and move normally through the rest of the intestine. In these cases the symptoms are the same as in a complete obstruction (vomiting and/or diarrhoea) but the symptoms are less severe and the risk of death from toxic shock is less.

Intussusceptions are rare in cats and tend to occur most commonly in kittens and young cats. The vet will often be able to feel the intussusception in the cat's belly when they are examining the belly with their hands. In many cases the vet will want to confirm their suspicion that an intussusception is the cause of the problem by taking X-rays, and often also barium X-rays, as discussed earlier in this chapter. An ultrasound scan of the belly may also help to confirm their suspicions. Once the intussusception has been confirmed as the cause of the problem then surgery will be required to correct the problem. The surgery may consist of simply pulling the stuck piece of intestine out of the other piece of intestine in the same way that a telescope is extended. However, if there has been a lot of damage to that piece of intestine then it will have to be cut out and the remaining sections of intestine will then be stitched back together. After the surgery these cats will need to be starved for about 6 to 12 hours to allow the intestine to rest and heal and then they should be fed only bland foods as discussed earlier. These bland food types should be offered to the cat in several small portions daily for the next week until normal intestinal function has resumed. Once normal stools have been seen for two days then the bland food should be mixed with the cat's normal food for a few days to gradually wean them back onto their usual diet.

2b Irritable bowel syndrome and colitis

Colitis and irritable bowel syndrome are well known conditions in human beings. Most of us know someone who suffers from one of these conditions and they will describe a large range of possible symptoms to us. The name colitis is actually only a description of the problem rather than a diagnosis of what causes the problem. The word colitis can be broken down into two parts: "itis" means simply inflammation and "col" is derived from colon. Thus colitis means inflammation of the colon. Irritable bowel syndrome is equally vague and implies simply inflammation and irritation of any part of the bowel (intestine). The wide variety of symptoms that sufferers will describe is due to variations in the amount of inflammation and to which portion of the bowel that is affected. The most extreme form of this condition in human beings is called Crohn's disease; thankfully this most extreme form does not seem to occur in cats.

The most common cause of irritable bowel syndrome is a dietary intolerance. This means that an individual may be intolerant to certain types of food. Think about people you know who may say to you that they cannot eat dairy products or products containing wheat or nuts. This is because these products produce an allergy-type reaction in their intestines in much the same way that pollen may produce an allergic reaction and inflammation in the nose of hay fever sufferers. Thus people with dietary intolerances have allergic reactions to certain food types which cause inflammation in their intestines. The severity of this allergic reaction and the portion of the intestine that is affected will determine the symptoms. If the inflammation is in the stomach or upper intestine then the symptoms will be vomiting and stomach cramps, whereas if the inflammation is in the lower portion of the intestine, the symptoms will be diarrhoea and stomach cramps. The more severe the inflammation, the more severe the cramping, vomiting or diarrhoea will be.

There is also no way of predicting which foods an individual will be intolerant (allergic) to; this can only be determined by eating various foods and then observing whether or not they cause a problem. There is no logical reason for one person having wheat intolerance but being fine when eating dairy products or vice versa. Similarly there is no logical reason why a certain type of cat food should cause irritable bowel disease in one cat but not in another. Once we suspect that irritable bowel syndrome is the cause of the vomiting and/or diarrhoea, we would have to either run tests to determine which foods cause the problem or simply experiment with different foods to identify which foods the cat can tolerate and which cause vomiting and/or diarrhoea.

Irritable bowel syndrome may cause inflammation in the stomach only. This is called "gastritis". In these cases the lining of the stomach becomes inflamed and produces more stomach acids than normal, inducing the same sensation as "heartburn" that many people suffer from. The symptoms in this instance would be vomiting and no diarrhoea. (We must bear in mind that the vomiting may simply be the result of "garbage disease" as discussed earlier, i.e. an isolated incident where a cat has eaten food that has spoiled or simply a type of food which they have not eaten before. If garbage disease is the cause of the vomiting then the symptoms will only occur only once or only very occasionally.) If bouts of vomiting recur regularly over the long term, then irritable bowel syndrome would be a very likely diagnosis.

The most common symptom of gastritis caused by irritable bowel syndrome is that the cats seem to vomit yellow bile, usually in the mornings. This is because the increased stomach acids have accumulated in the stomach overnight and "heartburn" will stimulate vomiting to get rid of this acid. These cats will also often eat grass to stimulate vomiting. I feel that it is a common misconception that normal cats eat grass. I think that cats eat grass only when they want to make themselves vomit. Cats eat grass for the same reason that people take antacids. When a person feels stomach discomfort or heartburn they know that it is due to too much acid in the stomach so they take antacids to neutralise the acids. Cats don't know about the use of antacids but instinct tells a cat with stomach pain and heartburn to empty its stomach to get rid of the acids and any other contents. Cats are unable to stick their fingers down their throats to make themselves vomit so they do the next best thing, which is to eat something that will irritate the stomach lining enough to stimulate vomiting. Once they have vomited out the excess stomach acids they immediately feel better and continue the rest of the day without any signs of illness or discomfort. This immediate return to feeling well after vomiting is an easy way to differentiate this type of vomiting from more serious causes of vomiting.

Irritable bowel syndrome in cats more commonly causes an inflammatory/allergic reaction in both the stomach and the upper portion of the intestines. The symptoms are thus usually vomiting and diarrhoea, although often only vomiting is noticed. These cases may start as vomiting and subsequently develop diarrhoea as the problem moves from the stomach into the small intestine.

If the small intestine is the main site of the irritable bowel syndrome, then the cat may often lose its appetite, may feel lethargic and look very unwell. When the vet feels the cat's intestines by examining the cat's belly with their hands, the intestines will often feel very hard and thickened. This hard and thick feeling is caused by the inflammation and the consequent spasms (cramps) in the intestines. If these symptoms recur regularly and, as a consequence, the cat starts to lose weight, then irritable bowel syndrome would be the most likely diagnosis.

Cats with irritable bowel syndrome affecting primarily the small intestine are usually very thin, seem hungry all the time, and tend to vomit soon after eating. They do not just vomit after meals but may vomit clear fluid or bile-stained (yellow) fluid several times a day. We would have to either run tests to determine which foods cause the problem or simply experiment with different foods to identify which foods the cat can tolerate and which cause vomiting and/or diarrhoea.

Colitis is another common form of irritable bowel syndrome in cats. By definition, the term colitis implies inflammation and irritation in the colon, which is the last portion of the bowel leading to the anus (bum). The symptoms of colitis are that these patients produce frequent small amounts of soft faeces and defecate/poo much more often than normal, and seem to strain to pass these small amounts of faeces. People often mistake this straining for constipation. The faeces are not only soft or runny but also contain a lot of mucous and appear very slimy. The other symptoms include a lot of flatulence ("farting") and occasionally bright red blood in the faeces (which may then look like strawberry jam), but the cats seem bright and alert and active and have a normal appetite. This is in stark contrast to cases of small intestinal diarrhoea where the cats look very sick and lethargic and lose their appetite.

Colitis symptoms may be the result of "garbage disease" as discussed earlier, this being the result of an isolated incident where a cat has eaten food that has spoiled or simply a type of food which they have not eaten before. In these cases the same treatment which was discussed for "garbage disease" will solve the problem, i.e. withhold food for 24 hours, then feed a bland diet until normal stools are passed. If the colitis symptoms recur regularly and, as a consequence, the cat starts to lose weight, then food intolerance and irritable bowel syndrome would be suspected. We would one again have to either run tests to determine which foods cause the problem or simply experiment with different foods to identify which foods the cat can tolerate and which cause diarrhoea.

Your vet may make a presumptive diagnosis of irritable bowel disease based on the symptoms the cat has and the way the intestines feel. The only way to confirm the diagnosis with 100% certainty is the same as applies to human beings, i.e. we would have to take biopsies from the stomach, the small intestine and the large intestine. In most cases the vet will not rush straight into abdominal surgery to take biopsies because this is an invasive procedure and may involve risks to the cat. So most vets will initially treat the cat for irritable bowel syndrome and assess the response to treatment. If all the problems resolve on treatment then they have confirmed their diagnosis. If the symptoms do not resolve then they may advise taking the biopsies to confirm that the cat does have irritable bowel syndrome and not a different condition with similar symptoms. This is always worth doing because the biopsies should confirm that the diagnosis is in fact correct and the cat is simply not responding to the treatment. Similarly, the results of the biopsies may actually disprove that the cat has irritable bowel syndrome but reveal the actual diagnosis so that appropriate treatment can be instituted.

The treatment for colitis and irritable bowel syndrome is very simple. The principle of the treatment is to feed no food for 24 hours and provide only water for drinking. The rationale behind this is that the stomach and intestines are trying to empty themselves out by vomiting and diarrhoea and if we keep feeding more food the stomach and intestines will not reach a point where they are satisfied that they have emptied themselves. Once the digestive system has emptied itself it must be allowed 24 hours to rest so we withhold food for this period of time. After the 24-hour fasting period, the cat should be fed a very bland food to start the digestive system working again. This is the same approach that we apply to ourselves when we have a tummy upset, i.e. we lose our appetite and will eat nothing for a day. When we do start eating again, we tend to eat bland foods like toast and tea until the digestive system resumes normal activity and then we return to our usual foods. The same concept applies to cats; after a fasting period of 24 hours, we should feed them only very bland food types, such as boiled or roasted chicken or turkey, white fish, or commercially prepared cat food produced specifically for cats with irritable bowel syndrome. The cat should be fed this bland food in small amounts offered three or four times a day, i.e. feed small amounts often. This will restart the digestive system without asking it to work too hard.

While this bland food is being fed to the cat the vet may also advise the use of cortisone/steroids to treat the inflammation in the bowel, either with tablets or injections. The cat should be kept on this bland diet, feeding small amounts often until the vomiting or diarrhoea has stopped and two normal stools have been passed. Once the vomiting and /or diarrhoea have resolved the cortisone therapy can be withdrawn. If the symptoms recur we can assume that the bland food we are feeding the cat is also not appropriate and thus several different types of food may need to be trialled until we know what the cat can and can't eat. In some severe cases the cat may have to stay on low dose cortisone treatment for the rest of their lives just as some people with irritable bowel syndrome have to.

Most people object to the use of cortisone because they are concerned about reported side effects. I frequently encounter this objection to the use of cortisone or "steroids" and when I ask why, most people do not have a clear reason other than that they have heard that cortisone can "cause side effects". There are indeed possible side effects when using cortisone but this is true for any medication. Any chemical can produce side effects if not used correctly. Consider our use of aspirin or paracetamol to treat pain like headaches in human beings. If we take the recommended dose, then we get all the benefits without the side effects. If we exceed the dose or the duration of treatment, then we are very likely to suffer unpleasant side effects. The same applies to vitamin tablets – take the recommended number of tablets as often as advised and you will be healthy but if you take one hundred vitamin tablets at a time they may in fact kill you. So, yes, cortisone may produce side effects, but if used correctly is unlikely to cause any significant problems. Cats are in fact very resistant to the side effects of steroids, i.e. they seem to derive all the benefits but very rarely develop any side effects. The most common side effect that can occur is that some cats on permanent steroid treatment may become overweight but this can usually be prevented or corrected by adjusting the dose of the treatment. A very rare side effect of steroid treatment in cats is it may cause diabetes mellitus (sugar diabetes). This is exceedingly rare but may be very serious and indeed even life-threatening if it is not treated. The indication that diabetes may have been induced is usually that the cat seems very unwell and eats and drinks very little or not at all within a few days of starting the steroid treatment. If you notice this happening in your cat, the vet will test their blood sugar levels. If they confirm that diabetes has been induced they will treat the cat for diabetes but this is usually only required until the steroid treatment wears off, when the cat will no longer be diabetic

The cortisone (steroid) we use to control irritable bowel syndrome in cats is the same thing that millions of human beings use all over the world to control their asthma without any side effects. The most commonly used cortisones are prednisone tablets or injectable steroids like dexamethasone or depo-medrone. This type of treatment is virtually identical to the natural steroid produced in all mammals' bodies by the adrenal glands, and when we take the synthetic form as tablets or injections, the effect is to temporarily increase the natural level of cortisone in the body. There are simple rules to be followed when using cortisone which, if followed, will prevent the development of any side effects. Should any side effects occur, they will resolve when the treatment is stopped. The rules are simple: where possible use very short courses of less than three consecutive days' treatment. If more than three days of treatment is required then do not stop the treatment abruptly when the symptoms have disappeared, instead reduce the dose gradually over one or two weeks until it is withdrawn. Use the lowest possible dose to control the symptoms in each individual. Every cat is unique and will require a different dose to control their vomiting and/or diarrhoea.

The most common side effects that people report to me when their cats are on cortisone treatment are that they are slightly hungrier and sometimes drink more water and pee more. This side effect will go away when the treatment is stopped and will cause no permanent effect on the body. It is a transient side effect which is only seen in some individuals while on this treatment. The worst-case scenario is potentially a cat who needs to take cortisone (steroids) regularly throughout their life. In this situation the individual may start to get fat after a prolonged course of treatment, which may have to be adjusted to compensate. This side effect may have to be weighed up against the alternative problems encountered in the individual without treatment for their allergy. The benchmark is: which of these two options affects the overall quality of life of the individual the least? If the cat is not treated and the vomiting and/or is so severe that the cat spends most of their life severely underweight and constantly, then I would personally rather treat that individual and accept that they become slightly overweight. I feel that this side effect of long-term steroid treatment causes less of an impact on the individual's quality of life than enduring a lifetime of relentless abdominal cramps and vomiting. If I could choose to be slightly overweight rather than endure intestinal discomfort, I would certainly do so.

A new product to control allergies is soon to be launched for cats. It is called cyclosporin and it has the same effect as steroids with no side effects in most individuals. It is still a very new type of treatment and we as vets are still waiting to see what the long-term effects of this treatment might be. I have found that it seems to be an excellent treatment, not only because it has not produced side effects in the cases where I have used it, but also that it seems to work in cases where steroids do not.

The worst-case scenario of having to accept weight gain in an individual on long-term steroid treatment is rarely encountered in practice. My feeling at the outset of a case of irritable bowel syndrome is to try to find an acceptable brand or type of food to control the symptoms before I accept that there is no alternative to a lifetime of intermittent treatment with cortisone.

2c Tumours in the walls of the stomach and/or intestines

Tumours are growths of abnormal cells in the tissues of the body. The most common type of tumour in the gastrointestinal system of cats is called lymphoma or lymphosarcoma. These tumours are very aggressive and appear and enlarge very quickly. The tumour develops from lymphatic cells in the walls of the stomach and/or intestine. The lymphatic cells in the gastrointestinal system form part of the lymphatic system of the body, which in turn forms the defence mechanism of the body (the immune system). Most of the lymphatic cells in the body are found in the lymph nodes, and these occur throughout the body. The lymph nodes are all connected to each other by lymphatic ducts, which are similar to veins and transport a fluid called lymph around the body. These ducts usually run alongside veins but are rarely seen because they are transparent. The lymph nodes and their interconnecting ducts form the lymphatic system.

Each lymph node is like a mini police station which is responsible for monitoring a specific part of the body for infection or disease. If a part of the body becomes infected or diseased, the problem is drained into the lymphatic vessels in the area and taken to the nearest lymph node. Once the problem is identified by the lymph node, it will produce antibodies to fight the problem. The lymph node will attempt to contain and cure the problem in that part of the body and prevent it spreading to the rest of the body. The simplest example of this would be your tonsils. The tonsils are lymph nodes in the back of your throat which monitor the mouth and throat for infections and disease. If you develop an infection, like a cold, the tonsils will react to the problem by swelling up and fighting the infection. If the tonsils are successful then all you will experience is the original infection in the mouth or throat and swollen tonsils. If the tonsils prevent the infection from spreading then you will not feel unwell. If the tonsils are unable to contain and resolve the infection, the infection may move past the tonsils to the rest of the body. If this happens then the lymph nodes patrolling each part of the body will react as the infection moves into those parts of the body. If many lymph nodes throughout the body become activated in the fight against an infection a fever will often develop, making the person feel unwell. An example of this is when we develop a fever with flu and all the lymph nodes in the body become swollen. The swollen lymph nodes tell us that the immune system is aware of the virus spreading throughout the body and that it is actively trying to contain and kill the virus. Once the lymph nodes have killed the virus, they shrink back to their normal size and continue monitoring the body for new infections.

There are clumps of lymphatic cells in the walls of the stomach and intestines which monitor the gastrointestinal tract for infections and disease. These clumps of cells are called Payer's patches. In addition to these clumps of cells, each part of the gastrointestinal system is monitored by a network of lymph nodes which act as backup for the Payer's patches. This is a very efficient network of police stations to monitor the gastrointestinal system but it has one potential flaw: if a tumour develops in this network it may very quickly spread through it, causing a very rapid spread of cancer throughout the body's entire lymphatic system. This is precisely what happens in cases of intestinal lymphoma, i.e. cancer cells develop in one of the Payer's patches or intestinal lymph nodes and the cancer cells are carried by the lymphatic ducts to many other Payer's patches and lymph nodes along the intestinal system. The end result is that by the time we are aware that there is a cancer present it has already spread to many parts of the system.

Once a lymphoma has started to grow in the wall of the stomach or intestine it gets progressively larger until it forms a lump. The lump may then become large enough to bulge inwards into the intestine to the extent that food and ingesta cannot squeeze past the lump. The final effect is the same as if the cat had an obstruction in the intestine, preventing ingesta from passing along the intestine. The most common point at which cats develop lymphoma cancerous lumps is in the region of the ileocaecal valve, the valve connecting the small intestine to the large intestine. The effect of a lump in this area is usually vomiting because the intestine assumes it has a blockage in the small intestine and tries to vomit it out. In the early stages of the condition the cat may not appear very unwell and the only symptoms are a loss of appetite and vomiting while the cat remains fairly active and normal in other respects. As the cancer lump enlarges and spreads along the lymphatic system the cat will start to feel unwell and will lose weight quickly and vomit more often.

The vet will often diagnose the condition quite easily in these more advanced cases because the lump in the intestine can be easily felt when the cat is examined. In earlier cases the vet will often only find that the intestines feel "harder" than normal. This finding does not, however, inevitably mean that the cat has intestinal cancer as many other conditions like irritable bowel syndrome may also make the intestines feel "harder" than normal. So if the vet feels a lump in the intestine or suspects that the hardened intestines may be associated with a tumour process they will often advise tests to investigate further. These tests may involve blood tests, X-rays and ultrasound scans but usually the final step is to perform abdominal surgery to directly see what the problem is and what needs to be done. If the surgery reveals only that the intestinal wall is thickened and "harder" than normal then the vet will usually take biopsies for analysis by a histopathologist.

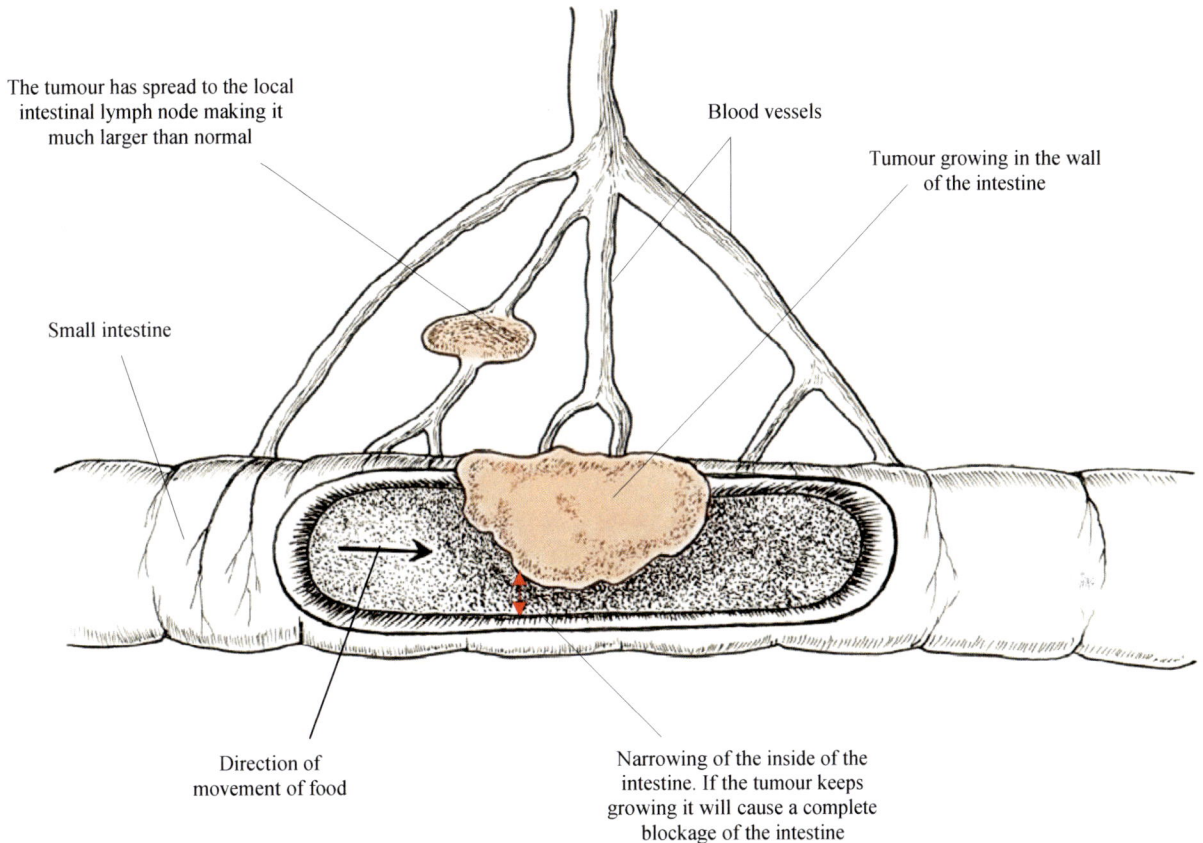

The tumour has spread to the local intestinal lymph node making it much larger than normal

Blood vessels

Tumour growing in the wall of the intestine

Small intestine

Direction of movement of food

Narrowing of the inside of the intestine. If the tumour keeps growing it will cause a complete blockage of the intestine

Fig. 11 – Cross-section of a tumour growing in the small intestine. The tumour obstructs the normal movement of food.

If the vet finds an obvious lump in the wall of the intestine which is acting like a blockage they may remove the affected portion of the intestine and send it to a histopathologist. In very advanced cases the vet may find not only the obstructive mass in the wall of the intestine but also many other smaller masses in other parts of the intestine and evidence that many of the local lymph nodes are enlarged. This may suggest that the tumour process has spread throughout the intestinal system and since one cannot remove all the intestines, the vet is only able to biopsy the abnormal-looking tissue. A specialist histopathologist would be asked to examine the abnormal tissue and they will provide a final diagnosis. It is often worth having the tissue analysed by a histopathologist even if it seems to be an obvious case of cancer for two reasons. The first reason is that the abnormal tissue may not be cancerous, i.e. the cause of the problem may be something other than cancer even though it looks like cancer to the naked eye. The second reason is that if it is cancer we need to know exactly what kind of cancer it is so that we know whether chemotherapy or radiation therapy would benefit the cat after surgery.

The tragedy of a final diagnosis of intestinal lymphoma is that it usually responds very poorly to surgery and chemotherapy and most cases will be fatal in less than nine months even if we use chemotherapy after surgery. So the dilemma we face once we have confirmed the diagnosis is what to do for the cat. The options are limited, i.e. try chemotherapy, or try symptomatic treatment to keep the cat comfortable for as long as possible, or humanely put the cat to sleep. The final decision is very personal to each individual person put in this position. I feel that each option is acceptable and the crux of the matter is the day-by-day welfare of the cat. If we use chemotherapy we should only continue the chemotherapy for as long as the cat has a good quality of life. If we use symptomatic treatment we usually use steroids to reduce the swelling caused by the cancer and this makes the cat feel better despite having cancer. Once again we should only continue this approach as long as the cat has a decent quality of life. Many people do not want to put themselves and their cat through the emotional and physical trauma of treating a terminal condition and would ask me to put the cat to sleep while they are still feeling okay to avoid future suffering. All three options are reasonable and the decision should be made by you and your vet after considering all the possibilities.

3 Vomiting and/or diarrhoea as a symptom of diseases/conditions in other organs

Vomiting and or diarrhoea may be symptomatic of diseases and conditions affecting other organ systems which then cause a knock-on effect and disturb the normal functioning of the stomach and intestines. In these instances the symptoms of vomiting and diarrhoea are not the primary problem but are symptoms associated with problems in other organs.

Examples of diseases and conditions which may produce a variety of symptoms possibly including vomiting and diarrhoea are:

- Pancreatitis
- Hyperthyroidism
- Kidney failure

3a Pancreatitis

The pancreas is a gland which is attached to the stomach and the first part of the small intestine leading from the stomach (the duodenum). The pancreas has two functions –it contains cells which produce insulin for the body and it contains cells which produce the digestive enzymes for digesting food in the intestines. The pancreas has a tube (pancreatic duct) which connects it to the small intestine and carries the digestive enzymes made by the pancreas into the intestines. The name pancreatitis is actually only a description of the problem rather than a diagnosis of what causes the problem. The word pancreatitis can be broken down into two parts: "itis" simply means inflammation and "pancreat" is derived from pancreas. Thus pancreatitis means inflammation of the pancreas. Because the pancreas actually touches the stomach and/or small intestines, inflammation in the pancreas may "jump" to those organs and so create inflammation in other parts of the gastrointestinal system.

The causes of pancreatitis in cats are not understood. Some researchers think that it may be due to bacteria in the intestine moving through the pancreatic duct into the pancreas causing an infection in the pancreas but this has not been proven. Most cases of pancreatitis occur for no apparent reason.

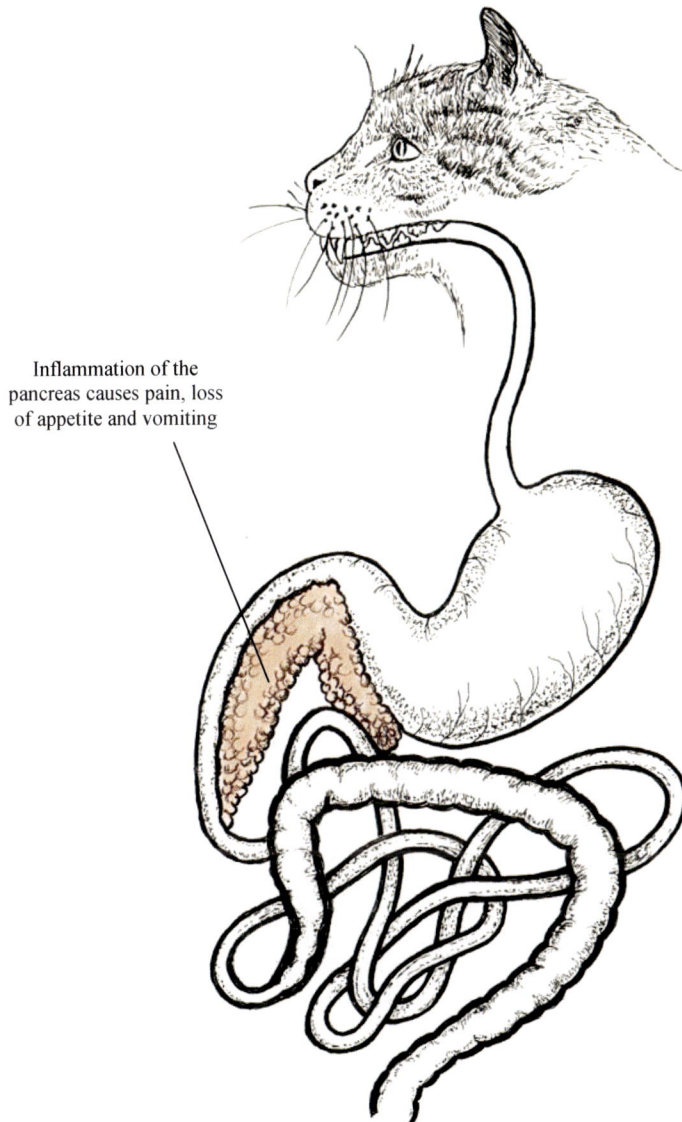

Inflammation of the pancreas causes pain, loss of appetite and vomiting

Fig. 12. – Pancreatitis

New research suggests that long-term, low-grade, intermittent pancreatitis is one of the most under-diagnosed conditions affecting cats. This means that it is much more common than we think and the reason that it is not identified more often is that the tests we traditionally use to diagnose this condition often simply fail to pick it up. This is because pancreatitis is traditionally diagnosed on blood tests but the blood test is one originally developed to diagnose the condition in human beings and is not accurate in cats. The increased use of ultrasound scanners in cats has revealed that many cats do in fact have pancreatitis even though blood tests suggest that they don't. A further problem is that it takes significant expertise to identify pancreatitis when performing an ultrasound scan of a cat's abdomen so vets in general practice may fail to make the diagnosis despite doing a scan. Specialists are often needed to accurately diagnose the condition via ultrasound scanning.

When pancreatitis occurs the pancreas becomes severely inflamed and the resulting symptoms range from just a loss of appetite, to severe pain in the cat's belly, to severe vomiting. The large range of symptoms that sufferers experience is due to the fact that the symptoms are determined by the amount of inflammation that occurs. In most cases there is only long-term low-grade inflammation with occasional vomiting, usually after eating meals. The inflammation in the pancreas causes the pancreas to swell and some of the digestive enzymes that it produces leak out of the cells that produce them. These digestive enzymes do not know the difference between the body's own tissues and food that has been eaten and they will start to try to digest the cells of the pancreas. This makes the pain and inflammation in the pancreas even worse and as the pancreas becomes more swollen, more digestive enzymes leak out and this vicious cycle makes the problem progressively worse. The pancreas is situated very close to the liver, stomach and intestines, and the inflammation may spread to these areas causing even more pain and discomfort. The inflammation in the stomach and intestines causes vomiting usually immediately after meals but often also between meals. The diagnosis may be confirmed by performing blood tests but often requires ultrasound scans of the pancreas.

Fortunately the treatment for pancreatitis is the same as general treatment for most cases of vomiting and diarrhoea so the cat can be effectively treated without making an exact diagnosis of pancreatitis. The treatment for pancreatitis involves withholding food for a day. The reason for this is that the pancreas is stimulated to release digestive enzymes into the intestine every time food arrives in the stomach. Thus, if these patients are allowed to eat, more digestive enzymes will be released every time they swallow food. The effect of this is that every time they eat or drink, more digestive enzymes will leak out of the inflamed pancreas and more damage will be inflicted on the pancreas and adjacent organs and the symptoms will become worse. The idea behind withholding food and water is thus to prevent more digestive enzymes being released by the pancreas, giving the pancreas a chance to repair itself and stop leaking enzymes. The other benefit of withholding food is that by doing so the pancreas is allowed to rest and this allows time for the inflammation to subside. If we were to continue feeding these cats, the pancreas would have to continue working and thereby inadvertently keep damaging itself, obtaining no chance to heal. In severe cases the cat should be maintained on intravenous fluids via a drip line to avoid dehydration and shock while food and water are withheld. The other components of their treatment are anti-inflammatories and antibiotics.

In cats, pancreatitis is often present in tandem with long term irritable bowel disease as discussed earlier and fortunately the long-term management for both conditions is the same.

3b Overactive thyroid function (hyperthyroidism)

Hyperthyroidism may produce a wide range of symptoms including vomiting and diarrhoea. Please refer to the chapter on weight loss for a full discussion of this condition.

3c Kidney failure (renal failure)

Kidney failure may produce many symptoms including vomiting and diarrhoea. To make sense of this, think of the kidneys simply as filters for the body even though they fulfil a great many other functions. If the filters are not removing waste products from the blood then the waste products will accumulate despite the body's attempts to reroute some of them, like urea, to other organ systems for elimination. These waste products, like any other waste products in your car or swimming pool for example, will damage the system if they are not removed.

If the kidneys are failing, the level of urea rises in the bloodstream and the body tries to eliminate the problem by other routes. The other options for elimination of high levels of urea are via the stomach and intestines or via the lungs. The process via the lungs involves releasing the urea into the air in the lungs thereby allowing its elimination when air is breathed out of the body. The problem with this route is that the exhaled urea is caustic and burns the lining of the mouth and lungs. The other alternative route of urea elimination, via the stomach and intestines, causes much the same problem. The urea released into the stomach and intestines may burn the lining of these organs and cause sufficient pain there to make the cat stop eating and, in more severe cases, the cats may also vomit and develop diarrhoea. Please refer to the chapter on weight loss for a full discussion of this condition.

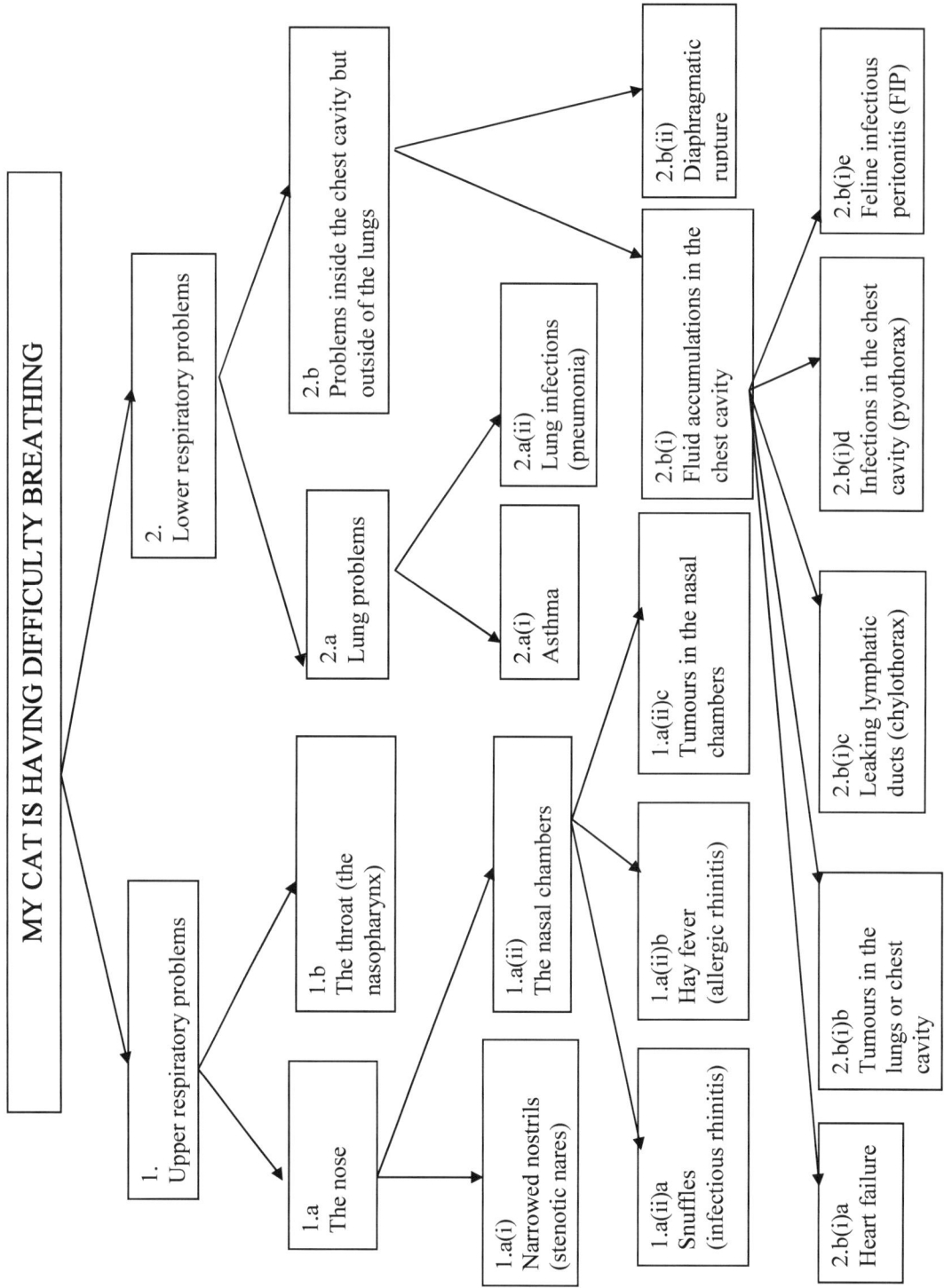

MY CAT IS HAVING DIFFICULTY BREATHING

1. Upper respiratory problems

- **1.a** The nose
  - **1.a(i)** Narrowed nostrils (stenotic nares)
  - **1.a(ii)** The nasal chambers
    - **1.a(ii)a** Snuffles (infectious rhinitis)
    - **1.a(ii)b** Hay fever (allergic rhinitis)
    - **1.a(ii)c** Tumours in the nasal chambers
- **1.b** The throat (the nasopharynx)

2. Lower respiratory problems

- **2.a** Lung problems
  - **2.a(i)** Asthma
  - **2.a(ii)** Lung infections (pneumonia)
- **2.b** Problems inside the chest cavity but outside of the lungs
  - **2.b(i)** Fluid accumulations in the chest cavity
    - **2.b(i)a** Heart failure
    - **2.b(i)b** Tumours in the lungs or chest cavity
    - **2.b(i)c** Leaking lymphatic ducts (chylothorax)
    - **2.b(i)d** Infections in the chest cavity (pyothorax)
    - **2.b(i)e** Feline infectious peritonitis (FIP)
  - **2.b(ii)** Diaphragmatic rupture

5

My Cat Is Having Difficulty Breathing

Cats are obligate nose breathers. This means that cats always breathe through their noses and refuse to breathe through their mouths except in dire circumstances. Most causes of laboured breathing in cats are very serious and potentially life-threatening. If you notice that your cat is having difficulty breathing you should seek veterinary advice and assistance immediately. If your cat is panting like a dog it is a dire emergency and you should take them to your vet immediately.

When a vet is presented with a cat who is having difficulty breathing they will act very quickly and ask you some of the following questions while they are examining your cat:

- How long have the symptoms been present?
- Does the cat seem well despite the difficulty breathing, i.e. is the cat still eating meals and are they alert and active?
- Is there any discharge from the nostrils, i.e. do they have a runny nose?

Most of the information the vet needs to make the diagnosis in these cases will be obtained by examining the cat and by performing a variety of diagnostic tests. The answers you give to their questions will help guide their thoughts which will go something like this:

The respiratory system in cats is anatomically the same as in human beings. The start of the respiratory system is the nostrils which lead into the nose. Inside the nose (the nasal chamber) are very thin plates of bone which are rolled up to resemble scrolls of paper. These scrolled bones are called the turbinate bones. The turbinate bones are covered with a thin layer of mucous membrane and the function of the turbinate bones is to remove dust from the inhaled air and to warm up the air before it moves into the body. The air moves through the nose into the larynx (the voice box) and from there it moves down the windpipe (the trachea) into the chest. The trachea runs over the top of the heart and splits into a left and right branch, or main stem bronchus. The left bronchus supplies the left lung and the right bronchus supplies the right lung. The bronchus is like the trunk of a tree which branches out into smaller and smaller branches forming the airways in the lungs. The smallest airways are called bronchioles which end in small round chambers called alveoli. It is in the alveoli that oxygen moves into the blood stream. The respiratory system can be regarded as consisting of two parts – an upper respiratory system and a lower respiratory system. The upper respiratory system consists of the nostrils, the nasal chambers, the larynx and the trachea. The lower respiratory system consists of the airways in the lungs.

The lungs lie on either side of the heart and are contained inside the chest cavity. The chest cavity is formed by the ribcage which has two functions. The ribcage is a strong solid structure which protects the heart and lungs and helps you to breathe. The back end of the ribcage is sealed off by a thin flat muscle called the diaphragm which separates the chest and the abdomen. The diaphragm's main function is breathing. The lungs fill the ribcage so that the outer surface of the lungs rests right up against the inside of the ribcage, leaving no air between the lungs and the walls of the ribcage. When we breathe in (inspiration), the walls of the ribcage move outwards slightly and the diaphragm muscle contracts to become flattened. This creates a type of vacuum in the chest between the lungs and the ribcage, effectively sucking air from the outside world into the lungs, which then expand to fill the chest. When we breathe out (expiration), the chest wall moves inwards and the air is squeezed out of the lungs. Thus during inspiration and expiration the lungs are always in contact with the chest wall even though they are not attached to the ribcage.

When the vet watches how your cat breathes they will try to decide which phase of respiration is more laboured, i.e. is the cat putting more effort into breathing in or more effort into breathing out. If the cat is having more effort breathing in then we will notice that they put more effort into expanding the chest because it is more difficult to suck air into the lungs. The cat literally seems to be trying to suck air into the chest but they breathe out normally. This is called an increased inspiratory effort and usually means that the problem is situated in the upper respiratory system. If the cat breathes in normally but seems to be forcing the rib-cage inwards during expiration then we would call this an increased expiratory effort and it usually indicates a problem in the lungs or chest cavity. The cat may even seem to make a soft grunting noise when they breathe out because they are trying so hard to force the air out of the lungs.

The vet will ask you if you have noticed a runny nose or a nasal discharge at home because cats lick their noses often and a runny nose may not be obvious when the cat is at the clinic. If the cat has a runny nose then the problem is probably situated in the nose and the cat will probably have an increased inspiratory effort. If the cat seems well despite the laboured respiration and if this labouring has been present for more than ten days, then the problem is likely to be less serious than respiratory problems which make the cat feel unwell and which seem to develop very quickly.

The vet will listen to your cat breathe. If the breathing sounds loud, noisy and "snuffly" or "nasal", they will suspect a problem in the nose. If the breathing sounds noisy and "throaty", they will suspect a problem at the back of the nasal chamber or in the throat. If the breathing sounds wheezy and/or is soft, shallow and fast, they will suspect a problem in the lungs or chest. The vet will listen to your cat's heart and lungs with a stethoscope. They will examine the nose, mouth and throat and the lymph nodes around the throat. They will also examine the rest of the cat and take their temperature. In most cases the vet will advise chest X-rays and possibly an ultrasound scan of the chest to see the heart and lungs.

I will discuss the most common causes of laboured breathing as two categories, i.e. upper respiratory problems with an increased inspiratory effort and lower respiratory problems with an increased expiratory effort.

1 Upper respiratory problems

Problems in the upper respiratory tract which interfere with breathing usually cause an increased inspiratory effort which is noisy, i.e. the cat sounds "snuffly" like people do when they have a head cold. There is usually an associated discharge from the nostrils which may not have been noticed at home because cats are fastidious creatures and lick their noses regularly to keep them clean. The appearance of this discharge will usually give us some idea of what the problem is. A clear watery discharge usually suggests a viral infection or hay fever in the nose. A yellow or green discharge would suggest a bacterial infection. A blood-tinged or bloody discharge may suggest a tumour in the nose.

1a *The nose*

The nose can be functionally divided into three components; the nostrils, the nasal chambers and the nasopharynx (the back part of the nasal chambers leading to the voice box).

1a(i) Narrowed nostrils (stenotic nares)

The medical term for the nostrils is the nares. Certain breeds of cats like Persian cats have very flat faces. These breeds may have very narrow nostrils to the extent that the nostrils are nothing more than narrow slits. This is effectively a design flaw associated with these flat-faced breeds. I mentioned earlier that cats are obligate nose breathers, i.e. they will insist on breathing through their noses despite breathing difficulties. If the cat has very narrowed nostrils (stenotic nares) they will have difficulty breathing enough air in through the nostrils with every breath they take. They may thus make a snorting or whistling noise associated with an increased inspiratory effort with every breath. These individuals often seem to be "lazy" in that they are not very active but the reason for this is simply that they cannot breathe in enough air to be more active. This is an easy diagnosis to make simply by looking at the shape of the nostrils and the way the nostrils move when the cat breathes. Other than the noisy inspiration and apparently lazy lifestyle, these cats seem perfectly normal. The problem is usually present from birth and is easily corrected with a simple operation to widen the nostrils.

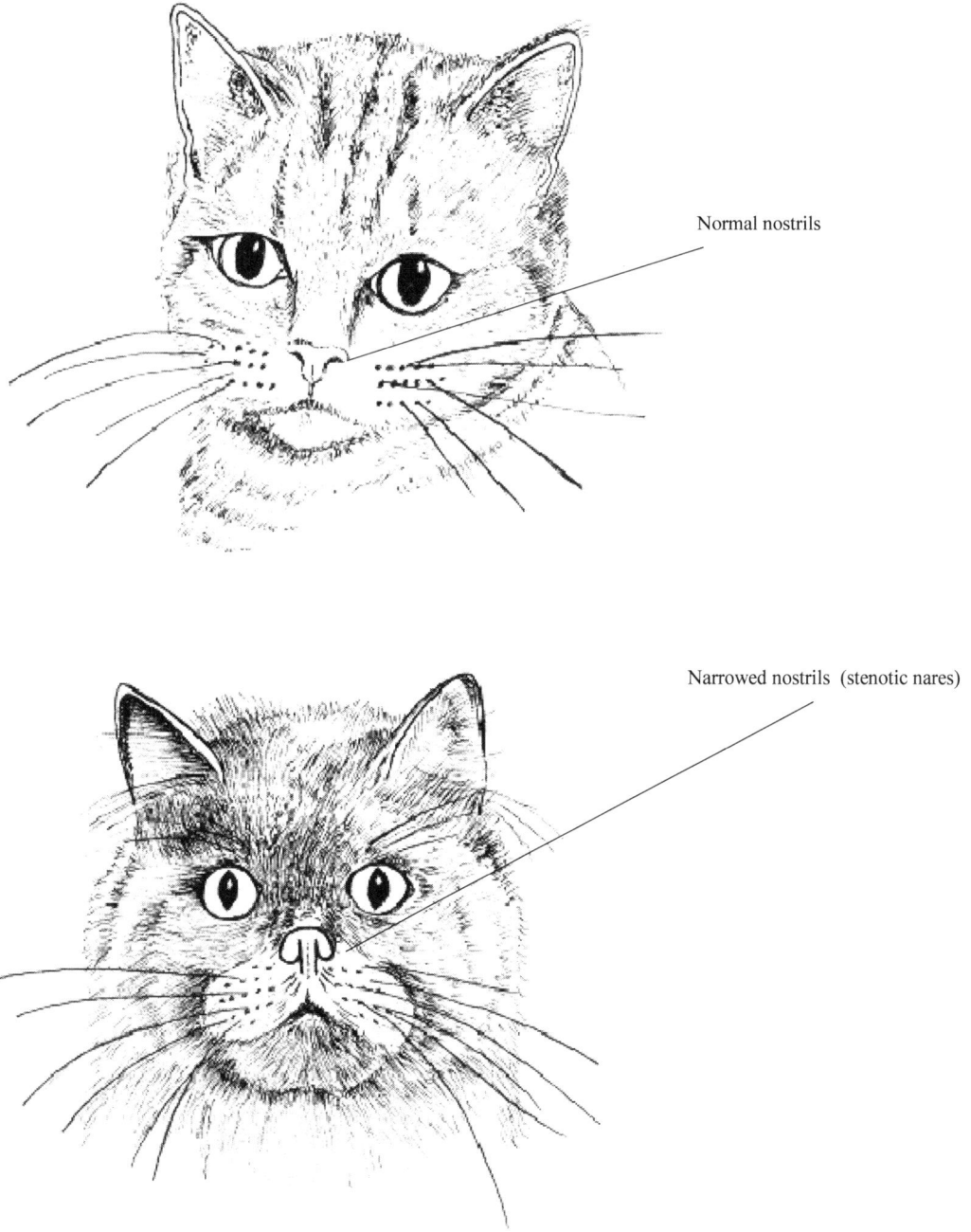

Normal nostrils

Narrowed nostrils (stenotic nares)

Fig 13. – Different facial anatomy of cat breeds with long and short noses.

1a(ii) The nasal chambers

The nasal chamber is a solid chamber within the skull and filled with the scroll-like turbinate bones. Any condition which causes inflammation and swelling of the mucous membranes covering the turbinate bones will impair the flow of air through these "scrolls", causing an increased inspiratory effort. Any condition which causes swelling of the mucous membranes in the nasal chambers is called rhinitis. "Rhin" is derived from the Latin word meaning nose and "itis" means inflammation, so rhinitis means inflammation in the nose. Rhinitis can be caused by infections, allergies and tumours in the nasal chambers so we need to accurately describe the problem as infectious rhinitis, allergic rhinitis (hay fever) or tumour-associated rhinitis.

1a(ii)a Snuffles (infectious rhinitis)

Infections in the nose are most commonly caused by viruses and bacteria. The most common viruses are the cat flu viruses called calici virus and rhinovirus. These viruses are very common in cats because they are very contagious. They are related to a large family of viruses called the herpes viruses. Most people think of venereal disease when they hear the word "herpes" but the herpes virus that causes venereal disease in human beings is only one type of herpes virus. Almost every species of mammal may become infected by a specific type of virus from the huge family of herpes viruses and each of these viruses causes very different diseases in different species. For example, cold sores, which some people develop in their mouth and on their lips, are caused by a herpes virus but not the same one that causes venereal disease.

The herpes virus which causes cold sores on people's lips is a good example of the typical behaviour of a herpes virus. People who suffer from cold sores will often develop cold sores for a while, which then disappear with time, only to reappear in a few weeks, months or years. This happens because the body is often unable to completely kill the virus, which then lies dormant in the body, hiding from the immune system. The next time that person feels tired or run-down the virus is then able to overcome the compromised immune system and flares up as cold sores on their lips again. Thus most individuals are never able to completely get rid of the herpes virus, which will intermittently flare up and cause symptoms.

The same process occurs in cats, i.e. infected cats often never completely get rid of the virus, which occasionally flares up and causes rhinitis. In cats the viruses usually only affect the nose, the mouth and the eyes because the virus likes temperatures slightly cooler than body temperature and so affects mucous membranes directly in contact with outside air as these areas are slightly cooler than body temperature. So the affected cat may have inflamed watery eyes, a runny nose and possibly ulcers on their tongue. The fluid running out of the nose is clear and watery if the infection is caused by the virus only, without secondary bacterial infection.

When the virus flares up the cats may feel unwell just as we do with a head cold. They may develop a fever and the inflammation in the nose may cause sneezing and a watery runny nose. Many cats will feel so unwell that they lose their appetite and stop eating food and stop all activity in favour of sleeping for several days. There is no treatment to cure a virus so your vet can only treat the symptoms, i.e. anti-inflammatory drugs to control the fever and inflammation. The infection usually goes away after 5–7 days but most vets will give your cat antibiotics during this time to ward off development of a secondary bacterial infection in the nose.

A secondary infection means that the bacteria were only able to infect the nose because the virus made the nose vulnerable to infection. If the virus had not weakened the nasal chamber, the bacteria would not have been able to cause an infection because the body's immune system would have been strong enough to kill the bacteria. If a secondary bacterial infection does develop then the nasal discharge will change to a thick greenish-yellow discharge and the cat may sound very "snuffly". The inspiratory effort will be laboured because they refuse to breathe through their mouths no matter how congested the nose becomes. This is why cats with recurring herpes infections with secondary bacterial infections are called "chronic snufflers" and the condition is called "snuffles". The presence of a secondary bacterial infection is usually very obvious because infected cats will often sneeze out large amounts of this yellow-green discharge onto your furniture and walls.

The vet will thus treat these cats with anti-inflammatories and antibiotics until the secondary bacterial infection is cured. Unfortunately, the problem will recur from time to time and the cat will usually need some treatment to help them through each episode.

The vet can confirm the diagnosis of viral infection using blood tests and viral cultures of swabs taken from infected cats. The secondary bacteria can also be identified by bacterial culture from swabs taken from the infected cat. In practice most vets will not need to run these tests in the initial stages of the problem but they may advise testing if the cat does not seem to be responding to treatment, or if the cat lives in a large community of cats like a breeding cattery where there may be concern about the potential to spread the disease to the other cats.

1a(ii)b Hay fever (allergic rhinitis)

Cats may develop hay fever just as people do. The symptoms in cats are the same as in humans, i.e. the inflammation and congestion in the nasal chambers causes a noisy "snuffly" inspiratory noise. There may be a clear watery discharge from the nostrils but this is often not seen as cats lick and clean their noses often. Allergic rhinitis is not common in cats and the way to differentiate between allergic rhinitis and viral rhinitis is to examine the rest of the cat. If the cat simply has hay fever then they will seem otherwise well, i.e. the appetite and activity levels and general behaviour remain as normal. In the case of viral rhinitis the cats seem unwell, with reduced appetites and reduced activity levels, i.e. the cat will seem to sleep a lot and eat less while they feel unwell just as we do when we have a cold or flu. A further distinction between the two conditions is that viral infections will usually cause a fever which can be confirmed by taking the cat's temperature. The definitive diagnosis of hay fever would require tests to confirm that there is no sign of infection in the nose and a biopsy of the mucous membranes inside the nose to confirm that these contain only allergy cells.

The treatment for hay fever is just the same as the treatment for any other allergic reaction in cats. Antihistamines have no effect on cats so if the hay fever is causing significant discomfort to the cat we would treat the problem using cortisone as required.

1a(ii)c Tumours in the nasal chambers

Tumours in the nasal chamber of cats are rare. The tumours which do occasionally develop in the nasal chambers of cats are invariably highly malignant and respond very poorly to any kind of treatment, including radiation and chemotherapy.

In the early stages of the tumour development, it can be very difficult to make the diagnosis because this can only be made by a histopathologist identifying cancer cells in a biopsy taken from inside the nasal chamber. In the initial stages of tumour development, one will often only see generalised inflammation inside the nose so the vet cannot be sure where to take the biopsy from because the tumour is not visible to the naked eye. The best the vet can do is to take a biopsy from the most inflamed part of the nasal chamber but this may not necessarily be the part with the early tumour cells in it.

In more advanced cases of tumours in the nasal chamber the diagnosis is easier to make because the tumour's position is revealed by X-rays and possibly MRI scans so the vet can be sure that they are taking the biopsy from the right spot. The clinical symptoms one would see in cases of nasal tumours usually only develop once the tumour has developed to a fairly advanced stage. The initial sign is nasal congestion with a noisy "snuffly" inspiratory sound and as the tumour progresses one may notice blood-tinged watery discharge from the nose which may develop into obvious nose bleeds. As the tumour expands inside the nasal chamber it may cause an outward bulge from the nose, usually fairly close to one of the cat's eyes. This bulge is usually not painful when touched. Once the diagnosis has been made one can consider various treatment options but as mentioned earlier nasal tumours tend to be very malignant, fast-growing cancers and respond poorly to treatment.

1b The throat (the nasopharynx)

The nasopharynx is the internal back part of the nose where it leads to the throat and windpipe. The "floor" of the nasopharynx is the soft palate. Young cats, usually less than one year old, may occasionally develop benign growths in the nasopharynx called nasopharyngeal polyps. The polyp will make the cat's breathing sound like they are gargling a large lump of phlegm or mucous in the back of their throat but they will seem otherwise well and active with a good appetite. The vet would suspect a polyp if they heard this noise in a young cat. The vet would then suggest anaesthetising the cat so that they can look into the back of the throat above the soft palate. If a polyp is present it is usually very easy to remove and when the cat wakes up from the anaesthetic their breathing is immediately normal again. These polyps are rare and almost always completely benign, i.e. they are not cancerous.

2 Lower respiratory problems

Laboured breathing caused by problems in the lower respiratory system, i.e. the lungs and chest cavity, are usually far more serious than upper respiratory problems. The symptoms are very different too, i.e. the breathing is fast, shallow, quiet (not noisy), and laboured. The expiratory effort is usually increased but in severe cases both inspiratory and expiratory effort are increased. The affected cat usually becomes very unwell very quickly. As the problem progresses the cat literally seems to be gasping for air and ultimately may start to pant like a dog. These symptoms indicate a severe life-threatening problem and you should contact your vet immediately.

Lower respiratory problems are the result of problems in the lungs, heart or chest cavity. I will discuss each of these categories individually. When the vet examines your cat with symptoms of lower respiratory disease they will usually only be able to tell you what is wrong after running some tests. The reason for this is that very different problems will all produce the same symptoms. The vet will need to identify the problem quickly because the very different causes of the symptoms will require very different types of treatment. The most important and usually the first test the vet will perform is an X-ray of the cat's chest. This will usually be followed by various laboratory tests, depending on what the vet sees on the X-ray.

2a Lung problems

2a(i) Asthma

Asthma is an increasingly common condition in cats, which very often remains undiagnosed in mild cases. Asthma in cats is exactly the same as asthma in human beings. The condition is the result of an allergic response to substances in the air that we breathe. The substances in the air that trigger the allergic reaction are called allergens. The most common allergens in cats and human beings are pollens and house dust mites.

The problem with these two types of allergens is that there is very little we can do to avoid them. There is no way of avoiding pollens in the summer and house dust mites are present in every home despite what we may do to eradicate them. The term house dust doesn't refer to the actual dust that you can see in a house. House dust means "dander". Dander is composed of the skin cells that fall off all living creatures every day. All living things shed old skin cells as the skin constantly renews itself and the effect is that millions of dead skin cells drop off into the house every day. These cells are microscopic and are eaten by microscopic house dust mites. The house dust mites produce faeces (poo) and these microscopic particles are breathed in by all the residents of your house. If a person or a cat becomes allergic to these particles they will cause asthma.

When an asthmatic person or cat breathes in allergens this triggers an allergic reaction in the lungs. The allergic reaction causes inflammation in the lungs, making the small airways in the lungs narrow as they become swollen. To make matters worse the lining of the airways produces more mucous than normal in an attempt to put up a protective barrier against what the lungs think is inflammation caused by an infection. The final effect is that the small airways in the lungs become narrower and clogged with mucous, so the affected individual will have difficulty breathing. The narrowed airways then contract and become even narrower so an asthma flare-up may therefore produce a wheezy noise during breathing because air is being forced through narrow airways.

The severity of the symptoms, i.e. how obvious the symptoms will be to you, depends on how severe the asthma is in your cat. In very mild cases you may not realise that the cat is asthmatic because when they feel wheezy and short of breath they will simply do less until they feel better. Thus many cats which sleep all day may in fact not be "lazy", they may simply be unable to breathe comfortably enough to be more active. If you observe the cat's breathing very closely you may notice that the breaths are faster and shallower than normal and occasionally the breathing may produce a soft wheezing sound. In severe cases the inflammation in the lungs may be so extreme that you will observe the cat fighting for breath, just as human beings with asthma do. The cat may obviously be putting more effort into breathing in and out but it will be evident that only small, rapid, shallow breaths are being taken.

The vet will take an X-ray of the cat's chest and will usually see things on the X-ray that suggest inflammation in the airways and other signs of asthma. The complicating factor in these cases is that asthma is not the only condition which causes inflammation in the airways. Infections like bronchitis and early pneumonia may look exactly the same on X-ray. The vet would ideally want to differentiate between asthma and infection-related inflammation by performing a bronchial lavage. This would be done by squirting a small amount of sterile saline via a catheter into the lungs and then sucking the saline back into a syringe. This fluid is then sent to a lab for various tests which include culturing and identifying infections in the lungs, or identifying allergic cells associated with asthma reactions, and identifying the possible presence of tumour cells. Thus the laboratory tests will usually identify the true cause of the inflammation. Although this test is the correct thing to do it is not always appropriate at initial presentation of the problem because restraining the cat to do the test may make their breathing worse and the added stress may be too much for them to deal with.

Most vets will make a presumptive diagnosis of an asthma attack based on the X-rays and the fact that the symptoms appeared very suddenly and very severely. The vet will treat the cat the same way people are treated when they have an asthma attack. The treatment may involve cortisone (steroid) injections to reduce the inflammation, bronchodilating injections to release the constriction of the airways, antibiotics to protect against infection, and placing the cat in an oxygen-tent filled with pure oxygen. Once the immediate life-threatening danger has passed the vet may then proceed with tests to confirm their diagnosis.

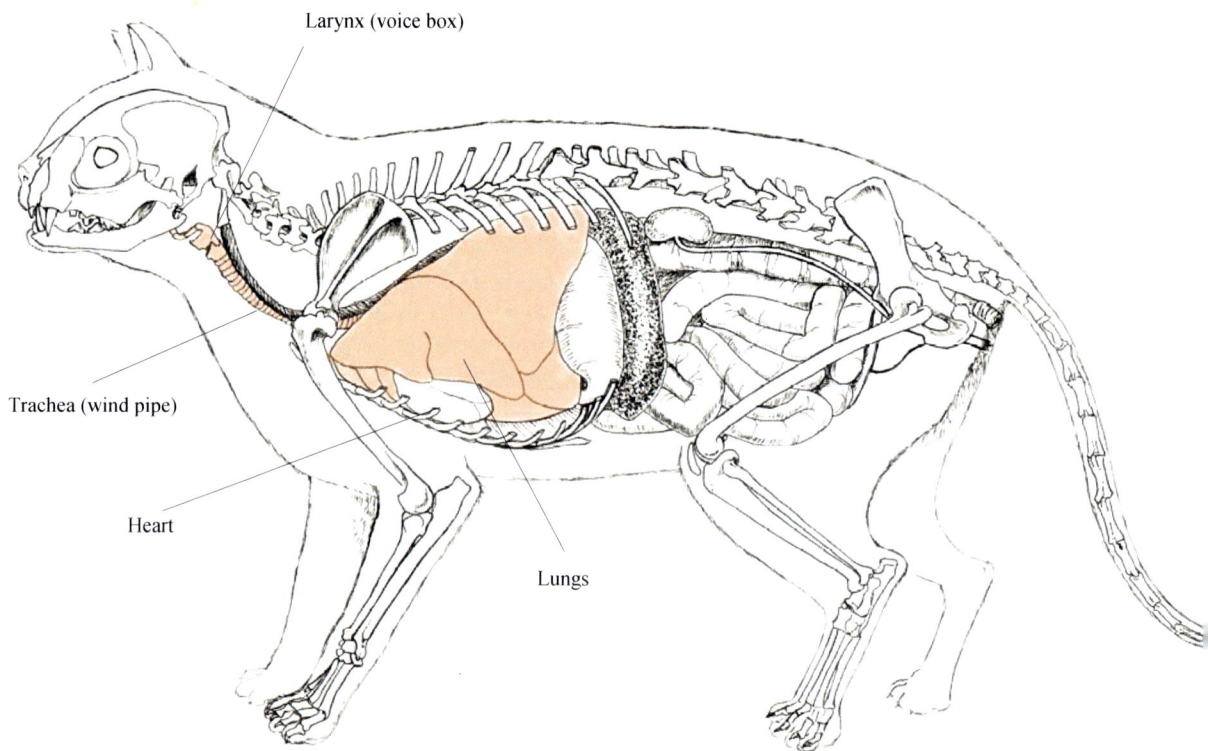

Fig 14. – Side view of a cat showing the normal size and
position of the respiratory organs.

The asthma may be a one-off event caused by something irritant the cat breathed in and in these cases the cat will not require long-term treatment. If, however, the tests reveal that the cat is a long-term asthmatic then we would want to treat them the same way human asthmatic patients are treated. Asthmatic cats can be treated daily or only when symptoms are apparent by using human asthma inhalers attached to a face mask and/or by using long-term low-dose treatment with cortisone (steroids). It is very important to treat these cats for as long as they suffer from asthma because without treatment they cannot live active comfortable lives.

2a(ii) Lung infections (pneumonia)

Viral and bacterial infections in the lungs will produce the same range of symptoms as asthma and the investigation (tests) and treatment are very similar. The major difference is that once laboratory tests have identified which virus or bacteria has caused the infection, they will also dictate exactly which antibiotic should be used. Pneumonia is not very common in cats so if it does occur one should confirm that the cat does not have a problem with their immune system. Conditions like feline leukaemia or feline AIDS may suppress the cat's immune system to the extent that they are more susceptible to infections in the same way that human AIDS patients are more susceptible to infections. Thus, if your cat is diagnosed with pneumonia you should request blood tests for feline AIDS and feline leukaemia infection. Feline AIDS and leukaemia are discussed in more detail in the chapter on weight loss.

2b Problems inside the chest cavity but outside of the lungs

As discussed at the beginning of this section your vet will always advise a chest X-ray when your cat is showing signs of a lower respiratory infection, i.e. the breathing is fast, shallow, quiet (not noisy), and laboured. The expiratory effort is usually increased but in severe cases both inspiratory and expiratory effort may be increased. The affected cat usually becomes very unwell very quickly. As the problem progresses the cat literally seems to be gasping for air and ultimately may start to pant like a dog. These symptoms indicate a severe life-threatening problem and you should contact your vet immediately.

2b(i) Fluid accumulations in the chest cavity

The X-ray may reveal that the chest cavity has filled with fluid. Fluid accumulating in the chest is called a pleural effusion. As discussed at the beginning of the chapter the chest is effectively a sealed rigid cage formed by the ribcage. If fluid accumulates in the chest the cage is not able to stretch and the only things that can change to accommodate this fluid are the lungs. As the fluid accumulates in the chest, the lungs are compressed and are gradually crushed by the fluid accumulation around them. The cat will thus have more and more difficulty breathing as the lungs are unable to expand and fill with air. Once the vet has identified that there is fluid in the chest they will need to remove the fluid and have it analysed to identify what it is and why it is in the chest. If the vet has an ultrasound scanner they may decide to scan the chest before draining off the fluid because the fluid improves the effectiveness of a scan. The idea behind the scan is to look for any abnormalities that may explain why the fluid has accumulated. The vet will only do the scan if the cat's life is not in immediate danger because of the fluid in the chest. If the cat's condition is too serious to delay draining the chest the vet will forego the scan.

The vet will initially remove the fluid with a needle and syringe or they will insert a chest drain. This is potentially dangerous for the cat because if they jump around or fidget while the needle is in their chest the tip of the needle may damage their lungs. Fortunately most cats feel so unwell with this condition that they will allow the fluid to be drained without putting up a struggle. Once the fluid is drained off it is sent to a lab to be analysed. The cat will immediately feel better once the fluid has been drained off but it may take a few days before the crushed lungs are able to fully expand again.

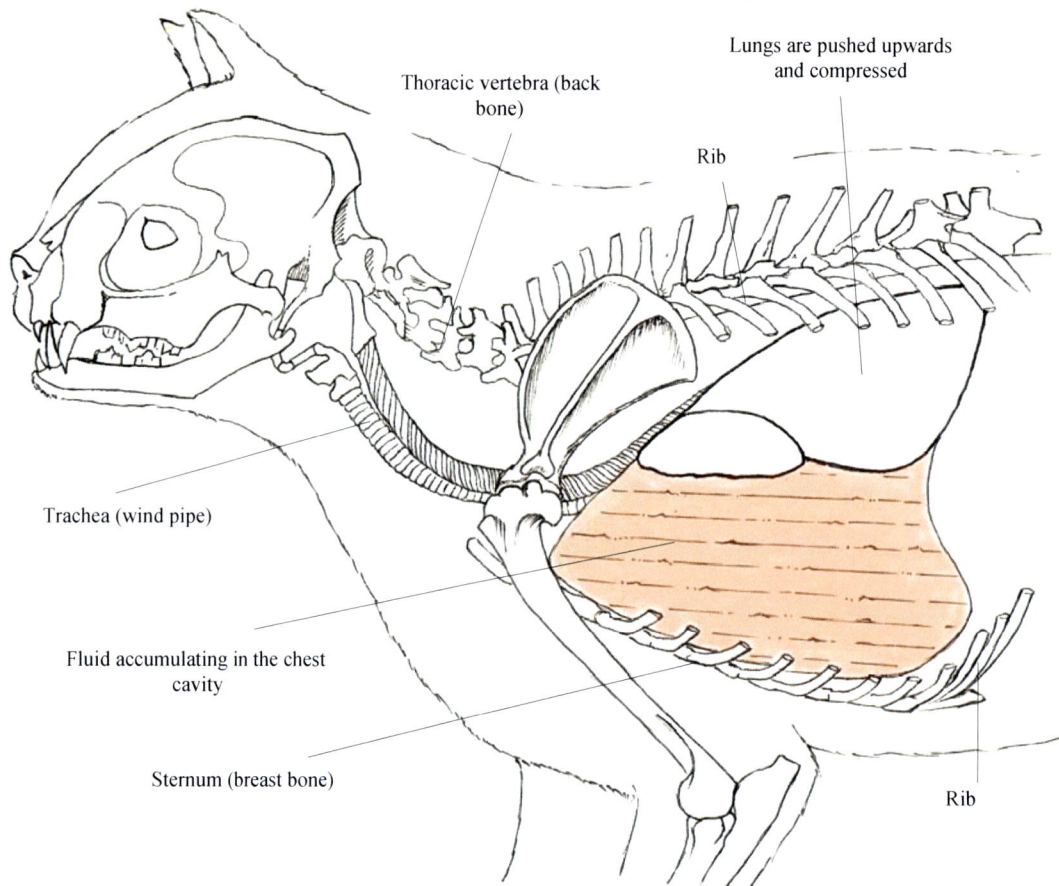

Fig 15. – Side view of the chest with ribs cut away to expose chest cavity. Fluid may accumulate in the chest cavity for a variety of reasons. The effect of the fluid in the chest is always the same i.e. the lungs are compressed and the cat will have great difficulty breathing. In severe cases, affected cats will start panting like a dog.

I usually take another chest X-ray immediately after draining the chest and then every day after this to ensure that the lungs are re-expanding and that more fluid is not re-accumulating while I am waiting for the test results. Once the fluid has been drained off the cat will be given supportive treatment which may include rest in an oxygen tent, antibiotics, anti-inflammatories and diuretics. Diuretic treatments are designed to make patients produce more urine and the body responds to this demand by re-routing any remaining fluid in the chest cavity to the kidneys to make more urine. If a chest drain has been put into the cat's chest it will usually be left in position until the lab results are back and follow-up X-rays confirm that the fluid is not re-accumulating.

Once the fluid (pleural effusion) has been analysed and identified we will usually be able to explain why it was produced and why it accumulated in the chest and then we will be able to adjust the treatment accordingly. The most common causes of pleural effusion (fluid) are:

- Heart failure
- Tumours in the chest cavity or lungs
- Leaking lymphatic ducts
- Infections (pus)
- Feline infectious peritonitis (FIP)

Each of these conditions produces a specific type of fluid accumulation and each condition requires a specific type of treatment. I will discuss each condition individually.

2b(ii)a Heart failure

Heart conditions may cause congestive heart failure. The name congestive heart failure accurately describes the problem, i.e. the fact that the heart is failing causes congestion in or around the lungs or other parts of the body. Heart failure means that the heart is failing to work as well as it should.

The heart is simply a pump which pumps blood around the body. The heart, the blood and all the veins and arteries and capillaries in the body form the cardiovascular system (circulatory system). One can think of the circulatory system as a system of pipes which carry liquid throughout the body. The liquid (blood) is pumped through this system of pipes (blood vessels) by a pump (the heart). The pipes which lead away from the pump are called arteries and the pipes which lead back to the pump are called veins. The arteries are connected to the veins by very small pipes called capillaries. The left side of the heart pumps blood to and from the body and the right side pumps blood to and from the lungs. The right side thus pumps blood into the lungs where oxygen is absorbed and carbon dioxide is released. The blood is now full of oxygen and returns to the heart .The left side of the heart then pumps the blood to the rest of the body where the oxygen is absorbed by the cells of the body. The carbon dioxide released by the body's cells moves into the blood to be carried back to the lungs to be breathed out as waste. The arteries, veins and capillaries thus lie in between the alveoli and air tubes in the lungs.

Heart failure simply means that the pump in the circulatory system is not working properly. This means that the liquid (the blood) does not move through the pipes properly either. The result is that, as the pump fails, it pumps less fluid forward each time it pumps. Because the total amount of fluid in the pipes remains the same, this means that fluid returning to the pump isn't pumped through as quickly as it should be because more fluid is arriving at the pump than is being pumped away from it. Compare this to a dam which is used to pump water to irrigate fields. If heavy rains cause the dam to fill up faster than the dam pumps can empty the water into the fields, the dam will fill up and overflow. A similar process happens in the case of heart failure and fluid builds up in the pipes returning to the pump. As more fluid accumulates in these pipes (the veins), they start to overflow, leaking clear fluid ("water") out of the veins which then accumulates in and around the organs in the body. If this "water" accumulates in the chest cavity around the lungs it will compress the lungs making it difficult for the cat to breathe. The overflow of water is the result of congestion in the veins which is why the condition is called congestive heart failure.

The vet will determine the cause and type of heart condition and will treat the symptoms. It is important to stress that all treatments for heart conditions simply help the heart to function better and alleviate the symptoms caused by the failing heart. The treatment does not "fix" the problem. The only way to "fix" most heart conditions would be to replace the heart (pump) with a brand new pump. This is not realistic because replacing a heart is not as simple as replacing a pump in a piece of machinery. So the treatment the vet uses will be chosen depending on the exact nature of the problem with the pump.

The most common heart condition in cats is hypertrophic cardiomyopathy (HCM). In this condition the heart muscle forming the walls of the heart chambers becomes thickened, usually most obviously on the internal surfaces of the heart chambers. This reduces the volume of the chambers as the heart muscle becomes thicker and as a result less blood can be pumped by each heartbeat. This leads to the "damming up" and "overflow" effect discussed earlier causing fluid to accumulate in the chest cavity.

Another increasingly common heart condition is restrictive cardiomyopathy. This condition is not very well understood but its net effect is to restrict movement of the heart muscle thus reducing the quantity of blood pumped with each heartbeat, which again causes fluid to accumulate in the chest cavity.

The third and least common heart condition is dilated cardiomyopathy. In this condition the heart muscle becomes stretched and loses its ability to contract properly. The end result is once again that fluid "dams up" and accumulates in the chest cavity and compresses the lungs.

Most cats will need to have their heart scanned with an ultrasound scanner to identify what the heart problem is.

Most cases of congestive heart failure are treated with a combination of medications. The most common medicine that appears in most combinations of treatment is a diuretic. Many people call diuretic tablets "water tablets". This is because diuretic tablets work by making the body produce more urine and thus pee more often. If the diuretic makes the kidneys produce more urine, the kidneys will have to take more "water" from the blood to make this extra urine. So because "water" has been extracted from the blood there is less fluid for the heart to pump around the body and so less fluid accumulates in the veins while waiting to be pumped by the heart. The end result is that the heart has less work to do and less congestion develops because less blood is accumulating in the veins and so less water is leaking out of them. Once less water is leaking out of the veins, less water accumulates in the airways and so the cough either becomes less severe or goes away entirely.

The normal size and shape of the heart in the chest cavity.

Normal thickness of the wall of the heart

The walls of the heart are much thicker than normal

Normal size of the heart chamber (left ventricle)

The heart chamber is much smaller than normal

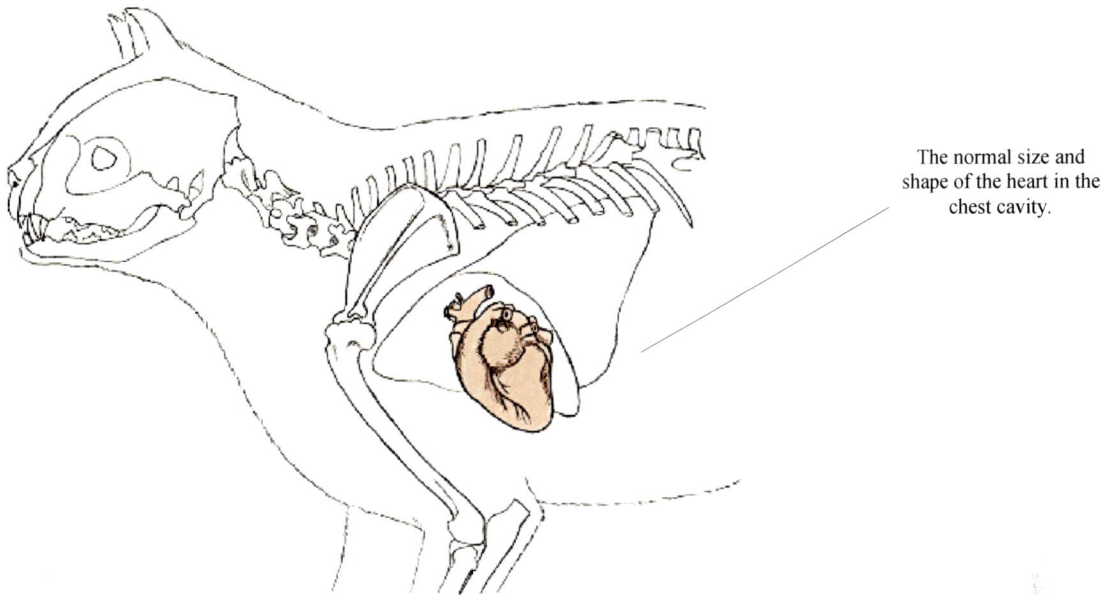

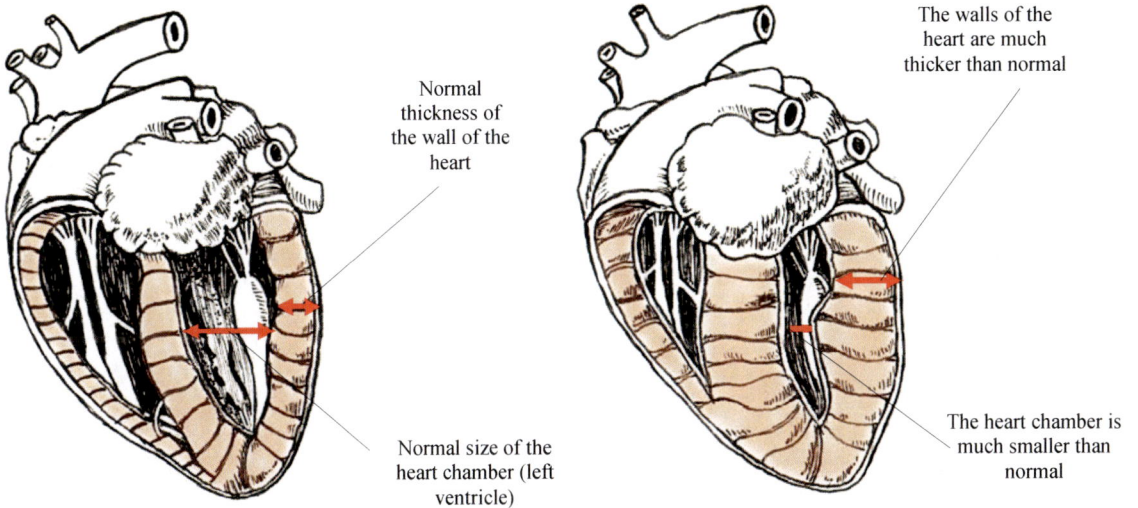

Cross-section of a normal heart

Cross-section of a heart with hypertrophic cardiomyopathy. From the outside this heart may appear normal in size and shape but the inside is very abnormal.

Fig 16. – Comparison between a normal heart and a heart with hypertrophic cardiomyopathy

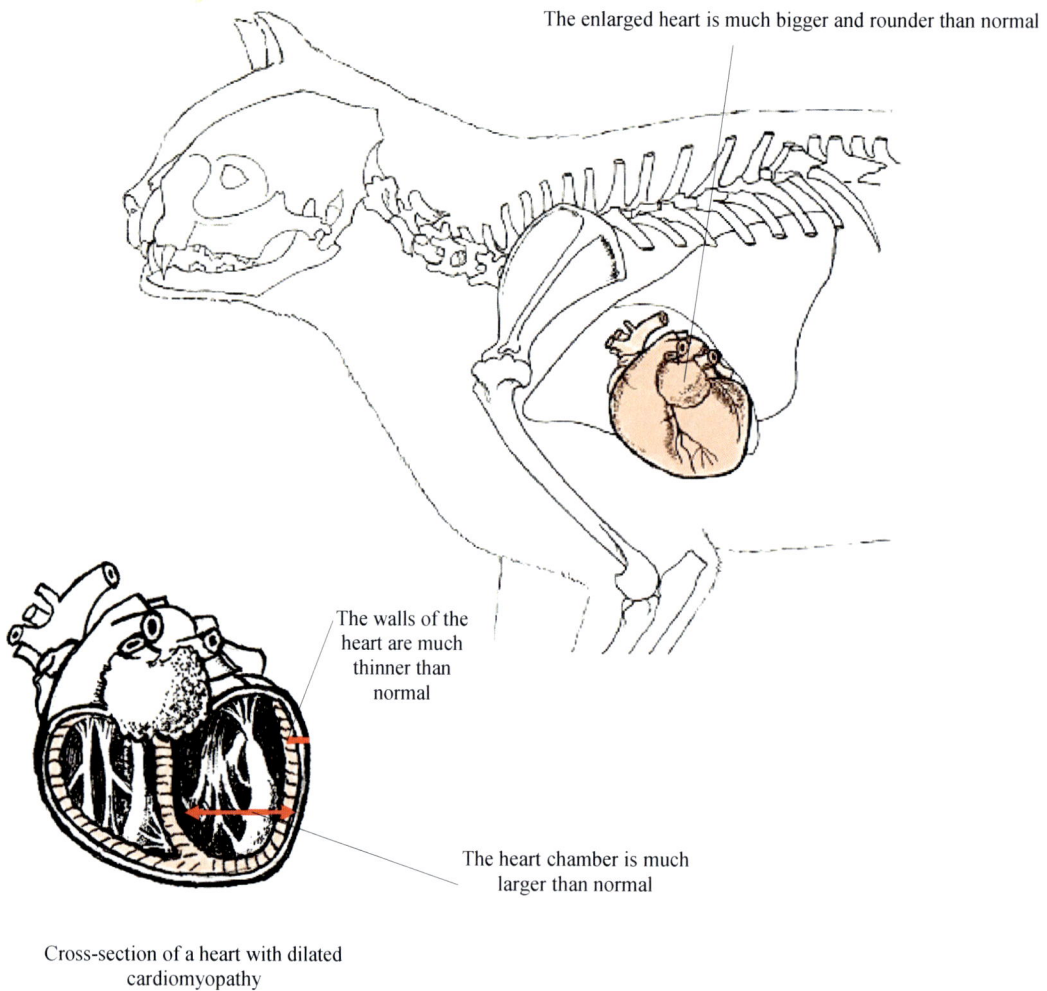

The enlarged heart is much bigger and rounder than normal

The walls of the heart are much thinner than normal

The heart chamber is much larger than normal

Cross-section of a heart with dilated cardiomyopathy

Fig 17. – Dilated cardiomyopathy

The other medications used will help the heart function through different methods and the choice of medicine depends on the precise problem with the heart muscle. The combination of treatments used is intended to help the heart in as many ways as possible so that it can function at optimum efficiency.

Heart failure is a gradual process which progressively worsens over a period of months to years. When the heart (the pump) initially starts to fail (work less efficiently), the patient will not be aware that there is a problem. This is because the body is able to activate a variety of compensatory mechanisms which effectively manufacture natural, internal medications to treat the problem. It is only when the body runs out of this naturally produced medicine that the patient will start to show symptoms of heart failure. In human beings the body runs out of this internally produced medicine very quickly so we show symptoms of heart failure at an early stage in the process. Imagine that heart failure goes through ten stages, numbered one to ten, with one being the initial stage and ten being the final stage before death. The reason that the patient dies after stage ten is that the heart problem is so severe that it cannot respond to treatment any more. In human beings the naturally produced medication runs out at about stage two so when the doctor prescribes medicine to treat the problem, the heart will be able to respond to the medicine until it reaches stage ten. When this happens the heart is so worn out that it can no longer respond to the medicine and the person dies. This gives us the impression that human beings respond very well to heart medication and that we can live for a long time on this medication. Cats, on the other hand, medicate themselves very successfully right up to stage nine. This means that heart failure symptoms like fluid accumulating in the chest only appear when the heart is already at stage nine of the failure process. Thus even though we then start the appropriate treatment when the symptoms appear, the heart is actually almost at the point where it cannot respond to treatment. This therefore creates the impression that cats do not respond to heart medication as well as human beings do. The truth is that they do in fact respond just as well as we do but they are so efficient at producing their own medicine that by the time symptoms appear and treatment is indicated, the heart has already reached the stage where it is no longer able to respond to any medication. So they have actually been living with the condition for just as long as the human heart-failure patient, the only difference being that people need to take tablets from stage two whereas cats medicate themselves up to stage nine. When either the person or the cat reaches stage nine they are both unable to respond to medication and will die at stage ten.

This brings me to the crux of the problem when we try to treat a cat with heart failure and fluid accumulating in the chest. The reason that the cat has suddenly developed this fluid accumulation in the chest is that the body has abruptly run out of naturally produced medicine. We can drain this fluid away and start the correct treatment but most of these cats are now at stage nine of the heart failure process when the heart is at the stage where it cannot really respond very well to the medication because it is so worn out. The result for the cat is that they don't generally respond very well to the medicine we give them and the fluid usually re-accumulates within a few weeks. At this point the cat will once again develop very sudden and very severe breathing problems as the lungs are crushed by the accumulation of fluid. We can drain the fluid again and again but it will simply re-accumulate faster and faster despite treatment until the heart reaches stage ten and can no longer respond to treatment, and the cat will die. My feeling is therefore that I would recommend draining the chest only once or twice and once the cat has reached stage ten I would advise humanely putting them to sleep. Otherwise, the death they are facing is effectively death by suffocation, which is a dreadful way to go. I would discuss all these points with the cat owner and the intention would be to let the cat go before they are in a constant state of suffering.

2b(i)b Tumours in the lungs or chest cavity

Many types of tumours may develop in the lungs and chest cavity. These tumours may cause fluid to accumulate in the chest through a variety of different mechanisms. The symptoms of tumour fluid accumulating in the chest will be the same as for all the other types of pleural effusions, i.e. rapid, shallow, laboured respiration. The vet will be able to identify the presence of a tumour by using a combination of tests like X-rays, ultrasound scans, MRI scans and analysis of the pleural effusion. Once we know that a tumour is causing the accumulation of fluid in the chest we need to identify the exact type of tumour to determine what we can do about it. Some tumours can be removed surgically, some can be treated with radiation and/or chemotherapy and some will not respond to any treatment at all. Thus the vet will need to get a biopsy of the tumour so that they can advise you on the best course of treatment.

2b(i)c Leaking lymphatic ducts (chylothorax)

There are thousands of lymph nodes situated throughout your body. The only lymph nodes that most people are commonly aware of are the tonsils. The other thousands of lymph nodes throughout the body are exactly the same but they are not readily visible. The lymph nodes are all connected to each other by tubes called lymphatic ducts, which transport lymph fluid from one lymph node to another. Most lymphatic ducts run alongside arteries and veins but are never seen because they are transparent. Think of each lymph node as a police station and the ducts as information channels between the police stations. All the lymph nodes together effectively form the immune system which monitors the body for infection and disease. Occasionally one of the large lymphatic ducts in the chest may develop a leak and this lymphatic fluid (lymph) starts to accumulate in the chest cavity. The technical term for lymphatic fluid accumulating in the chest cavity is chylothorax. As more and more lymph accumulates it will start to compress the lungs and the cat will develop the typical breathing difficulties associated with a pleural effusion, i.e. rapid, shallow and laboured respiration. The initial investigation is once again an X-ray which reveals the presence of fluid in the chest which must be drained off and sent to a laboratory for identification and analysis. Once the lab has identified the fluid as lymphatic fluid the vet will need to determine why a lymphatic duct is leaking in the chest. This is very difficult to do and may require many complicated tests and possibly even exploratory chest surgery. Many of these cases simply resolve themselves, i.e. the leak seems to repair itself, meaning there is no need for further investigation but if this does not happen we must find and repair the leak otherwise the fluid will simply keep re-accumulating.

2b(i)d Infections in the chest cavity (pyothorax)

The fluid that accumulates in the chest cavity may be pus. The initial symptoms are much the same as for any other type of pleural fluid, i.e. the cat develops breathing problems and the breaths are rapid and shallow and the cat looks very unwell. Most cats with pus accumulating in the chest cavity will have a high temperature associated with the infection. The technical term for pus accumulating in the chest is pyothorax. Once the vet has taken the initial X-rays and has identified that the cause of the problem is a pleural effusion they will drain the fluid off the chest. It will be very obvious to the vet that the fluid is pus but they will still send the fluid for analysis because they need to know which bacteria is causing the infection and which antibiotic will cure it. Once the vet has drained the pus from the chest the lungs will start to re-inflate and the cat will immediately feel a bit better. Cats with such large accumulations of pus in the chest are usually very ill because of the septic effect of the pus.

The pus in the chest cavity has a toxic effect on the body and these cats will usually need intensive care to avoid toxic or septic shock. They will need to be connected to a drip line to flush the toxins out of their body and support the blood pressure. I would also immediately start the cat on a combination of two antibiotics and an anti-inflammatory drug to bring down the fever while waiting for the laboratory report. Most of these cats will need to have a chest tube inserted into the chest and kept there for several days. This tube is used to rinse out the inside of the chest with saline solution and antibiotics to clear any re-accumulation of pus. In most cases of pyothorax we are unable to find any sign of penetrating wounds or injuries to the chest to explain how the infection started. So more often than not the cause of the problem is never identified but if we can get the cat through the toxic shock stage and successfully clear the infection most of them never have a relapse.

2b(i)e Feline infectious peritonitis (FIP)

Feline infectious peritonitis is a viral infection that causes large amounts of straw-coloured fluid to accumulate in the body. The fluid usually accumulates in the abdomen but may accumulate in the chest. If the fluid accumulates in the chest the lungs will be compressed and the cat will develop the symptoms associated with any pleural effusion, i.e. rapid, shallow and laboured breathing. The infection also causes a high temperature (fever) so the cat will appear very sick. Once the vet has taken the initial X-rays and has identified that the cause of the problem is a pleural effusion they will drain the fluid off the chest. If the fluid is yellow or straw-coloured and the cat has a fever the vet will be immediately suspicious that the cat may be infected with the FIP virus. Once the vet has drained the fluid from the chest the lungs will start to re-inflate and the cat will immediately feel a bit better. The vet will send the fluid and blood samples to a laboratory for analysis.

The FIP virus, once it has infected a cat, may move into any organ in the body. The laboratory tests on the fluid and blood samples will give a high probability that the cat is infected with the virus but often the only way to prove that FIP is the cause of the problem is to take a biopsy from tissue which contains the virus. This may be difficult to achieve if it is not clear which organs are affected but the vet will usually recommend a liver biopsy because the virus often settles in the liver in addition to any other organs which may be infected. Once the vet has made a diagnosis of FIP the long-term outlook for the cat is poor. Some cats will recover from the infection but in most cases it is fatal.

2b(ii) Diaphragmatic rupture

The diaphragm is a broad thin muscle which separates the chest from the abdomen. It is the most important muscle used for breathing. If a cat is subjected to a severe shunting injury like being hit by a car, this thin muscle may rupture/tear and any variety of abdominal organs like the liver, the spleen, the stomach and the intestines may be pushed through this tear into the chest cavity. Once the diaphragm has been ruptured and abdominal organs slide forward into the chest cavity, the lungs will in turn be pushed forwards in the chest cavity. The net effect is that the abdominal organs compress the lungs and the diaphragm is unable to assist in the breathing process. The lungs are therefore not able to expand and fill with air so the clinical symptom we will see is that the cat has laboured breathing and is only able to take rapid shallow breaths. If many abdominal organs are shunted into the chest the cat's breathing may deteriorate and we will see that the breathing has been reduced to short rapid gasps or panting like a dog. The vet will take X-rays of the chest as a standard first step in dealing with any case of lower respiratory tract symptoms. The X-ray will reveal the presence of a torn/ruptured diaphragm and it will also reveal which abdominal organs have been displaced into the chest and the extent to which the lungs are able to expand.

It takes a significant impact to produce this injury so the cat should be thoroughly examined for any other injuries. Even if no other injuries are found, careful examination of the cat's claws will usually reveal that their tips are torn or scuffed. This happens when the impact shunts the cat across the ground and the cat tries to cling to the ground with their claws. As they slide across the ground the claw tips are scuffed and torn. If other injuries are found the vet will prioritise the importance of each injury in terms of how life-threatening it is. Usually the diaphragmatic rupture is the highest priority and should be dealt with first. If possible the vet will want to take a few hours to stabilise the cat as the trauma may have induced shock. To address this the vet will usually start an intravenous drip line to provide cardiovascular support and place the cat in an oxygen tent. Once the cat's condition is stable the vet will schedule surgery to repair the torn diaphragm. The cat is usually unable to breathe by themselves so the anaesthetist will need to breathe for the cat until the surgeon has placed the abdominal organs back in the abdomen and has sutured the torn diaphragm. Once the chest has been re-sealed the cat should be able to breathe by themselves and most cats recover uneventfully after surgery.

6

MY CAT HAS AN EYE PROBLEM AND/OR A RUNNY NOSE AND/OR IS SNEEZING

This chapter should really be split into one on eye problems and one on nose problems individually, but this would mean that there would be a lot of repetition in the two chapters. This is because many conditions which affect the eyes will also affect the nose and vice versa. I have therefore tried to combine two chapters into one which means that you will need to read the whole chapter even if it seems obvious to you that the problem specifically affects only the eyes or only the nose. I have tried to separate the two systems to some extent to make the task of referencing the symptom easier.

1 The nose

The cat's nose can be regarded as consisting of three parts just like a human nose. These are the nostrils, the nasal chamber and the nasopharynx (the back of the nose leading into the throat).

The nasal chamber is the space leading from the nostrils to the back of the throat. The floor of the nasal chamber is the hard and soft palate that also acts as the roof of the mouth. The back of the nasal chamber opens into the back of the throat where the air breathed in moves into the opening of the voice box (trachea). The nasal chamber is divided into a left and right chamber leading back from the left and right nostril respectively. There is a thin plate of bone called the vomer bone that forms the wall between the left and right nasal chambers. Inside each nasal chamber there are turbinate bones, positioned one on top of the other. Each turbinate bone is like a rolled-up piece of paper that is positioned lengthways along the nasal chamber, and is covered by a mucous membrane. The front opening of this rolled-up wafer-thin bone is just inside the nostril and the back opening of each turbinate bone leads to the back of the throat. The turbinate bones warm up air before it is passed to the lungs and also filter out particles in the air such as dust particles.

MY CAT HAS AN EYE PROBLEM AND/OR A RUNNY NOSE AND/OR IS SNEEZING

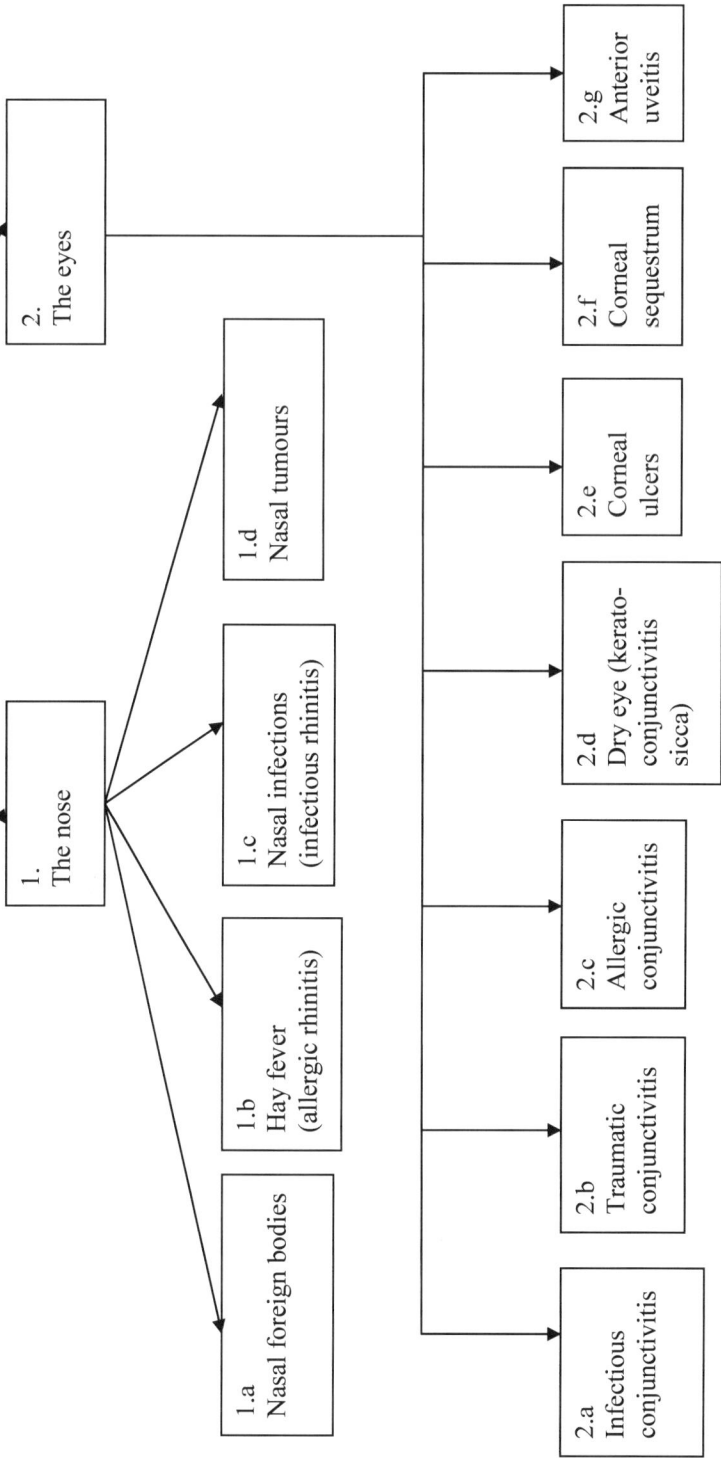

```
                        ┌─────────────┐
                        │ 1.          │
                        │ The nose    │
                        └─────────────┘

┌──────────────┐  ┌──────────────┐  ┌──────────────┐  ┌──────────────┐
│ 1.a          │  │ 1.b          │  │ 1.c          │  │ 1.d          │
│ Nasal        │  │ Hay fever    │  │ Nasal        │  │ Nasal        │
│ foreign      │  │ (allergic    │  │ infections   │  │ tumours      │
│ bodies       │  │ rhinitis)    │  │ (infectious  │  │              │
│              │  │              │  │ rhinitis)    │  │              │
└──────────────┘  └──────────────┘  └──────────────┘  └──────────────┘
```

```
                        ┌─────────────┐
                        │ 2.          │
                        │ The eyes    │
                        └─────────────┘

┌──────────────┐ ┌──────────────┐ ┌──────────────┐ ┌──────────────┐ ┌──────────────┐ ┌──────────────┐ ┌──────────────┐
│ 2.a          │ │ 2.b          │ │ 2.c          │ │ 2.d          │ │ 2.e          │ │ 2.f          │ │ 2.g          │
│ Infectious   │ │ Traumatic    │ │ Allergic     │ │ Dry eye      │ │ Corneal      │ │ Corneal      │ │ Anterior     │
│ conjunctivitis│ │ conjunctivitis│ │ conjunctivitis│ │ (kerato-     │ │ ulcers       │ │ sequestrum   │ │ uveitis      │
│              │ │              │ │              │ │ conjunctivitis│ │             │ │              │ │              │
│              │ │              │ │              │ │ sicca)       │ │              │ │              │ │              │
└──────────────┘ └──────────────┘ └──────────────┘ └──────────────┘ └──────────────┘ └──────────────┘ └──────────────┘
```

The ethmoid bone is a sponge-like structure at the back end of the nasal chambers that is covered by a special type of mucous membrane which provides our sense of smell. This mucous membrane lines all the small nooks, crannies and small tubes inside the ethmoid bone. The reason for the bone's sponge-like structure is that it allows the mucous membrane to cover a much larger surface area than if the membrane simply covered a solid piece of bone the same size as the ethmoid bone.

The nasopharynx is the internal back part of the nose where it leads to the throat and windpipe. The "floor" of the nasopharynx is the soft palate.

The nasal sinuses are hollow "air pockets" in the skull bones. The most important of these are called the frontal sinuses and they are found in the frontal bone forming the forehead. These "air pockets" are hollow chambers in the skull bones that are lined with a mucous membrane and are connected to the nasal chambers. People who suffer from hay fever and sinusitis will be well aware of the frontal sinuses because allergic inflammation in these sinuses causes the feeling of congestion, headaches and the "bunged-up" feeling associated with hay fever.

The symptoms of sneezing and/or discharge from the nostrils tell us that there is inflammation and irritation in the nasal chambers and their turbinate bones. This irritation and inflammation can be caused by allergic inflammation (hay fever), infections, tumours or particles such as dust, pieces of grass, etc. which have become stuck in the mucous membranes in the nasal chamber or turbinate bones. Inflammation in the nose is called rhinitis.

When a vet examines a cat which is sneezing and/or has a discharge from the nostrils, the vet's questions will help them to explain the cause of the problem. The problem that the vet will face during the consultation is that very often the final diagnosis can only be made after various tests have been performed because many different causes of sneezing and nasal discharge will often produce exactly the same symptoms.

The vet's thoughts and questions will proceed along the following lines.

- Is the cat just sneezing or is there also a discharge from one or both nostrils?
- If there is a discharge from the nostrils is it coming from one or both of the nostrils?
- What does the discharge look like?
- How long have the symptoms been present?
- Did the symptoms appear very suddenly or did they gradually develop over a longer period of time?
- Apart from the sneezing and/or discharge does the cat seem fit and well or do they appear ill?
- Are the nostrils or the muzzle of the cat painful when touched?
- Is the cat still eating food?

If the cat is just sneezing and there is no nasal discharge and the symptoms developed gradually over a period of a few days or weeks then the irritation in the nose may be to due to allergic inflammation (hay fever) or mild infection. If the cat suddenly started sneezing frequently and very forcefully and there is no nasal discharge then it is quite likely that a foreign body, like a piece of grass, has recently lodged in the nasal chamber or nasopharynx. If the sneezing started very suddenly after the cat ate grass then it is very likely that a blade of grass has lodged in the nasopharynx.

If the cat has a nasal discharge then we must try to determine if it is coming from one or both nostrils and we must try to determine what the discharge looks like. If the discharge is mostly pus and coming from only one or both nostrils then one might suspect an infection in the nasal chamber. This infection may be due to a foreign body being lodged in the nasal cavity for more than several days or it may be due to a viral or bacterial infection. Bacterial infections may cause a pus-like discharge from one or both nostrils and the amount of sneezing may vary from a lot of sneezing to none at all. If there is a clear watery discharge from one or both nostrils then one might suspect a viral infection or allergic inflammation (hay fever). If the discharge is a clear fluid which contains blood and is coming from only one nostril and has developed over a period of several days to several weeks, then one might consider the presence of a tumour in the nasal chamber. If the cat appears very ill or if the nostrils or the muzzle are painful then one would consider severe infection or possibly a tumour to be the cause of the problem.

The standard way of testing a cat with sneezing and/or a nasal discharge consists of several steps. The tests will need to be done with the cat sleeping under a general anaesthetic and will be done in the following order. The first step is to take X-rays and if possible an MRI scan of the nasal chambers, the nasal sinuses and the bones of the skull. The next step is to take a swab from the inside of the nasal chambers to send to a laboratory to check for different types of bacterial and fungal infection and to determine the best treatment for the infection. The next step is to look inside the nasal chambers between the turbinate bones with an endoscope. The final step is to take a biopsy from the nasal turbinate bones for analysis by a specialist laboratory.

Once the results of the tests are known the vet should be able to make an accurate diagnosis. The most common frustration in cases of sneezing and/or nasal discharge is that, in 20% of cases, the tests will not give the vet a diagnosis. This means that despite performing all the tests discussed earlier, one in five of these cases will not be explained. These cases are then often treated symptomatically, usually with antibiotics and anti-inflammatories. If the symptoms do not resolve within a few weeks then all the tests should be run again to try once more to establish a definite diagnosis. There can be several different reasons for the failure of the tests to provide a diagnosis: endoscopes cannot reach and examine every part of the nasal chamber; very early tumours may not be detected on X-rays and MRI scans; and biopsies may not contain representative tissue samples. The majority of cases will however yield a specific diagnosis after the appropriate tests have been performed.

The variety of possible explanations for sneezing and/or a nasal discharge will be discussed individually.

1a Nasal foreign bodies

Many cats will occasionally eat grass. Many people think this is "normal" behaviour for cats but I think this usually means that there is a stomach problem. I think that cats eat grass only when they want to make themselves vomit. The reason that cats eat grass is the same reason that people take antacids. When a person feels stomach discomfort or heartburn they know that it is due to too much acid in the stomach so they take antacids to neutralise the acids. Cats don't know about the use of antacids but natural instinct leads the cat with stomach pain and heartburn to want to empty their stomach to get rid of the acids and any other contents. Cats are unable to stick their fingers down their throats to make themselves vomit so they do the next best thing which is to eat something which will irritate the stomach lining enough to stimulate vomiting. Once they have vomited out the excess stomach acids they immediately feel better and continue the rest of the day without any signs of illness or discomfort. This immediate return to feeling well after vomiting is an easy way to differentiate this type of vomiting from more serious causes of vomiting.

One will notice that when cats eat grass they specifically eat tough, course blades of grass with sharp edges. This is because this type of grass is most likely to irritate the stomach enough to induce vomiting. If you run your fingers along this type of grass you will feel that the hairs on the blade of grass are very sharp and snag the skin on your fingers and may even cut them. So when a cat eats these blades of grass the hairs on it may cause it to become lodged in the cat's throat. The cat will try to retch to remove the blade of grass and this may push the piece of grass into the nasopharynx, which is the back of the nose above the soft palate. The cat now has a highly irritating object stuck in the back of the nose which they can't swallow and which they can't cough or sneeze out. The result is that the cat produces a throaty snorting type of sound as they try to snort the piece of grass forwards and out of the nostrils. In the early stages of this problem this will often be the only symptom but if the grass has been lodged for a few days it may cause a more severe reaction in the back of the nose and the cat may develop a discharge that is either watery or contains pus and may stop eating food. The vet will suspect a lodged blade of grass on the basis of the strange throaty snorting sound. The only way to investigate this problem is to anaesthetise the cat and to look into the back of the throat and pull the soft palate out of the way to see the nasopharynx. Once the blade of grass has been found the vet will simply pull it out and the symptoms will resolve. If the piece of grass has caused an infection the vet will usually prescribe a course of antibiotics.

1b Hay fever (allergic rhinitis)

This condition is usually diagnosed on the basis the biopsy taken from the nasal turbinate bones and the vet will prescribe treatment for the allergy. Many cats suffering from allergic reactions in the nose will have similar allergic inflammation in the eyes, causing reddened eyes, often with a slight watery discharge. This watery discharge is actually an overflow of excessive tear production caused by the inflammation in the eyes. The inflammation may also cause a runny nose, i.e. there is a thin watery discharge from the nostrils. Apart from the inflammation in the eyes and nose the cat will seem perfectly well and will have a normal appetite and normal activity levels. For a full discussion of the treatment options for allergy please refer to the allergy section in the chapter on itchy skin. Although this type of allergy is different from a skin allergy, the concepts for treating allergies are the same.

1c Nasal infections (infectious rhinitis)

Infections in the nose are most commonly caused by viruses and bacteria. The most common viruses are the "cat flu" viruses called calici virus and rhinovirus. These viruses are very common in cats because they are highly contagious. They are related to a large family of viruses called the herpes viruses. Most people think of venereal disease when they hear the word "herpes" but the herpes virus that causes venereal disease in human beings is only one type of herpes virus. Almost every species of mammal may become infected by a specific type of virus from the huge family of herpes viruses and each of these viruses causes very different diseases in different species. For example, cold sores, which some people develop in their mouth and on their lips, are caused by a herpes virus but not the same one that causes venereal disease.

The herpes virus which causes cold sores on people's lips is a good example of the typical behaviour of a herpes virus. People who suffer from cold sores will often develop cold sores for a while, which then disappear with time, only to reappear in a few weeks, months or years. This happens because the body is often unable to completely kill the virus, which then lies dormant in the body, hiding from the immune system. The next time that person feels tired or run-down the virus is then able to overcome the compromised immune system and flares up as cold sores on their lips again. Thus most individuals are never able to completely get rid of the herpes virus, which will intermittently flare up and cause symptoms. The same process occurs in cats so infected cats often never completely get rid of the virus which occasionally flares up and causes rhinitis.

In cats the viruses usually only affect the nose, the mouth and the eyes because the virus likes temperatures slightly cooler than body temperature so affects mucous membranes directly in contact with the outside air, as these areas are slightly cooler than body temperature. When the virus flares up it may thus affect not only the nose but also the eyes, mouth and throat. The affected cat may therefore have inflamed watery eyes, a runny nose and possibly ulcers on its tongue. The fluid which runs out of the nose is clear and watery if the infection is caused by the virus only without secondary bacterial infection. When the virus flares up the cats may feel unwell just as we do with a head cold, they may develop a fever, and the inflammation in the nose may cause sneezing and a watery runny nose. Many cats will feel so unwell that they lose their appetite and stop eating food and stop all activity in favour of sleeping for several days. There is no treatment to cure a virus so your vet can only treat the symptoms, using anti-inflammatory drugs to control the fever and inflammation. The infection usually goes away after five to seven days but most vets will give your cat antibiotics during this time because it may well develop a secondary bacterial infection in the nose. If the cat refuses to eat food or drink water while they are ill the vet may advise giving them food and water via an intravenous drip. This is done for two main reasons. Firstly, the cat needs the energy from food to have the strength to fight the infection and needs liquids to prevent dehydration. Secondly, if some cats don't eat for more than a few days they may develop serious complications like liver failure due to hepatic lipidosis. This concern regarding damage to the liver seems only to apply to cats living in North America.

A secondary infection means that the bacteria were only able to infect the nose because the virus made the nose vulnerable to infection. If the virus had not weakened the nasal chamber the bacteria would not have been able to cause an infection because the body's immune system would have been able to kill the bacteria. If a secondary bacterial infection does develop then the nasal discharge will change to a thick greenish-yellow discharge, the cat may sound very "snuffly", and the inspiratory effort will be laboured because they refuse to breathe through their mouths no matter how congested the nose becomes. This is why these cats with recurring herpes infections with secondary bacterial infections are called "chronic snufflers" and the condition is called "snuffles". The presence of a secondary bacterial infection is usually very obvious because infected cats will often sneeze out large amounts of this yellow-green discharge onto your furniture and walls. A secondary bacterial infection may similarly develop in the eyes, causing watery pus to accumulate and discharge from the eyes. Bacteria like Chlamydia may cause primary bacterial conjunctivitis without the presence of any viral infection. Primary or secondary bacterial infections look the same and are both treated with antibiotic eye drops.

The vet will thus treat all cats with these symptoms with antibiotics until the primary or secondary bacterial infection is cured. Unfortunately, the problem may recur from time to time and the cat will usually need further treatment to help them through each episode.

The vet can confirm the diagnosis of viral infection using blood tests and viral cultures of swabs taken from infected cats. The primary or secondary bacteria can also be identified by bacterial culture from swabs taken from the infected cat. In practice most vets will not initially need to run these tests but they may advise testing if the cat does not seem to be responding to treatment or if the cat lives in a large community of cats like a breeding cattery where there may be concern about the risk of spreading the disease to the other cats.

1d Nasal tumours

Two types of tumours may develop in the nasal chamber – benign tumours and malignant tumours (cancer).

Benign tumours in the nasal chambers are often called nasal polyps. These are growths that are not cancerous, i.e. they do not spread to the rest of the body and they do not cause massive damage in the site where they grow. They are therefore not life-threatening but may cause discomfort and secondary infections in the nasal chamber because, as they grow, they obstruct the nasal chamber and may damage the adjacent turbinate bones or the vomer bone. These tumours are often easily removed using an endoscope and if they do not regrow this will solve the problem.

However, the most common tumours in the nasal chambers are malignant. The most common of these tumours is called a nasal carcinoma. This type of cancer causes massive damage to the bones of the nose and face and may spread to the rest of the body. If these tumours are diagnosed early enough, before they have spread or caused a lot of damage, the vet may discuss the option of radical surgery followed by a course of radiation therapy. This is called radical surgery because large sections of the nose and face may need to be removed and this may cause significant disfigurement of the cat's face. The surgery may be painful and dangerous as large amounts of blood may be lost during the surgery and the cat may require one or more blood transfusions. Some cats have survived nasal cancer because of early diagnosis and prompt effective treatment and, after recovery, are unaffected by any disfigurement the treatment may have caused. The surgery and the radiation therapy may, however, not cure the problem so each individual case of nasal cancer should be fully discussed as promptly as possible with a cancer specialist. Most nasal cancers are terminal, i.e. they will ultimately claim the cat's life because they do not respond well to any type of treatment.

Initially, nasal tumours are not uncomfortable. Affected cats seem to have a blocked nose, i.e. they may sound "snuffly" and/or have a watery discharge from one or both nostrils and sneeze often. As the tumour enlarges it may distort the appearance of the nose by causing bulges or swellings and the nasal discharge may become blood-tinged. If the tumour obstructs one or both tear ducts, one or both eyes may seem "watery" and tears may flow out of the eye onto the cheek below.

Many people feel strongly about cancer in respect of the "futility" of any treatment, or feel that they would want the option of humane euthanasia for themselves in the event of a diagnosis of terminal cancer. Many people feel that it is not humane to ask their pets to accept the discomfort, pain or suffering that may be caused by some types of cancer. Others want to treat only the symptoms of the cancer; most importantly any pain or discomfort. Many will request euthanasia when the treatment is no longer able to eliminate pain and discomfort or when they feel that the quality of life has deteriorated despite symptomatic treatment. People have often watched friends or family members lose the battle against cancer. These people will often request humane euthanasia for their pets with cancer and I feel that this is a reasonable request in the face of a diagnosis with a terminal prognosis. I personally would not deny the request for euthanasia of a cancer patient because we are not all able to cope with the emotional strain of caring for a pet with a terminal condition. Many people, living with this "sword of Damocles" over their heads, succumb to stress and anxiety and this will often adversely affect the pets living with them. There is never a good time to say goodbye to a pet but sometimes, if they are on a downhill slide, it is better to let them go before they hit rock bottom.

2 The eyes

Cats' eyes may become red and inflamed for long or short periods of time. When one or both eyes seem inflamed and red one might also notice that there is a discharge from one or both eyes. The eyes may also seem itchy, causing the cat to rub their eyes with their paws. The eye or eyes may be so uncomfortable that the cat holds the eyelids closed. Inflammation that affects the surface of the eye is called conjunctivitis or keratitis. When you look at your own eye or your cat's eye, they have exactly the same structure. The structures that we can see are the whites of the eyes and the coloured part of the eye with the pupil in the centre. The white part of the eye is called the sclera, which is covered on its outer surface by a very thin transparent membrane called the conjunctival membrane. The term conjunctivitis simply means that this membrane is inflamed. The coloured part of the eye is called the iris and is actually situated inside the eyeball. The membrane between the iris and the outside world is also a transparent membrane and is called the cornea. The word keratitis means that the cornea is inflamed. So when one or both eyes are red and inflamed the eye can be examined to decide whether the conjunctival membrane covering the white part of the eye is inflamed (conjunctivitis) or the cornea over the coloured part of the eye is inflamed (keratitis). If both membranes are inflamed the condition is called keratoconjunctivitis.

Most cats with red and inflamed eyes have conjunctivitis. The name conjunctivitis simply means that the conjunctival membrane is inflamed but it does not tell us why it is inflamed. Most people think that the word conjunctivitis means infection in the eye. This is because the most common form of conjunctivitis in people, especially schoolchildren, is conjunctivitis caused by a bacterial infection which is usually contagious and may often spread from one person to another. In schools this type of conjunctivitis is often called "pink eye".

I feel that a diagnosis of just "conjunctivitis" is not good enough because it simply means that the membrane is inflamed and doesn't explain why it is inflamed. The most common causes of conjunctivitis are infection in the eye (infectious conjunctivitis), damage or irritation to the eye (traumatic conjunctivitis), allergic reactions like hay fever (allergic conjunctivitis), and corneal ulcers. These different types of conjunctivitis may occur together. For example, if a cat scratches their eye while playing in the garden, this will initially cause a traumatic conjunctivitis because the damage causes the conjunctival membrane to become inflamed. If the cat then keeps rubbing the eye, bacteria may then enter the damaged membrane and then bacterial conjunctivitis may develop at the same time. Thus by the time that the eye is examined the inflammation (conjunctivitis) will be caused partly by the scratch and partly by the infection.

Conjunctivitis and keratitis may occur as separate conditions or together at the same time in the same eye. One or both eyes may be affected. The causes of conjunctivitis and keratitis are usually the same and the only difference is in which part of the surface of the eye becomes inflamed. I find that although the causes of keratitis and conjunctivitis are usually the same, conjunctivitis is more common. Thus, when reading the next section, please bear in mind that the discussion of the types of conjunctivitis and their causes are equally applicable to keratitis and keratoconjunctivitis.

The standard way of investigating an eye problem is to carefully examine the eye with an opthalmoscope which is the same hand-held tool that a doctor will use to examine your own eyes. The vet may also take a swab from the surface of the eye which is then sent to a laboratory to identify the presence of a viral or bacterial infection and then identify the best treatment to use to eradicate that infection. Occasionally the vet may need to anaesthetise the cat to examine the eye more thoroughly using more specialist equipment. If the cat is sneezing and/or has a nasal discharge in addition to the eye problem the vet will also use this opportunity to examine the components of the nose and perform tests on it as discussed previously.

The variety of possible explanations for red, inflamed eyes with or without a discharge from the eyes will be discussed individually.

2a Infectious conjunctivitis

Infectious conjunctivitis is inflammation in one or both eyes caused by an infection in the conjunctival membrane. The infection is most commonly caused by a primary viral infection like the "cat flu" viruses, rhinovirus and calici virus discussed earlier in the chapter, or primary bacterial infection due to bacteria like chlamydia. The viruses cause inflammation in the eyes, nose, mouth and throat and may predispose these areas to secondary bacterial infections. There are many different types of secondary bacteria which may cause conjunctivitis and some of these may cause a discharge of pus from the eyes. This discharge is usually green or yellow and the dry pus on the eyelids may appear crusty. Infectious conjunctivitis may cause so much pain or discomfort in the eye that the cat may hold the eyelids tightly closed over the eyeball; this is called blepharospasm. The range of symptoms and treatments for viral and/or bacterial infections in the eyes and/or nose are discussed in the paragraphs on nasal infections earlier in this chapter.

Careful examination of any eye infection is always merited because the bacterial infection may be secondary to something other than a viral infection in the eye. A secondary infection means that the infection has developed because of a pre-existing problem in the eye like a scratch or a piece of grass lodged behind the eyelids. If there is a pre-existing problem then the infection will not be cured by antibiotic drops until the pre-existing problem is cured by, for example, finding and removing the piece of grass.

2b Traumatic conjunctivitis

Traumatic conjunctivitis means that the inflammation in one or both eyes has been caused by damage to the conjunctival membrane. This damage may be due to a scratch in the membrane, something flying into the eye like a toy or a piece of grass or dirt, abnormal eyelashes rubbing the conjunctival membrane or abnormal eyelids rolling into the eye. Once the conjunctival membrane has been damaged it tends to become red, inflamed and painful. The pain is often severe enough to make the cat hold the eyelids tightly shut over the eyeball. The damaged membrane is also susceptible to secondary infections so the damaged membrane may quickly also become infected. The eye must therefore be carefully examined to determine the cause of the damage. Most cases of traumatic conjunctivitis caused by bumps or scratches are quickly cured using eyedrops that contain anti-inflammatories and anti-biotics. These cases will quickly heal by themselves and the treatment simply alleviates the discomfort and pain during the healing process. If something like a piece of grass or seed is stuck in the eye or behind the eyelids then it must be found and removed otherwise the conjunctivitis will not go away.

If the cat has abnormal eyelashes or eyelids, the eyelashes or hairs on the eyelids may constantly rub and irritate the conjunctival membrane. The most common condition causing abnormal eyelids is called entropion. Entropion means that the eyelid is folded or rolled into the eye meaning that the normal hairs on the outer eyelid rub the surface of the eyeball and irritate the conjunctival membrane and/or cornea. This causes inflammation and pain and often secondary infections will develop. Eye drops will only partially and temporarily relieve the conjunctivitis in these cases. The only way to cure these cases is to operate on the abnormal eyelid to prevent it from rolling into the eye. This is done by removing a thin wedge of skin from the eyelid. This condition may affect any one or even all of the eyelids. This is, however, an uncommon condition in cats.

Very occasionally cats may have one or more abnormal eyelashes which grow towards the surface of the eye and scratch the surface of the eye. An abnormal eyelash is called an ectopic cilia. This scratching causes pain and invites secondary infections so the offending eyelashes need to be permanently removed surgically.

Many people are reluctant to consider surgery to cure the problem of conjunctivitis caused by abnormal eyelashes or abnormal eyelids but I feel strongly that it should be undertaken because the condition is very uncomfortable. Consider how uncomfortable your own eye feels when a speck of dirt or an eyelash is rubbing the surface of the eye; the level of discomfort is ten times worse for cats with these conditions and it persists until we perform the surgery. It must be terrible to have permanent pain in the eye so I would always recommend surgery in these instances.

2c Allergic conjunctivitis

People who suffer from hay fever will often also suffer from allergic conjunctivitis. This means that the allergy causes inflammation in the conjunctival membrane on the surface of the eye, which in turn causes the eyes to appear red and inflamed and to feel itchy. Cats may develop exactly the same allergy reaction in their eyes. These cats can be easily treated using "anti-allergy" eye drops, and homeopathic treatment with euphrasia is often also effective. The treatment only alleviates the symptoms so to cure the problem we must determine what substance is causing the allergy and what, if any, steps can be taken to avoid that substance. This is not always possible. For example, if the allergy is caused by pollen, then the cat will always suffer from allergic conjunctivitis during the pollen season and the best advice I can offer is to treat the condition during that season. If the allergy is caused by other factors, for example food, the condition can be cured by changing the type of food that the cat eats.

Many cats who suffer from allergic conjunctivitis will also have other "hay fever" symptoms like a runny nose and sneezing. This has been mentioned earlier in this chapter in the section on allergic rhinitis. Allergic conjunctivitis and/or rhinitis usually do not affect the cat's appetite or activity levels. This helps to differentiate allergies from viral infections which tend to make cats feel so unwell that they lose their appetite and sleep all day. Please refer to the allergy section in the chapter on itchy skin for a more detailed discussion of the causes and symptoms of, and treatments for, allergies in cats.

2d Dry eye (keratoconjunctivitis sicca)

The surface of the eye is a very delicate structure and it must be kept moist at all times. The body keeps the eye surface moist by constantly producing small amounts of tears that wash over the surface of the eye and drain away through small openings in the inner corner of the eyelids. This means that new tears need to be constantly produced and drained away every minute of the day.

There are many glands that produce the tears to keep the eye moist, the most important of which is the lachrymal gland, situated above and behind the eye. The lachrymal gland produces most of the tears needed by the eye and the gland drains the tears into the eye through a small tube called a duct. The second most important tear-producing gland is called the harderian gland, situated in the inner corner of the eye, tucked away under the third eyelid. The less important tear-producing glands are minute glands dotted along the edge of the eyelids between the eyelashes.

The tears produced by all these glands help to keep the surface of the eye clean and moist, rinsing the surface of the eye and draining away from it through small openings in the inner edges of both the upper and lower eyelids. These openings lead to small tubes called ducts. The ducts from the upper and lower eyelids join together to make one single duct called the naso-lacrimal duct. This leads from the eye and drains into the nose, which is why our noses run when we cry. Normally, when we are not crying, the amount of tears being drained into the nose is so small that we do not notice it.

If the tear-producing glands do not produce enough tears to keep the eye clean and moist then the membranes over the surface of the eye start to dry out. When the conjunctival membrane and the cornea are too dry then they become inflamed and may become painful. The surface of the eye no longer appears clean and shiny and instead one will notice that the surface of the eye appears dull, and sticky fluid clings to it. This sticky fluid may be white, grey, green or yellow. If this "dry eye" is not treated then the inflammation on the surface of the eye will become more and more severe and eventually that eye may go blind. The technical term for this condition is keratoconjunctivitis sicca which simply means that the cat has conjunctivitis (inflammation in the conjunctival membrane) and keratitis (inflammation in the cornea) because the eye surface is too dry (sicca means dry). This does not tell us why the tear-producing glands have stopped working. Research suggests that the main cause of this condition is a problem with the body's own immune system. This is called an autoimmune disorder and it means that the body's immune system is attacking its own cells for no apparent reason. It seems that the immune system simply fails to recognise that some tissue, for example the lachrymal gland, is normal tissue and it attacks it as if it were invading bacteria. As the attack on the cells continues, the cells become damaged and unable to work efficiently and may eventually die.

The diagnosis of a dry eye is made when the surface of the eye is seen to be dry, dull, inflamed and sticky. There are no other symptoms in other parts of the cat's body. The vet will confirm this diagnosis by testing the amount of tear production in the eye. This is called the Schirmer tear test and is quick and easy to do. The vet will place a special type of "blotting paper" against the inside surface of the lower eyelid and measure how much fluid is absorbed by the paper. This test reveals whether the eye surface has enough tear production and, if not, how severe the problem is. The vet will test both eyes even if only one seems affected because this condition often affects both eyes at different speeds.

The treatment for "dry eye" (keratoconjunctivitis sicca) is aimed at controlling the pain and inflammation with anti-inflammatory eye drops and using artificial tears to keep the eye moist. An additional type of eye drop containing cyclosporin has proved to be very effective at controlling and treating this condition, either on its own or in combination with other types of eye drops. I feel that it is important to treat this condition aggressively and keep treating it permanently as it is very uncomfortable and human beings with this condition confirm that without treatment they are in constant pain. Dry-eye is fortunately very rare in cats.

2e Corneal ulcers

The cornea is a thin, transparent membrane lying in front of the coloured part of the eye. Because the cornea is transparent, when we look at an eye we look straight through the cornea and see the iris behind it. People who wear contact lenses will know that the contact lens is placed on the cornea and will thus also know that the cornea is very sensitive to pain and may become inflamed if it is rubbed or irritated. The cornea is very thin, only about twenty cell layers thick, and has a very poor blood supply, which is why we cannot see blood vessels in it. Ulcers may develop in the cornea which may be either very shallow or very deep. A corneal ulcer may develop on any part of the cornea and looks like an ulcer with jagged edges, although sometimes it may be too small to be seen by the naked eye.

If the vet suspects that there may be an ulcer on the cornea they may put a drop of green dye in the eye. This dye will stick to the ulcer but not to any normal cornea so a green area appearing on the cornea will indicates the presence of an ulcer. If no green areas appear after insertion of the dye, then there is no ulcer. The dye is called fluorescein and is completely harmless to the eye, and the green spot will disappear a few hours later.

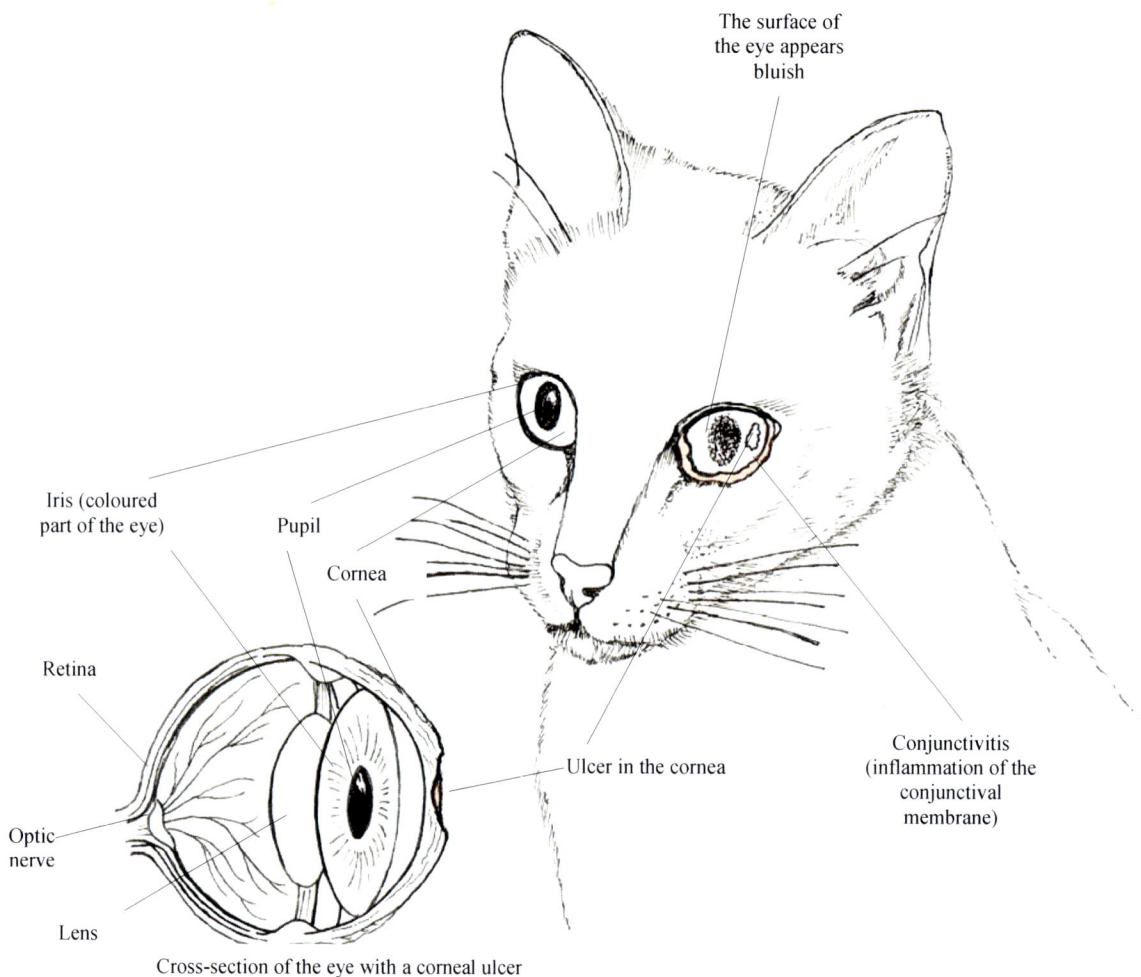

Labels on the cat head illustration:
- The surface of the eye appears bluish
- Conjunctivitis (inflammation of the conjunctival membrane)
- Iris (coloured part of the eye)
- Pupil
- Cornea

Labels on the cross-section illustration:
- Retina
- Optic nerve
- Lens
- Ulcer in the cornea

Cross-section of the eye with a corneal ulcer

Fig 18. – Conjunctivitis and a corneal ulcer in the left eye.

Once fluorescein dye has been placed in the eye there will sometimes be a green discharge from the nostril on the same side of the face. This is because the fluorescein dye mixes with the normal tears in the eye and drains away from the dye through the naso-lacrimal duct which drains tears from the eye to the nose.

The tears produced help to keep the surface of the eye clean and moist, rinsing the surface of the eye and draining away from it through small openings in the inner edges of both the upper and lower eyelids. These openings lead to small tubes called ducts. The ducts from the upper and lower eyelids join together to make one single duct called the naso-lacrimal duct. This leads from the eye and drains into the nose, which is why our noses run when we cry. Normally, when we are not crying, the amount of tears being drained into the nose is so small that we do not notice it.

Once a corneal ulcer has developed, the eye becomes very painful and often the surface of the eyeball becomes inflamed because of conjunctivitis and keratitis and the cat will keep the painful eye shut. Once a corneal ulcer has been diagnosed one should try to determine the cause. The ulcer may develop from a superficial cut or scrape on the surface of the cornea but most often no reason for the ulcer can be found. If the ulcer has developed from a cut or scrape to the cornea the vet should check to see that there is nothing lodged in the eye or behind the eyelids which may be causing the damage. Grass seeds, pieces of grass or twigs, etc. are all likely suspects. If an object is found it must be removed otherwise the damage will continue and the ulcer will not heal. If no object is found the vet should examine the eyelids to make sure that the ulcer has not been caused by abnormal eyelashes, entropion or keratoconjunctivitis sicca as discussed previously. If any of these conditions are identified then they must be corrected otherwise the damage to the cornea will continue and the ulcer will not heal. Thus once an ulcer has been identified one must try to find an explanation for the development of the ulcer. If an explanation is found then the underlying condition must be treated at the same time as treating the ulcer. If no underlying cause for the ulcer can be found the ulcer is treated as an unexplained corneal ulcer.

The treatment for a corneal ulcer should be started as soon as possible for two reasons; to prevent the ulcer from becoming larger and deeper, and to alleviate the pain caused by the ulcer. Treatment will depend on how deep the ulcer is. If it is very superficial then appropriate antibiotic eye ointment should be instilled in the eye at least three times daily. The vet may use eye ointment rather than eye drops because the ointment forms a protective and soothing layer over the surface of the eye whereas eye drops drain from the eye via the naso-lacrimal duct too quickly. The ulcer should heal very quickly over a period of one or two weeks. If the ulcer does not heal or if the ulcer is very deep and there is a risk that it may cause the eyeball to burst, then the vet may recommend an operation.

The simplest form of operation for a corneal ulcer is called a third eyelid flap. The third eyelid is something that most animals have but human beings don't have. The third eyelid is literally another eyelid which is hairless, covered by the conjunctival membrane and tucked away out of sight in the inner corner of the eye under the upper and lower eyelids. The operation involves pulling the third eyelid across the surface of the eye and temporarily stitching it to the upper eyelid so that it stays in position covering the eye. This is a simple and quick procedure and causes little or no discomfort to the cat. The effect of stitching the eyelid in this position is that it acts as a temporary bandage over the surface of the eye to allow the ulcer to heal. The stitches are removed after one or two weeks and the ulcer will almost always have healed in this time. If the ulcer has not completely healed when the stitches are removed then the vet may advise replacing the stitches and removing them in another week or two, or the vet may propose a different kind of operation. This alternative operation is called a conjunctival graft and is not as simple to perform. A conjunctival graft involves pulling a strip of the conjunctival membrane which covers the whites of the eyes over the ulcer in the cornea and stitching it to the cornea. I have found that it is rarely necessary to do this second operation as most cases heal with the simpler and cheaper operation of the third eyelid flap. If, however, the ulcer refuses to heal or if it is so deep that the risk of the eyeball bursting is very high then the conjunctival graft may be the only option.

2f Corneal sequestrum

A corneal sequestrum is a small, hard, round, black spot on the surface of the eye on the cornea. This hard, black spot is simply a piece of the cornea which has lost its blood supply and has died. This is similar to a skin injury like a cut which, when stitched, may develop a small area of skin which turns black and dies off. Eventually the dead piece of skin will fall off and the skin will heal. In the case of a corneal sequestrum there is usually no reason why that piece of cornea has lost its blood supply. The sequestrum is painful and the cat will keep their eye tightly closed. Treatment for this problem involves pain relief in the form of eye drops initially and, eventually, as the dead piece of cornea starts to lift off the surface of the eye, it can be removed. In some severe cases the vet may advise surgery immediately to remove the dead tissue and repair the cornea with a conjuntival graft. Other than pain in the eye the cat will have no other symptoms like coughing, sneezing or loss of appetite.

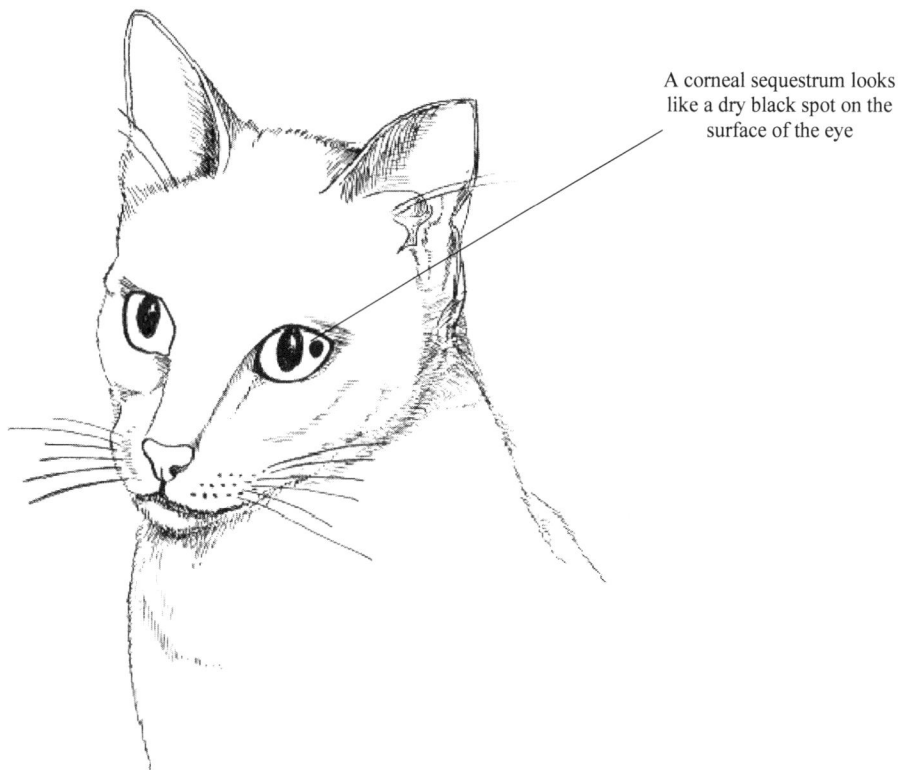

A corneal sequestrum looks like a dry black spot on the surface of the eye

Fig 19. – Corneal sequestrum in the left eye

2g Anterior uveitis

Anterior uveitis means that all the structures and membranes in the front part of the eyeball are inflamed. This means that the eye appears red because the cat has conjunctivitis and keratitis, and the inflammation also involves the structures inside the eyeball like the iris (the coloured part of the eye), the inside lining of the eyeball and the fluid in the eye. The cause of anterior uveitis is often not determined when cats are initially examined and vets often assume that the causes of this condition are largely similar to the causes of conjunctivitis and keratitis as discussed earlier. Thus treatment consists of antibiotics and anti-inflammatories used in eye drop form and often also in tablet form to ensure that the treatment reaches not just the surface of the eye but also the inside of the eyeball.

The most serious concern that the vet may have when they diagnose anterior uveitis is that the inflammation inside the eye will obstruct the normal flow of fluid inside the eye, and the eyeball may develop glaucoma. Glaucoma means that the eyeball is swollen and most often the pressure of the fluid inside the eyeball is much higher than normal. This high pressure causes severe pain and may permanently damage the inside of the eye and result in permanent blindness. Thus, if the vet diagnoses anterior uveitis they will want to regularly check the condition of the eye and the pressure in the eye because if glaucoma develops the best chance of saving the sight in that eye hinges on starting glaucoma treatment immediately. Treatment for glaucoma consists of specific types of eye drops and tablets and sometimes even advanced eye surgery.

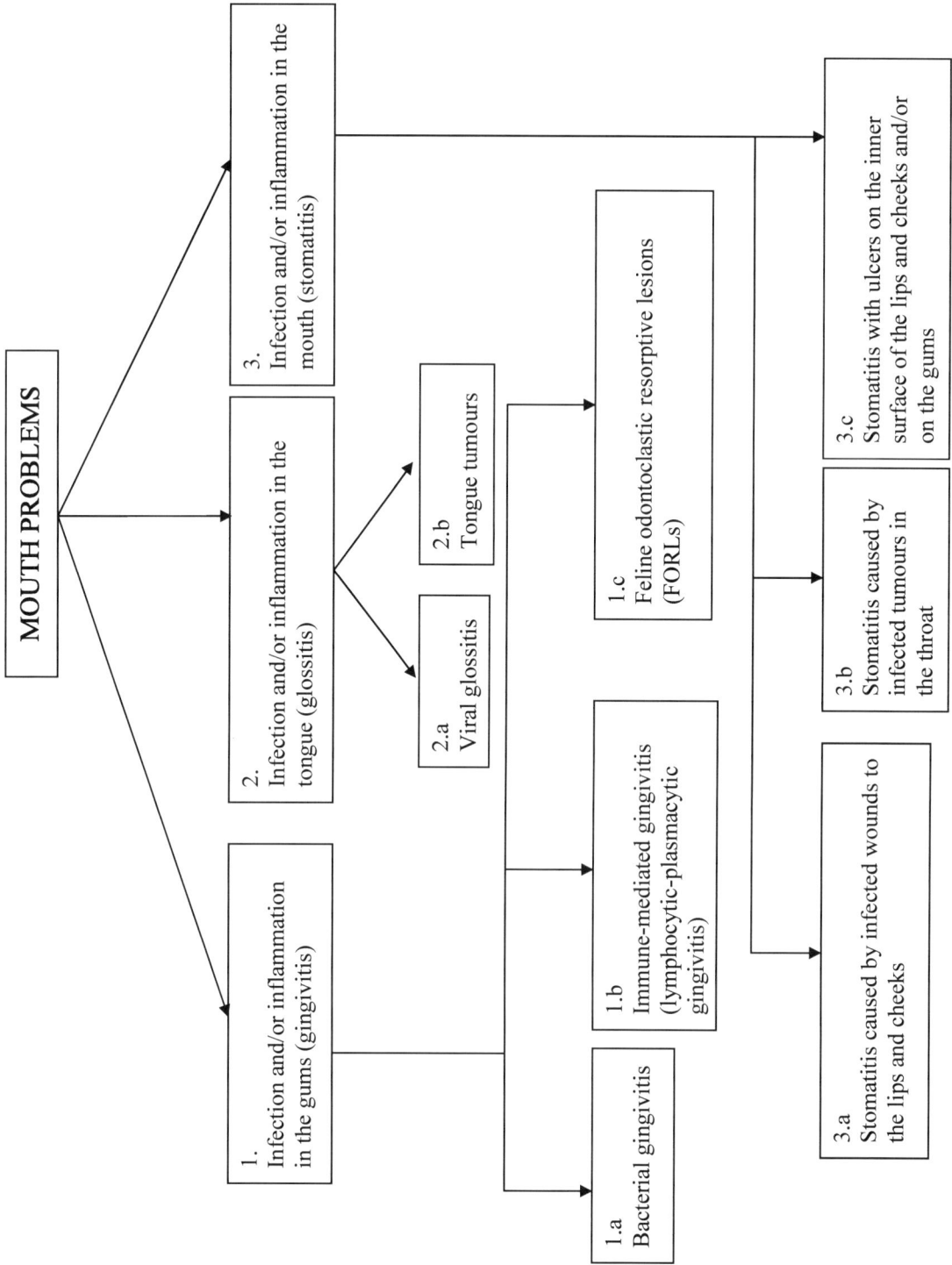

MOUTH PROBLEMS

1.
Infection and/or inflammation in the gums (gingivitis)

2.
Infection and/or inflammation in the tongue (glossitis)

3.
Infection and/or inflammation in the mouth (stomatitis)

1.a
Bacterial gingivitis

1.b
Immune-mediated gingivitis (lymphocytic-plasmacytic gingivitis)

1.c
Feline odontoclastic resorptive lesions (FORLs)

2.a
Viral glossitis

2.b
Tongue tumours

3.a
Stomatitis caused by infected wounds to the lips and cheeks

3.b
Stomatitis caused by infected tumours in the throat

3.c
Stomatitis with ulcers on the inner surface of the lips and cheeks and/or on the gums

7

MOUTH PROBLEMS

People often find that their cat's breath has become very smelly and unpleasant as they grow older. The most common reason for this is the same as for human beings who suffer from halitosis (smelly breath). Bacteria which live in the mouth cause smelly breath. The more bacteria there are in the mouth, the smellier the breath will be.

If you notice that your cat has smelly breath, try to look inside the mouth and see if there are any areas of infection and/or inflammation. The inside of the cat's mouth should look much like the inside of your own mouth, i.e. the teeth should be white and shiny and the tongue, gums and inside of the lips should be smooth, pink and shiny. Any areas that seem different from the rest of the inside of the mouth are probably abnormal and are probably the cause of the halitosis.

The mouth is full of bacteria and some of these bacteria cause plaque. Plaque is the "furry" texture you feel on the surface of your teeth with your tongue when you have forgotten to brush your teeth. The bacteria attach themselves to the surface of your teeth and most noticeably in the groove between the tooth and the gum. This groove is called the gingival sulcus. Most of us do not realise that the very edge of the gum lying against the tooth is not attached to the tooth. This edge of the gum actually just lies against the tooth, creating a groove between the gum and the tooth, usually less than one millimetre deep. Most of us have used a toothpick at some point in our lives to remove a piece of food stuck in this groove (like popcorn). The piece of food is easily seen because the groove is very shallow and most of the food protrudes from it.

This groove (the gingival sulcus) is the easiest place in the mouth for bacteria to live and grow. When we brush our teeth every day we remove most of the bacteria but as soon as you put your toothbrush down, the bacteria start growing again. Most people do not brush their cat's teeth every day so the bacteria aren't removed on a daily basis. The body's immune system wages war against bacteria in the mouth every minute of our lives and is very efficient at keeping the numbers of bacteria down even without daily brushing, so this is what most animals rely on to control oral bacteria.

Some individuals simply just have better teeth and gums than others do; this applies to both human beings and cats. This means that some individuals will naturally have healthier teeth and gums than others despite not brushing their teeth as regularly. This is because some individuals have more effective immune system patrols in their mouths and the conditions in their mouths are less favourable for the growth of bacteria. The conditions in your mouth are affected by the food you eat and the type of saliva (spit) that you produce.

We are all well aware that eating a lot of sugar is not good for our teeth and gums and much the same concept applies to cats. Cats do not develop "rotten teeth" like we do despite what they eat. This is because their teeth have a different design and they are naturally resistant to tooth decay. The food that a cat eats does, however, affect the health of the teeth and gums in other ways. The natural diet of cats would be small animals like rodents and birds. When eating their prey cats would chew through skin, bone and gristle. Cats who eat only soft moist cat foods and never chew dry food or tough gristly food will have more bacteria in their mouths. This is simply because chewing dry foods and gristle does help to scrape bacteria off the teeth. The second reason is that chewing for a longer period of time changes the acidity level of the saliva which makes it more effective at killing plaque bacteria. Human beings get the same benefit from chewing gum, i.e. as we chew gum we constantly produce saliva and after producing saliva for about ten minutes the acidity level of the saliva changes, making it much more efficient at killing oral bacteria. Thus cats who spend more time chewing and salivating will have fewer bacteria in their mouths. Some individuals simply just have a better acidity level in their saliva all the time so they will have naturally healthy teeth and gums. And they are less likely to have smelly breath because as their saliva rinses the gingival sulcus it kills the bacteria hiding there.

Thus large numbers of bacteria in the mouth cause smelly breath (halitosis). The most common area for bacteria to accumulate in the mouth is in the gingival sulcus where they cause gingivitis. Bacteria may occasionally also accumulate at other sites in the mouth where they cause infections. Infections in the tongue are called glossitis and infections in areas of the mouth other than the tongue or the gums are called stomatitis. The most common causes of stomatitis (infection in the mouth) are infected bite wounds in the cheeks or lips, or infected tumours in the throat, or infected ulcers on the inner surface of the lips or on the gums. The most common causes of glossitis (infection in the tongue) are viral infections affecting the tongue or infected tumours under the tongue. Thus halitosis (smelly breath) may be caused by

- Infection and/or inflammation in the gums (gingivitis)
- Infection and/or inflammation in the tongue (glossitis)
- Infection and/or inflammation in mouth (stomatitis)

I will discuss each of these three areas separately.

1 Infection and/or inflammation in the gums (gingivitis)

We have determined that smelly breath is caused by bacteria living in the mouth, especially the bacteria living in the gingival sulcus (the groove between the gum and the tooth). The more bacteria there are in the groove, the more the breath will smell. Bacteria which accumulate in this groove cause gingivitis. Gingiva is the medical term for the gums, and the suffix "itis" means inflamed, thus gingivitis simply means inflammation of the gums. Initially gingivitis is seen as a dark red or purple band of colour on the edge of the gum lying against the tooth. The three most common conditions associated with gingivitis in cats are:

- Bacterial gingivitis
- Immune-mediated (lymphocytic-plasmacytic) gingivitis
- Feline odontoclastic resorptive lesions (FORLs)

All three of these conditions look very similar, i.e. the edge of the gum lying against the tooth becomes inflamed and takes on a red or purple colour. The three causes of inflammation are quite different and I will discuss each one separately.

1a Bacterial gingivitis

The most common cause of gingivitis is the accumulation of bacteria in the gingival sulcus; this is called bacterial gingivitis. These bacteria cause plaque to form on the surface of the tooth and if this plaque is not removed it will turn into tartar, a very hard substance similar to cement. Once plaque has turned into tartar, it can only be removed by a dentist or a vet as it is very tightly stuck to the tooth. The dentist or the vet removes this substance when you go for a "dental scale and polish". The process of removing tartar is called "dental scaling".

Tartar is often visible on one or more of your cat's teeth as a brown deposit on the surface of the tooth. Once a deposit of tartar has formed on a tooth the lump of tartar will continue to enlarge until it is removed. The enlarging mass of tartar pushes into the groove between the tooth and the gum and makes the groove deeper which then invites more bacteria to live and breed there. As this process continues, the groove and the bacteria move deeper and deeper inwards into the tooth socket in the bone of the jaw. Ultimately the tooth root may become loose and the tooth will fall out. This process of bacteria and infection moving deeper into the gum and ultimately into the tooth socket is called periodontal disease or periodontitis. Periodontal disease results in infections around the tooth roots and this causes the tooth to lose its attachment to the tooth socket in the jaw bone and to fall out. Thus if we do not constantly remove plaque and tartar the teeth will be lost. The tartar thus also makes the breath smellier as it invites more bacteria to live in the mouth.

The most common cause of smelly breath is thus bacteria, plaque and tartar on the teeth. Some individuals are more prone to these problems than others but you can help your cat by ensuring that they eat and chew properly to reduce the number of bacteria in the mouth. You can further help them by brushing their teeth every day and if you do notice tartar developing in the mouth, ask the vet to remove it.

Once the vet has removed the tartar you must continue brushing and encouraging your cat to chew coarse food to slow down the reappearance of plaque bacteria.

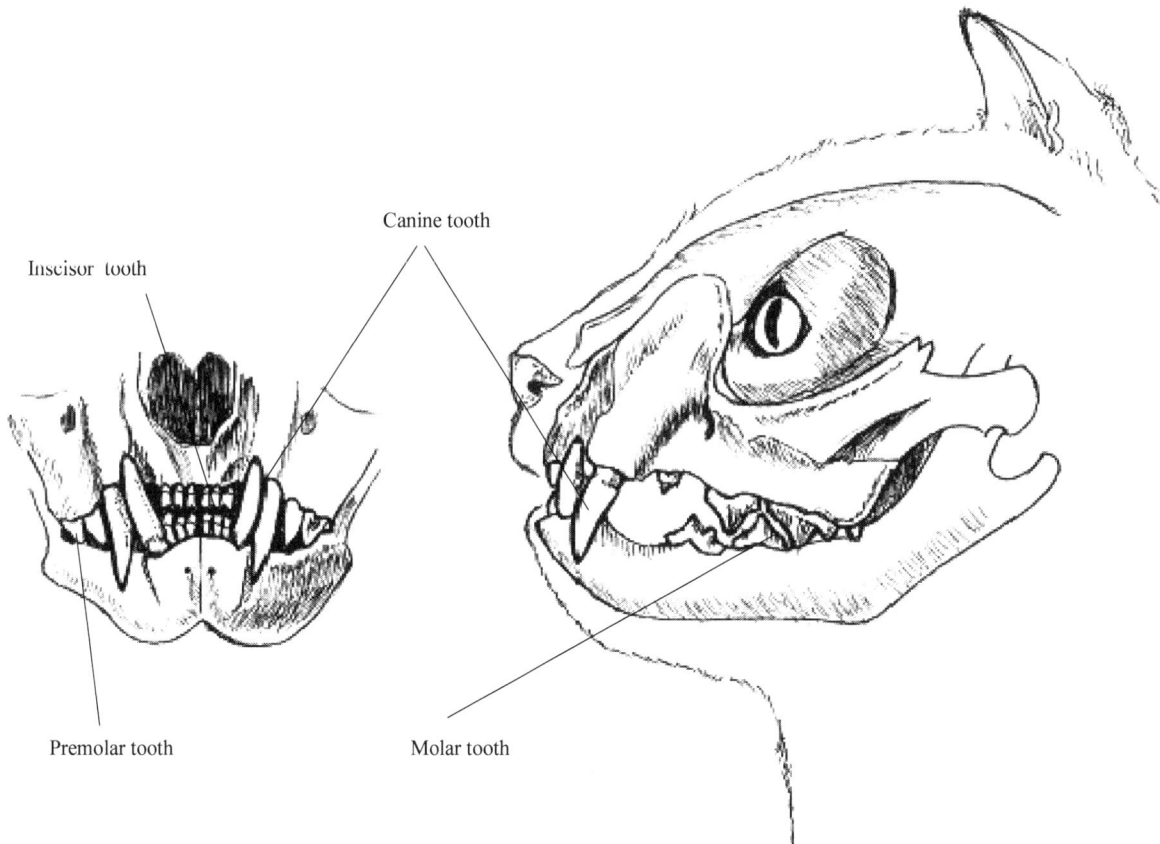

Fig 20. – Normal anatomy of the teeth and skull

This is because, just like us, the minute you leave the dentist's chair after a scale and polish, the war against the bacteria starts again immediately. Cats, just like us, will need to have their teeth professionally cleaned regularly and, again just like human beings, some cats will need more frequent cleaning than others. Most modern commercial cat food manufacturers produce cat food with dental health in mind. They design the formulation of the food to try to keep the teeth and gums healthy and produce special types of food for those cats which seem especially prone to gingivitis. This is a step in the right direction but none of these foods is as efficient as chewing natural prey so, although some types of food are better than others, there is as yet no particular food that will guarantee permanently healthy teeth and gums.

Fig 21a. – Normal gums will look like your own. The gums should be pale pink and shiny with no yellow tartar accumulation on the surface of the teeth.

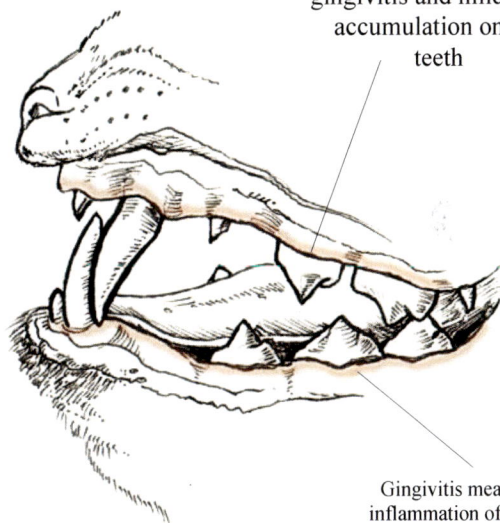

Fig 21b. – Early gingivitis and mild tartar accumulation on the teeth

Gingivitis means inflammation of the gums

Severe gingivitis

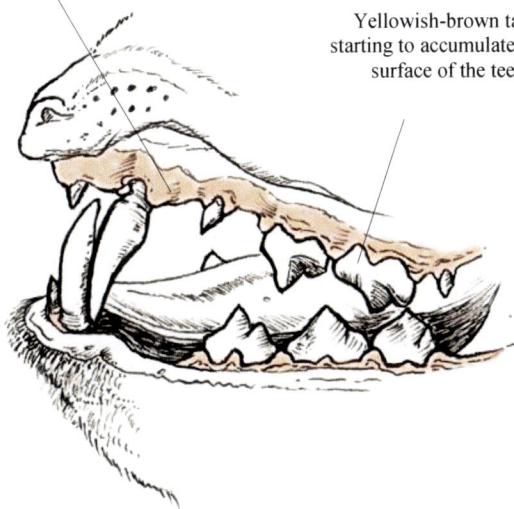

Yellowish-brown tartar starting to accumulate on the surface of the teeth

Fig 21c. – Advanced gingivitis and periodontal disease with large deposits of tartar. The gums are very inflamed and the gum margin is receding

1b Immune-mediated (lymphocytic-plasmacytic) gingivitis

As discussed at the beginning of the chapter, even the healthiest mouth is full of bacteria and most of these bacteria live in the gingival sulcus against the surface of the teeth. These bacteria do not cause any significant harm if the body's immune system is able to control them successfully. The immune system detects the bacteria in the gingival sulcus and kills them. The bacteria are constantly breeding and producing more bacteria so the intention of the war waged by the immune system is simply to keep the numbers of bacteria as low as possible.

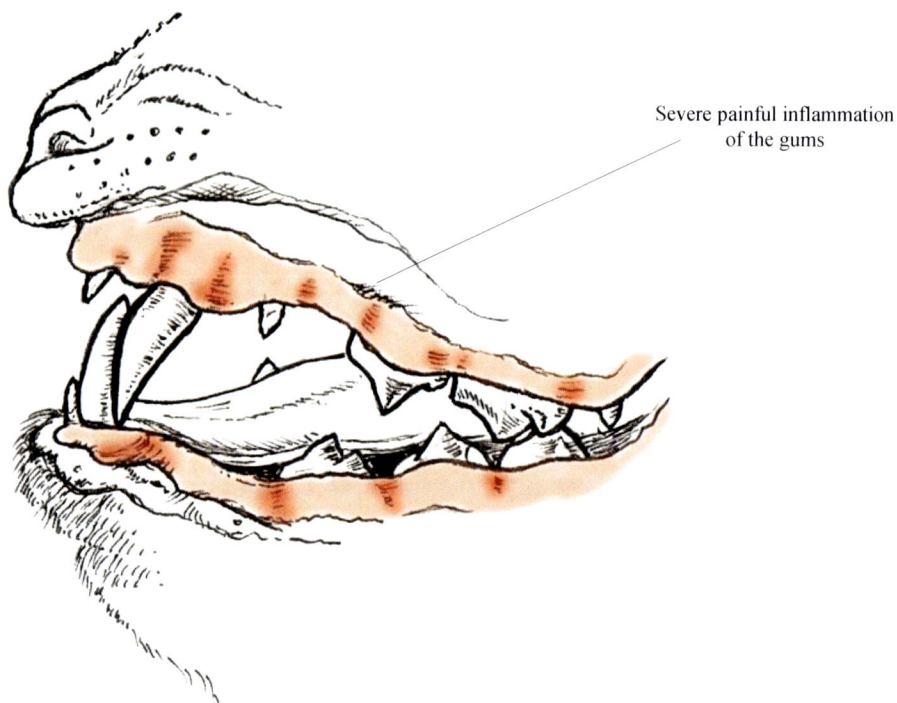

Severe painful inflammation of the gums

Fig 22. – Immune-mediated (lymphocytic-plasmacytic) gingivitis

In some cats the immune system "overreacts" to the bacteria in the gingival sulcus. The immune system attacks the bacteria more aggressively than it needs to and this overreaction causes inflammation in the gums. Thus it is the overreaction of the immune system to a normal amount of bacteria in the gingival sulcus that causes the gingivitis. This is similar to hay fever in human beings where the immune system in some individuals overreacts to pollen in the nose, causing severe inflammation. In these individuals it is the body's own immune system which is causing the inflammation because it is overreacting to normal amounts of pollen. If the overreaction of the immune system causes the gingivitis, the condition is called lymphocytic-plasmacytic gingivitis because the cells which are sent to fight the bacteria are called lymphocytes and plasmacytes. This diagnosis can only be made by taking a biopsy from the affected gum. When the biopsy is examined under a microscope one will see an excessively large number of these cells considering the number of bacteria. The swelling in the gums, i.e. the gingivitis, causes the gingival sulcus to swell open so allowing more bacteria in. This aggravates the problem because the immune system then sends even more lymphocytes and plasmacytes to fight the problem, provoking the overreaction still further. This overreaction is often so severe that the inflammation in the gums causes significant pain in the gums and these cats may find it difficult to eat. One will notice that the affected cat is hungry but is nervous about eating and chewing food because it causes them pain. They will sometimes gulp the food down with the minimum of chewing to avoid the pain but in severe cases may start to lose weight because the pain is so extreme that they simply refuse to eat enough.

The treatment for this condition will centre on treating the cause and the effect, i.e. the first component of treatment is to reduce the number of bacteria and the second component is to reduce the immune system's reaction to those bacteria. The easiest way to reduce the number of bacteria in the gingival sulcus is simply to use antibiotics. The problem with this approach is that although the antibiotics will efficiently kill the bacteria, the bacteria will simply come back when the antibiotic treatment is stopped. Thus while the cat is on antibiotics the immune system overreaction will be less severe but when the antibiotics are stopped the gingivitis will reappear because the immune system simply starts overreacting again. An alternative approach is to use medication to reduce the response of the immune system. In the case of human beings with hay fever this is achieved by using antihistamines and/or cortisone. These medicines work by effectively inhibiting the immune system and so reducing the force of the overreaction. In the case of cats with lymphocytic-plasmacytic gingivitis, antihistamines produce no effect so the only option we have is to use cortisone. This can be administered by using courses of tablets or long-acting injections. The problem with this treatment approach is also that it only works while the treatment is applied, i.e. when the cat is on the treatment the problem is resolved or reduced to a tolerable level but when the treatment is stopped the overreaction simply reappears. Thus we will often apply a combination of these two treatment approaches. The vet will advise a long-term strategy to control the number of bacteria in the mouth by suggesting regular dental check-ups and regular dental scaling and polishing to remove the offending bacteria, alternating with courses of antibiotics to kill the bacteria in between dental check-ups. They will also advise types of food which reduce the growth of the bacteria and the formation of plaque and tartar. In addition to these steps the cat may need occasional treatment with cortisone, or other medications like cyclosporin, to reduce the immune system overreaction. Most people are resistant to the regular use of cortisone because they have heard about the risk of side effects. Please refer to the chapter on itchy skin for a full discussion of the do's and don'ts and pros and cons of regular or long-term cortisone (steroid) use.

If all of the above treatment strategies are insufficient to control the problem an ultimate solution may be to remove all the teeth. This is an extreme solution to the problem but in severe cases it may be the only option. The reason this works is that the bacteria live in the gingival sulcus against the surface of each tooth. If the teeth are removed the gums will heal up and thus there is no longer a groove for the bacteria to live in. If there is nowhere for the bacteria to live and hide there will no longer be areas in the gums filled with bacteria and the immune system response will not be activated. Most people are very resistant to the idea of removing all the teeth and I think this is because we place a high value on our teeth in terms of appearance, i.e. we want to keep our teeth because it does not look nice if we have no teeth. We all want a beautiful smile with white and shiny teeth for cosmetic reasons even though we can live quite happily without our teeth simply by changing what we eat. Cats do not care what their mouth looks like. Cats are not concerned with the cosmetic appearance of their mouths, they are only concerned with their ability to eat and be free of mouth pain.

If we have to remove all their teeth the cat does not care about their appearance. Once the gums have healed up after the teeth have been removed, most cats are happily able to eat their usual diet, i.e. cats who prefer eating dry cat food will continue eating dry food and cats who prefer eating soft wet food will also continue doing so. Even without their teeth most cats are quite happy to eat dry kibble food because their gums are so hard and strong. If they do have any trouble eating the dry kibble we can simply add a bit of water to soften the food or change to wet tinned food. Cats are so unaffected by losing all their teeth that the hunters keep on hunting and the fighters keep on fighting despite having no teeth. So although removing all the teeth may seem to be an unacceptable option to us as human beings it seems completely unimportant to cats. Cats function perfectly normally without any teeth at all and in fact are much happier having no teeth than having painful teeth and gums. If medications and dental treatments are ineffective at controlling lymphocytic-plasmacytic gingivitis or if the doses required are causing unacceptable side effects then removing all the teeth is definitely the right thing to do.

1c Feline odontoclastic resorptive lesions (FORLs)

The name of this condition sounds quite daunting but is really quite simple. "Feline" means that the condition occurs in cats. "Odontoclastic" means that the condition causes parts of the teeth to dissolve. "Resorptive" means that the way the affected part of the tooth is dissolved is that it is reabsorbed into the body's blood supply. "Lesions" mean that the effects of this process cause specific abnormalities that can be seen and easily identified.

To understand this condition we have to understand the anatomy of the teeth. Each tooth is divided into three parts – the tooth root, the tooth neck and the crown of the tooth. The root is obviously the part of the tooth in the tooth socket sunk into jaw bones. The crown of the tooth is the part of the tooth that we can see in the mouth and the part that chews food. The tooth neck is the part of the tooth at the gum-line which connects the tooth crown to the tooth root. The outside of the tooth is covered in enamel. Inside the enamel the tooth is made of dentine and inside the dentine is the pulp cavity. The pulp cavity is the chamber inside each tooth which contains the nerves and blood vessels which supply the tooth.

The name of this condition is long-winded and vague because we simply do not fully understand it. As discussed earlier in this chapter the immune system is constantly fighting a war against bacteria living in the gingival sulcus lying against the surface of each tooth. The gingival sulcus runs along the tooth neck and the war is fought against bacteria lying there. The reaction of the immune system fighting against bacteria involves many different kinds of infection-fighting cells and many different types of chemicals. Some of these chemicals seem to have the side effect that they can dissolve the tooth enamel and dentine. Because these chemicals are concentrated in the gingival sulcus there is constant contact between these chemicals and the neck of each tooth. In most cats these chemicals do not damage the tooth but in some cats they start to dissolve the enamel and dentine in the tooth neck. As this part of the tooth is dissolved the gum will react by producing a flap of gum to patch the hole forming in the side of the tooth. As the tooth neck is dissolved, the affected part of the tooth becomes painful because the nerves inside the tooth are being exposed. The flap of gum does help to cover the exposed nerve to some extent but the tooth is still painful when food or the tongue or the lips touch the tooth in the affected area. This dissolving process cannot be stopped once it has started and eventually so much of the tooth neck will be dissolved that the crown of the tooth will snap off. This will expose all of the nerves in the tooth, making the remains of the tooth very painful. Eventually the gums will grow over the exposed tooth roots and the tooth nerve recedes and the condition is no longer painful. One or many of the teeth may be affected and ultimately all the crowns of the affected teeth will snap off and the remaining roots are covered by the gums.

We do not know why this process happens in some cats and not in others. There is no treatment to stop or fix the damage once the process has started. The only help we can offer the cat is to remove the affected teeth. We remove the tooth because that solves the problem of pain in that tooth even though the problem would eventually solve itself when the crown snaps off. The reason we advise removing the tooth is that the natural process takes a long time, leaving the cat in pain for some time until the crown snaps off and the gums grow over the remaining roots. The vet will advise removing the affected tooth if it is painful when touched. The affected tooth is easily identified by the presence of a flap of gum growing up from the gingival sulcus and lying against the side of the tooth. This flap is very small and one must look closely to identify it. Once you have identified a flap of gum on the side of a tooth you can assess for pain by touching the flap with your finger tip. If the cat feels pain the jaw will twitch or the cat will jerk their mouth away from your finger. If there seems to be no pain when the affected tooth is touched then it may not need to be removed immediately but eventually all of these lesions become painful and when that happens I would advise removing the affected tooth. Various types of treatments have been tried including "fillings" like we have in our teeth but none of them save the tooth.

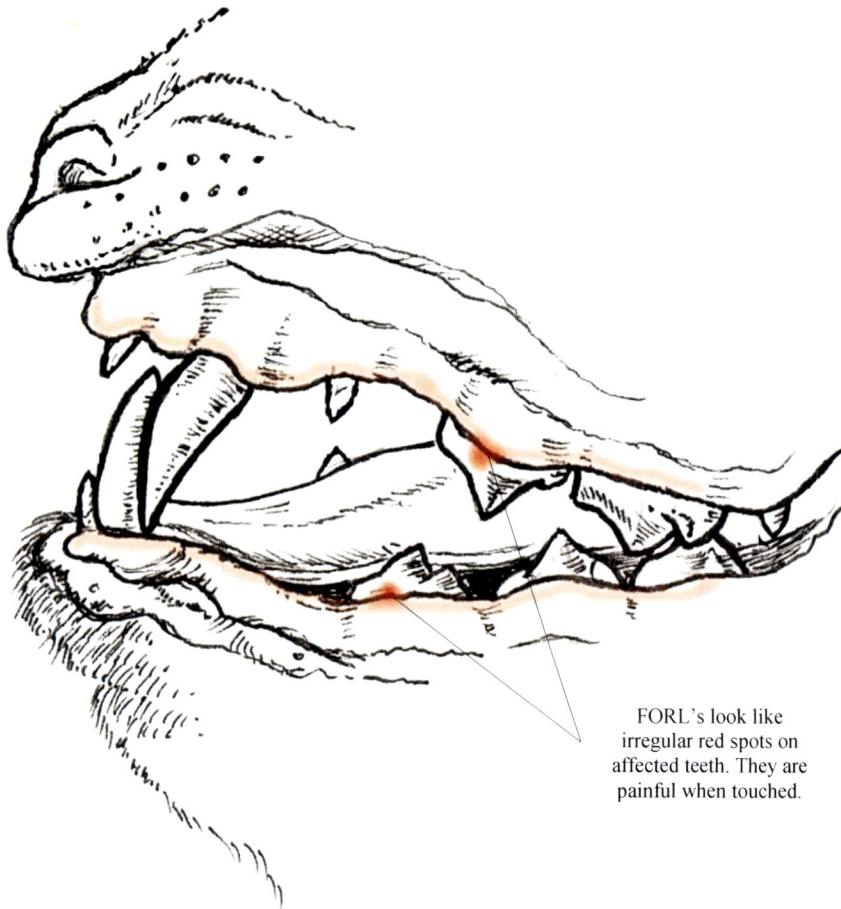

FORL's look like irregular red spots on affected teeth. They are painful when touched.

Fig 23. – Feline odontoclastic resorptive lesions (FORL's)

2 Infection and/or inflammation in the tongue (glossitis)

Infections affecting the tongue may affect the upper surface or the underside of the tongue. Bacterial infections cause smelly breath and usually bacterial infections in the tongue are secondary to another problem affecting the tongue. This is because the immune system in the mouth is very good at controlling oral bacteria and often the only way the bacteria can gain enough advantage over the immune system to multiply into an infection is if something else is wrong in the mouth. This is similar to your skin which is covered with millions of bacteria; the defence systems in the skin are able to prevent these bacteria causing an infection. But if the skin is cut or scratched, the bacteria will be able to gain an advantage and move into the cut to cause an infection. This is called a secondary bacterial infection, i.e. something has to happen first to give the bacteria enough advantage to gain a foothold and cause an infection.

The most common condition affecting the top of the tongue sufficiently to invite a secondary bacterial infection is infection with the "cat flu" viruses, i.e. viral glossitis. The most common condition affecting the underside of the tongue sufficiently to invite secondary bacterial infection is a tumour on the underside of the tongue, i.e. tumour-induced glossitis. These two conditions will be discussed separately.

2a Viral glossitis

The two most common viruses causing "cat flu" are calici virus and rhinovirus. These viruses and the infections they cause have been discussed in the section on nose and eye problems – please refer to that chapter for a more detailed discussion regarding these viruses. In addition to all the other symptoms they may cause, these viruses may occasionally cause ulcers to develop on the upper surface of the tongue. These ulcers are painful and affected cats will be reluctant to eat and often drool thick, ropy saliva. If these ulcers become infected by a secondary bacterial infection the mouth may become very smelly. The diagnosis of and treatment for this problem have been discussed in the chapter on eye and nose problems.

Fig 24. – Painful tongue ulcers are usually caused by viral infections

2b Tongue tumours

Cats may occasionally develop very aggressive cancers on the underside of the tongue where it is attached to the floor of the mouth. These tumours develop very suddenly and progress very rapidly. The first symptom people usually notice is that the cat is having difficulty eating food. When you examine the mouth in these cases remember to look under the tongue. In the initial stages the tumour may look like an ulcer or it may look like a small piece of abnormal tissue on the underside of the tongue where it attaches to the floor of the mouth. These tumours grow very rapidly and soon cause the tongue to become swollen and the symptoms we then see are difficulty eating and drooling saliva (spit), and the mouth starts to smell as bacteria accumulate in the mouth because the cat can't swallow normally. Eventually the bacteria in the mouth may cause a secondary infection in the base of the tongue and this causes a very smelly mouth. These cancers are highly aggressive and usually fail to respond to any attempts to treat them. They tend to keep enlarging very rapidly and within four weeks the cat is unable to eat or drink and the only option we are left with is to humanely put the cat to sleep to end their suffering.

3 Infection and/or inflammation in the mouth (stomatitis)

The most common causes of stomatitis (infection in the mouth) are infected bite wounds in the cheeks or lips, or infected tumours in the throat, or infected ulcers on the inner surface of the lips or on the gums.

3a Stomatitis caused by infected wounds to the lips and cheeks

Cats have very small teeth and claws and when they fight each other they tend to pepper each other with small puncture wounds. The dirt and bacteria on the tips of the teeth and claws are thus pushed through the skin into the tissue beneath. The actual puncture wounds are very small and tend to seal off very quickly. The result is that the dirt and bacteria deposited under the skin tend to develop into abscesses just as a thorn or splinter would do. If the puncture wounds are inflicted on the cheeks of the cat they may develop an abscess in the cheek, which will progressively enlarge until it bursts. Sometimes cheek abscesses will burst on the inside of the cheek and the pus will discharge into the mouth causing smelly breath. If you find a discharging abscess on the inner surface of the cheek the cat will need antibiotics to cure the infection. These abscesses are not always painful but, if they are, the vet will advise painkiller medication in addition to the antibiotics.

3b Stomatitis caused by infected tumours in the throat

Cats may occasionally develop tumours in the throat in the same way that people do. Tumours in the throat are almost always very malignant cancer and are usually fatal. The cancer in the throat looks like a large lump in the back of the throat and as it enlarges it will interfere with the cat's ability to swallow. The result is that the initial symptom will be difficulty eating. As the cancer grows we then see difficulty eating and drooling saliva (spit), and the mouth starts to smell as bacteria accumulate in the mouth because the cat can't swallow normally. Eventually the bacteria in the mouth may cause a secondary infection in the tumour and this causes a very smelly mouth. These cancers are highly aggressive and usually fail to respond to any attempts to treat them. They tend to keep enlarging very rapidly and within a few weeks the cat is unable to eat or drink and the only option we are left with is to humanely put the cat to sleep to end their suffering.

3c Stomatitis with ulcers on the inner surface of the lips and cheeks and/or on the gums

Ulcers on the inner surface of the lips and cheeks or on the gums have a greyish-yellow appearance and are very painful. These are generally as a result of kidney failure in old age. The reason for this is that one of the functions of the kidneys is to eliminate a waste product called urea. If the kidneys are failing, the level of urea rises in the bloodstream and the body tries to eliminate the problem by other routes. The other options for elimination of high levels of urea are via the stomach and intestines or via the lungs. The process via the lungs involves releasing the urea into the air in the lungs thereby allowing its elimination when air is breathed out of the body. The problem with this route is that the exhaled urea is caustic and burns the lining of the mouth thereby causing ulcers. These are very painful and often develop secondary bacterial infections, so the cat stops eating and may drool thick, ropy saliva. The other alternative route of urea elimination, via the stomach and intestines, causes much the same problem. The urea released into the stomach and intestines may burn the lining of these organs and cause sufficient pain there to cause the cat to stop eating and in more severe cases the cat may also vomit and develop diarrhoea. In both of these instances the cats tend to appear lethargic and depressed as these processes make them feel very unwell in addition to the obvious pain and discomfort. Thus if your cat has smelly breath and you can see greyish-yellow ulcers on the inside surfaces of the lips and/or on the gums the vet may suggest blood tests to check for kidney failure. Kidney failure is discussed more fully in the chapter on losing weight.

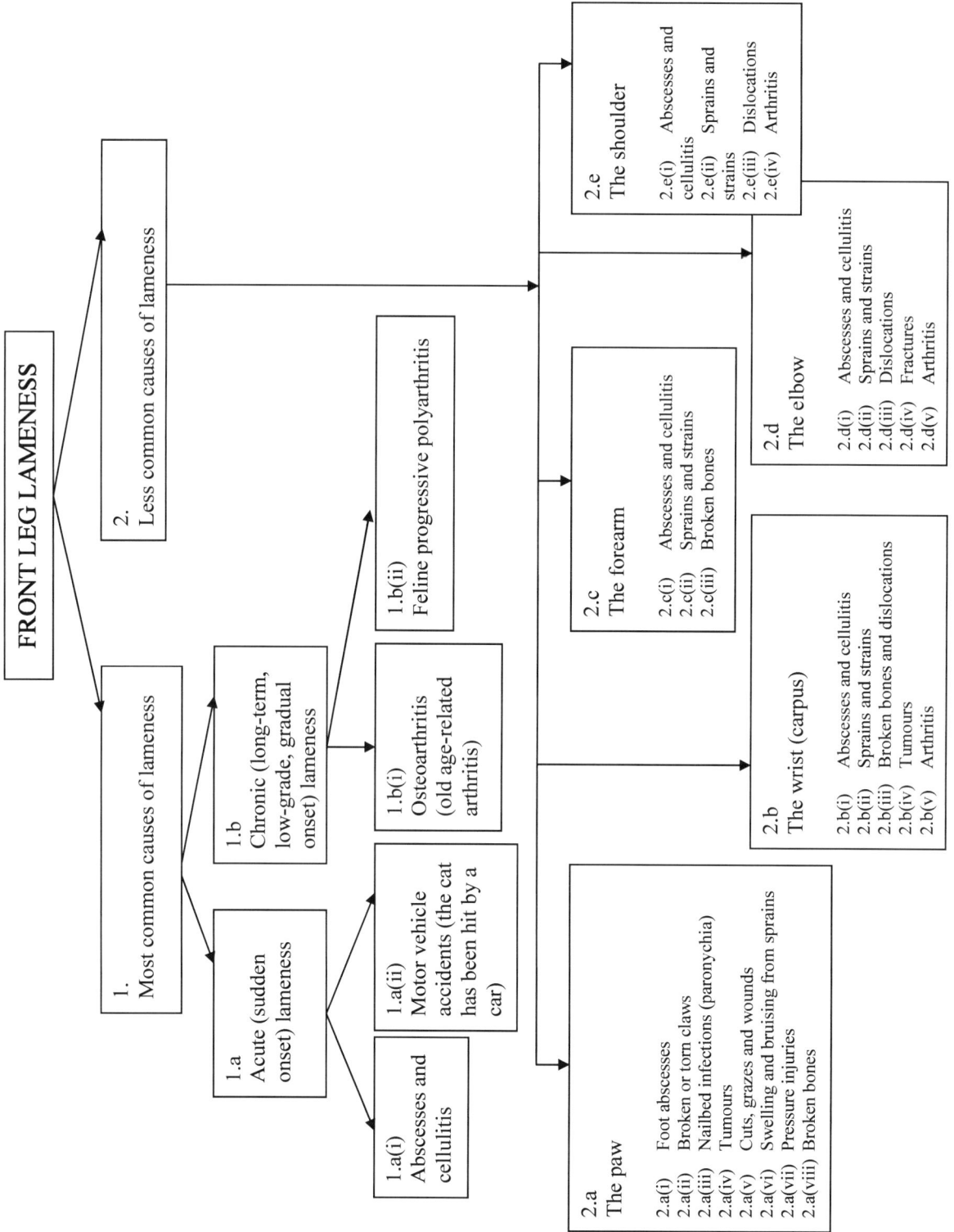

FRONT LEG LAMENESS

1. Most common causes of lameness

2. Less common causes of lameness

1. Most common causes of lameness

1.a Acute (sudden onset) lameness

- 1.a(i) Abscesses and cellulitis
- 1.a(ii) Motor vehicle accidents (the cat has been hit by a car)

1.b Chronic (long-term, low-grade, gradual onset) lameness

- 1.b(i) Osteoarthritis (old age-related arthritis)
- 1.b(ii) Feline progressive polyarthritis

2. Less common causes of lameness

2.a The paw

- 2.a(i) Foot abscesses
- 2.a(ii) Broken or torn claws
- 2.a(iii) Nailbed infections (paronychia)
- 2.a(iv) Tumours
- 2.a(v) Cuts, grazes and wounds
- 2.a(vi) Swelling and bruising from sprains
- 2.a(vii) Pressure injuries
- 2.a(viii) Broken bones

2.b The wrist (carpus)

- 2.b(i) Abscesses and cellulitis
- 2.b(ii) Sprains and strains
- 2.b(iii) Broken bones and dislocations
- 2.b(iv) Tumours
- 2.b(v) Arthritis

2.c The forearm

- 2.c(i) Abscesses and cellulitis
- 2.c(ii) Sprains and strains
- 2.c(iii) Broken bones

2.d The elbow

- 2.d(i) Abscesses and cellulitis
- 2.d(ii) Sprains and strains
- 2.d(iii) Dislocations
- 2.d(iv) Fractures
- 2.d(v) Arthritis

2.e The shoulder

- 2.e(i) Abscesses and cellulitis
- 2.e(ii) Sprains and strains
- 2.e(iii) Dislocations
- 2.e(iv) Arthritis

8

FRONT LEG LAMENESS (LIMPING)

1 Most common causes of lameness

The most common causes of lameness in one or both front legs can be divided into two categories:

- Sudden onset (acute) lameness
- Long-term, low-grade, gradual onset (chronic) lameness

Acute lameness means that the cat is suddenly lame, i.e. they were not lame yesterday but are lame today. Chronic lameness means that the cat has been becoming gradually lame over a long period of time.

The anatomy of the cat's front leg has the same components as our own arms and hands and one should think about them as functioning in much the same way as our own. The bones, joints, tendons, muscles and ligaments are virtually identical to our own. The two big differences are that cats do not have collarbones in the sense that we do i.e. they have a very underdeveloped collarbone which is not attached to the shoulder and is not easily felt by anyone other than by vets. The second big difference is that they walk on the tips of their toes, not on the palms of their hands as we do when we are on our hands and knees.

When an owner finds that their cat is lame I encourage them to feel and examine the front leg in the same way that you would examine your own arm if it were painful. I start from the toes and feel each bone and joint systematically as I progress toward the top of the leg. What you are looking for are signs of pain, heat and abnormal movement. A good tip when you examine a lame leg is to compare what you think may be abnormal to the same area on the other leg. As a general rule of thumb in the case of cats, assume the lameness is caused by an abscess or an emerging abscess until you have proved that it is due to some other cause.

1a Acute (sudden onset) lameness

The most common cause of trauma to the front leg is a cat fight which often leads to abscesses in the front leg and paw and the second most common cause is motor vehicle accidents.

1a(i) Abscesses or cellulitis as a cause of lameness

When your cat appears home and is suddenly lame, assume that they have an abscess or are developing an abscess as the most likely explanation for the lameness. The first thing to do is examine the leg with your hands rather than with your eyes. I will explain what I mean by this later in this section but first it is important that you understand what an abscess is and how it develops.

The world of cats is a very violent place. You may think you own your garden around your house but cats have no perception of property ownership in the way that we do. Any cat living near you will own their own piece of territory and our fences play no role in determining the boundaries of each cat's territory. Cats obtain and keep their territory by fighting other cats for possession of that territory. Your cat does not have automatic ownership of your garden just because they live in your house. They will have to stake their claim for ownership of your garden and they will have to defend it against other local cats trying to expand their territory. Your cat may, for example, own half of your garden and half of your neighbour's garden while the rest of your garden may be owned by another cat. When your cat strays into another cat's territory or vice versa there will very likely be a fight to defend the territory.

Cats fight differently from dogs. When dogs fight they rip large holes and gashes into each other. These wounds appear very dramatic and severe but they do offer one good feature, which is that the wound is large enough to allow natural drainage. Drainage from a wound is very important in that the wound can ooze just as your own cuts and grazes do. This oozing from wounds is the body's way of removing dirt and bacteria (infection) from a wound. Only when the body is satisfied that the dirt and bacteria have been removed will the wound heal. If a wound heals before all the bacteria have been removed there is a high risk that an abscess will develop under the skin. Cats, unlike dogs, have very small teeth and claws and when they fight they tend to pepper each other with small puncture wounds. The dirt and bacteria on the tips of the teeth and claws are thus pushed through the skin into the tissue beneath. The actual puncture wounds are very small and generally seal off very quickly. The result is that the dirt and bacteria deposited under the skin tend to develop into abscesses just as a thorn or splinter would do. The abscess will progressively enlarge until it bursts.

The initial stage in the development of an abscess is called cellulitis and this stage is very painful. Once the abscess has matured and is full of pus it will burst and once it has burst it is less painful. This process is similar to the process we have all experienced when developing a pimple on our face or nose. A pimple is simply a very small abscess. In the first stage of developing a pimple there may be nothing to see on the surface of the skin but the affected area is painful especially when touched; this stage is called cellulitis. Cellulitis means inflammation in the tissue under the skin and is painful because the inflammation causes the tissues in the area to stretch and this stretching effect is what hurts. During the cellulitis stage pus has not yet developed. If you then wait a few days one of two things may happen; either the painful area will simply stop being painful and the problem will disappear, or the painful area will develop into a ripe and yellow pimple full of pus. This stage is still painful because the accumulation of pus under the skin is still causing the surrounding tissues to be stretched but once the pimple is popped it is less painful. The pain subsides when the pimple is popped because this allows the pus to drain away, reducing stretching of the tissue in the area. An abscess behaves in exactly the same way but on a larger and more dramatic scale.

The most painful stage in the development of an abscess is the cellulitis stage and this is the most difficult time to diagnose the appearance of an abscess because the affected area is simply painful without any other obvious clues as to the cause of the pain. If the cellulitis develops into a full-blown abscess full of pus, the painful area is more easily identified as a painful swelling which is soft to the touch; the painful area feels like a balloon filled with water. As the pus accumulates under the skin the pus has the effect of "poisoning" the skin covering the abscess. This causes the hair follicles that anchor the fur in that area to lose their grip on the hairs they produce. In practice this means that if you suspect a painful swollen area under the skin is an abscess, simply tug the fur overlying the swelling. If a tuft of hair is very easily and painlessly pulled out then you know that the swelling you are feeling is indeed an abscess.

If the abscess is not lanced to drain out the pus, then the pus will continue poisoning the skin overlying it until a circular piece of skin dies off and a hole appears over the abscess to drain the pus out. Thus if we do not lance the abscess it will eventually "lance" itself. The reason that we always lance an abscess once we have identified it is that it immediately reduces the pain and starts the healing process because the body can only start healing a wound once the dirt and infection in the wound have drained away. The second reason for lancing the abscess is that, if it is left to lance itself by making a piece of skin die off and fall away, an unnecessarily large hole will be created and the wound will take longer to heal than if it is simply lanced with a small incision. The third reason we always lance an abscess is that it may sometimes take a long time to lance itself, thus allowing a very large amount of pus to accumulate for several days. A large amount of pus trapped in the body has a toxic effect on the body and makes the cat feel very unwell with a high fever. In severe cases of accumulations of large amounts of pus the toxic effect on the body may even be life-threatening.

In the cellulitis stage of the formation of an abscess there is no benefit in trying to lance the area because there is no pus yet to drain away. The problem at this stage is simply hard and painful swelling, i.e. the affected area feels very firm in contrast to the feel of an abscess which feels soft and "spongy" like a balloon filled with water. At this stage the immune system is fighting the infection and very often it will win the fight and the problem simply goes away without a proper abscess ever appearing.

A good indication that cellulitis has been caused by puncture wounds from teeth or claws is that there may be small scabs over the painful swollen area. I look for these scabs with my fingertips rather than with my eyes. I very gently feel the surface of the skin with my fingertips by moving up the leg against the direction of hair growth. This means my fingers lift the fur from the skin and my fingertips are moving under the hairs and feel the surface of the skin. If you run your finger over the leg in the direction of hair growth then you will feel only the surface of the fur coat and not the skin. Once you have found a small scab or even a tuft of fur matted with blood or ooze from the puncture wound, then you have found the site of the injury. You should remove a small amount of fur overlying the puncture wound by plucking the fur out or trimming it away with scissors. This is done so that you can monitor the puncture wound and keep it clean.

The vet will usually use painkillers and antibiotics to assist the immune system in the fight against the bacteria. If an abscess containing pus has been identified, then the vet will lance the abscess to drain it. The vet will once again prescribe painkillers and antibiotics to clear the infection and they will ask you to clean the incision they made to lance the abscess twice daily. They will stress to you that you must remove the scab trying to form at the incision twice a day otherwise the incision will simply seal off and the abscess will simply refill as the pus is no longer draining out. In practice the vet will usually advise dabbing the scab which forms at the incision site with wet cotton wool. Warm tap water is quite sufficient for the purpose because the intention is simply to dab the scab until it is so soggy that it falls off. In this way the opening into the abscess is kept open and the pus can keep draining out. You should do this twice daily for a week to prevent the incision sealing off and the abscess recurring.

1a(ii) Motor vehicle accidents (the cat has been hit by a car)

Cats are free spirits and their inquisitive nature means that they constantly roam and explore their environment. This inevitably means that your cat will cross roads in their search for adventure. Cats have no road sense and often run in front of cars travelling on the roads around your house. If they are struck directly by a car they are usually killed outright and we are presented with the trauma of finding our cats dead on the road often with horrific external injuries. If the cat is struck a glancing blow by a car then they may simply suffer painful bruising or broken bones. If your cat returns home after an adventure in the great outdoors and is obviously lame then you need to consider whether the lameness is due to the pain caused by fight wounds or being struck by a car. The first thing to consider is just how lame the cat is. If they are still walking and taking some weight on the affected leg despite the pain then it is unlikely that any bones have been broken. If the affected leg is not taking any weight and is either being carried up off the ground or is being dragged on the ground then there is quite possibly significant damage to the leg in terms of damage to bones and/or the nerve supply to the leg.

The first and most obvious thing to do is to examine the leg by feeling all parts of the leg with your hands. If the leg is floppy and swinging like a pendulum then there is almost certainly a broken bone so be very gentle when you feel the leg. I examine the leg by starting at the paw and working my way upwards toward the top of the leg. The first thing to examine is the claws; if the tips of the claws look ragged and frayed like miniature mopheads then it is very likely that the cat has been involved in a car accident. The reason the tips of the claws look ragged in these cases is that as the cat is shunted by the car, they slide and skid over the road and will extend their claws to try to get a grip and stop the slide. Obviously the tarmac is too hard for them to dig their claws into so the road surface acts like a massive piece of sandpaper and shreds the tips of the claws. If you find that the tips of the claws are ragged then you can assume that something, like a car, has shunted the cat across a rough surface. The ragged claw tips are not painful per se so we must continue examining the leg to find where the leg has been injured by the shunting impact.

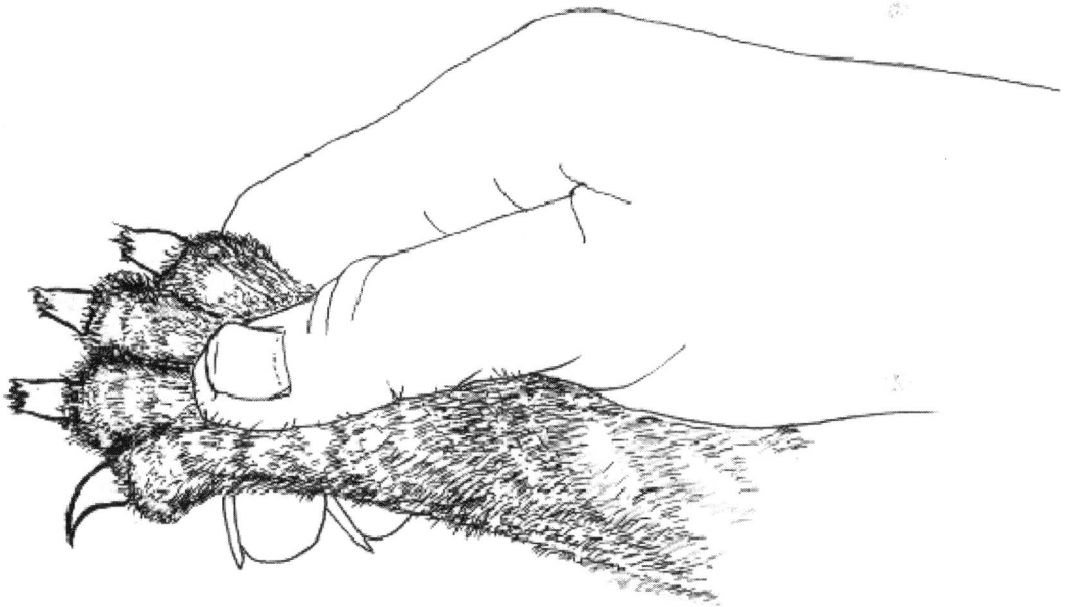

Fig. 25 – Torn nails are usually an indication that a cat has been
hit by a car or has had a very near miss

Continue examining the leg by systematically examining every part with your hands. The anatomy of the cat's front and back legs is virtually identical to your own anatomy so simply imagine you are examining a human being's arm or leg. Feel each toe individually and then examine the bones leading up to the next joint which will be the wrist (carpus). Continue upwards by feeling the bones in the forearm (the radius and ulna bones). Examine the elbow by flexing and extending it and then continue upwards toward the shoulder joint along the upper arm bone (the humerus). Examine the shoulder by bending and flexing it and then feel the shoulder blade which extends to the top of the leg. Be very gentle initially and be careful because when you find the painful part the cat may hiss and spit and may lash out at you. When you examine the parts of the leg simply try to move all the joints in their natural type and range of movement and check that the bones between the joints are solid, i.e. the leg should not bend in between the joints. At the same time run your fingers against the direction of hair growth to feel the surface of the skin to check for superficial injuries like cuts and grazes or scabs caused by bite and fight wounds as discussed previously.

In conclusion, if you find that your cat is suddenly lame and has frayed claws then assume they have been struck by something that has shunted them across the road. The shunting injury may simply have caused deep and painful bruising or sprained a joint or it may have broken bones or more seriously damaged joints. If bones are broken the cat will be unable to stand on the leg and it will often swing like a floppy pendulum and the leg can be bent at points between the normal joints in the leg. If a joint has been damaged the leg won't swing like a pendulum but rather it is held off the ground and the joint is painful when you try to bend and straighten it. It would always be prudent to have your vet double-check the cat's lame leg and the rest of the cat's body when you identify frayed claws as these trauma cases may also involve damage to other body parts other than the obviously lame leg. The treatment for the damage will depend on the exact type of damage you and your vet identify and will be discussed later in this chapter.

When people talk about arthritis what they mean is long-term low-grade pain and inflammation in one or more joints usually associated with growing older. The word "chronic" means that the arthritis is a long-term problem. The classic example of this is the arthritis we develop in the joints of our fingers as we grow old. To be pedantic, the word "arthritis" is actually a very vague term meaning simply inflammation in a joint. The term "arthritis" does not explain why the joint is inflamed. Thus if you sprain your ankle it would be technically correct to say that your ankle has acute (sudden onset) arthritis because the sprain has caused inflammation. For the sake of simplicity I will use the word "arthritis" as it is used in common everyday speech to imply long-term low-grade inflammation in one or more joints.

There are two common types of arthritis in cats. The first type of arthritis is osteoarthritis which is the technical term for old age-related arthritis caused by the wear and tear on the joint as it is used throughout life.

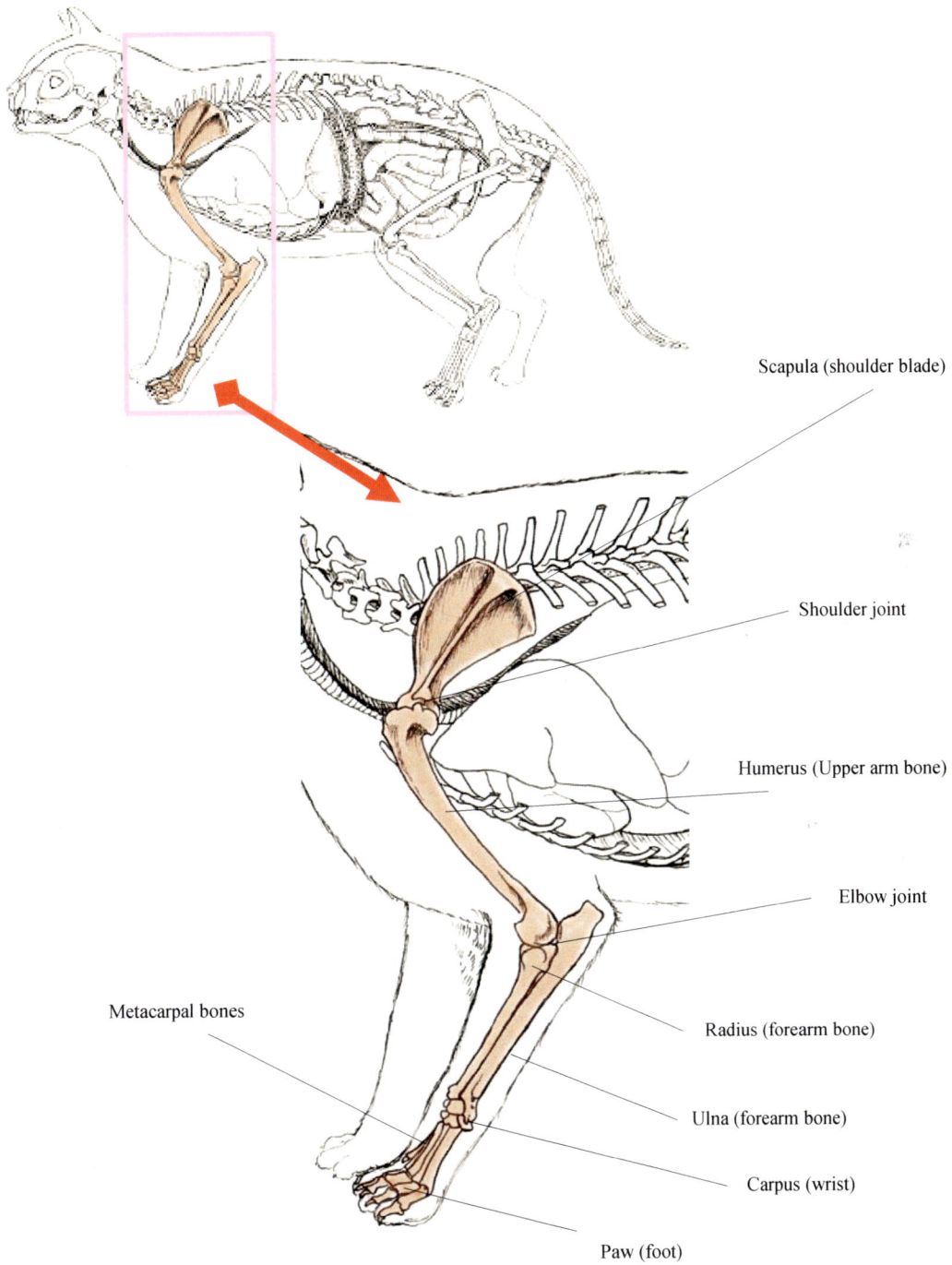

Scapula (shoulder blade)

Shoulder joint

Humerus (Upper arm bone)

Elbow joint

Metacarpal bones

Radius (forearm bone)

Ulna (forearm bone)

Carpus (wrist)

Paw (foot)

Fig 26. – Anatomy of the front leg

1b Chronic (long-term, low-grade, gradual onset) lameness

The joints will wear out in old age just as an old door hinge wears out over time. The second type of arthritis is feline progressive polyarthritis which is the cat equivalent of rheumatoid arthritis and may develop at any age although it is most commonly seen in older cats. The name of this condition in cats sounds complicated but is actually very simple when broken down; "feline" means relating to cats; "progressive" means literally that the condition is progressive and will gradually become worse over time; "poly" means more than one joint is affected; and "arthritis" means that the affected joint becomes inflamed and thus painful.

The effects and symptoms of both types of long-term arthritis in cats are very similar but the treatments are different so I will discuss each condition individually.

1b(i) Osteoarthritis (old age-related arthritis)

Factors that cause acute arthritis may develop into chronic arthritis. Arthritis may develop after a joint has been injured or infected. The types of injuries which may cause acute or chronic arthritis are sprains, fractures, dislocations, etc. Injuries to joints should thus be treated as quickly and efficiently as possible to try to prevent long-term permanent arthritis developing in that joint. We are all familiar with the concept of someone injuring a joint and then either having permanent low-grade discomfort in that joint, or the injury may have seemed to heal well but as we get older the joint may cause discomfort due to the delayed onset of arthritis. Arthritis may also develop in a joint which is not anatomically perfectly formed, i.e. it is dysplastic. Dysplasia is the technical description for a joint which is not perfectly formed. Most people are familiar with the term hip dysplasia, most commonly seen in certain breeds of dogs like German Shepherd dogs, which means that the hips are not properly formed, but any joint in any type of animal may suffer from dysplasia. If a joint is dysplastic then it will wear out faster than a normally formed joint. This process of wearing out causes arthritis. Most commonly, however, arthritis develops simply due to ordinary "wear and tear" in a normal joint due to old age.

The process of chronic osteoarthritis is often referred to as degenerative joint disease (DJD). Chronic arthritis causes thickening of the tissues around the joint, making the affected joint feel larger and thicker than normal. This thickening is caused by "scar tissue" forming around the joint. The bones forming the joint will develop irregular thickenings called osteophytes and the lining of the joint capsule will be permanently inflamed and thickened. These three changes represent the body's attempt to heal and strengthen the affected joint. These changes often make the arthritis worse as they will continue permanently and lead to the pain of the arthritis becoming progressively worse. The second effect of these three processes is that the joint will lose its full range of movement. This happens because the "scar tissue" laid down around the joint will make it less flexible, rendering the joint less able to perform its full range of movements.

The ends of the bones forming moving joints are covered with a layer of cartilage called articular or joint cartilage. This cartilage is very smooth and is essential for smooth movement of the joint. This joint cartilage has very few nerve cells supplying it and this relatively nerve-free layer is essential in covering the bone ends which have a good nerve supply. The best way to understand this concept is to consider the forces acting on the ends of the bones when they are bearing weight during walking or standing. When we walk or stand our entire body weight is pressing down on our joints. The reason this doesn't cause pain is the layer of numb cartilage covering the ends of the bones (the articular cartilage). If we didn't have this layer of articular cartilage then the ends of the bones would be pressed together by our body weight and as the bone ends have a good nerve supply this would cause severe pain. Even limited areas of damage to this articular cartilage allow small areas of bone to be exposed and pressure on this exposed bone causes pain. The process of arthritis causes erosions in the articular cartilage and this contributes significantly to the pain in the affected joint.

The bone ends forming the joint are held together by the joint capsule which effectively forms a sealed bag around the bone ends. The purpose of the joint capsule is not only to hold the ends of the bones forming the joint together but also to produce joint fluid, which fills the joint. The joint fluid in turn serves two main purposes, namely to serve as lubrication for the joint in the same way that oil lubricates a door hinge and, secondly, to carry nutrients to feed and maintain the articular cartilages and other structures inside the joint. This joint fluid is called synovial fluid and is produced by the synovial membrane, which is the inside layer of the joint capsule. To my knowledge there are no man-made lubricants for machinery which are as efficient as synovial fluid in terms of lubricating moving parts. Many cats with arthritis do not produce enough joint fluid to feed and lubricate the affected joint and this leads to increased grinding of the joint cartilage which further contributes to the pain and progression of the arthritis.

Once the processes of chronic arthritis have been present for a few months or years the affected joint will feel thicker than the same joint on the other leg. When a joint with chronic arthritis is flexed and extended one will notice that it may not be able to bend or straighten as much as a healthy joint does. During bending and straightening one may also notice a "crunchy" sound or feeling in the joint. This "crunchy" sensation is called crepitus. Once the process of chronic arthritis has started, the changes in the joint are irreversible. The changes in fact will become more severe as time goes on. This process of arthritis is identical to the process of arthritis in human beings as we grow old.

When the vet is faced with an arthritic joint the treatment they apply will have three objectives, i.e.

- Relieve the pain and inflammation in the joint
- Slow down the ongoing changes which worsen the arthritis over time
- Improve the range of movement of the joint

The first step is to find a suitable long-term anti-inflammatory drug that will alleviate the pain in the joint. The second treatment I use is the category of agents called mobility supplements (chondroitin sulphate and/or glucosamine). These are agents that help the joint to produce synovial (joint) fluid to maintain its lubrication and to promote natural healing of the eroded articular cartilages covering the bone ends. This is an important component of the treatment as these erosions expose the nerve endings in the bone, causing a lot of the pain and if we can repair these areas the patient will obviously require a lower daily dose of anti-inflammatories.

A change in lifestyle also benefits these patients in that overweight individuals should lose weight to take the extra strain off the joints and gentle controlled exercise should be encouraged to maintain the size and strength of the muscles of the affected leg to help support the joints. This programme of sustained, controlled exercise is effectively the same as a physiotherapy programme for human beings. The objective of this programme of activity (physiotherapy) is to keep the joints as flexible as possible and improve their range of movement as this will make movement easier and less uncomfortable for the cat.

The individuals who show very little or no pain can often be successfully treated using only natural remedies like glucosamine and chondroitin sulphate or natural oils like cod liver oil and evening primrose oil, or homeopathic remedies like sulphur, arnica and rhus tox. These remedies work by relieving the pain and, in the case of glucosamine and chondroitin sulphate, also help the joint to lubricate itself and repair the damage to the joint cartilage caused by the grinding action of the unstable bone ends.

If these products are not sufficient to alleviate the pain then they can be combined with long-term anti-inflammatory and painkilling medications. A major problem faced by vets all over the world is that there are currently no anti-inflammatory or painkilling medications available for long-term use in cats. This is in stark contrast to the wide range of medicines available for human beings and dogs to treat the pain of long-term osteoarthritis. The main reason that there are no licensed medicines for long-term pain relief in cats is that they are very sensitive to adverse reactions to anti-inflammatory and painkilling medicines. For example even a tiny dose of paracetamol will kill your cat despite being very safe to use on your baby. Other human medicines like ibuprofen and aspirin can also cause severe damage to cats. The result is that vets have been forced to try some of the dog arthritis medications on cats. In some cases this has led to disastrous and fatal side effects and in other cases some of these medicines appear to be safe if used at very low doses. My advice would be to consult your vet about current unofficial (unlicensed) use of some of the dog medicines in cats if osteoarthritis is causing severe pain. There are some natural remedies available to try to alleviate the pain of osteoarthritis and these include green-lipped mussel extract and curcumins. These remedies are not as effective as conventional anti-inflammatory medicines but they are not dangerous. One again, you should consult your vet about the state of current knowledge regarding the use of these remedies.

If one particular medication does not seem to help much then others should be tried until one is found that works for your individual cat. This trial and error period in which different medicines in different combinations are tried should be controlled and monitored by your vet, as there are many medicines that should not be used in combination with each other.

Most cats who have developed arthritis for whatever reason should be able to enjoy an active and happy life when the appropriate treatments are used. The process of developing arthritis is, just as in human beings, something one should expect in old age but one does not have to accept the pain or discomfort which may accompany the arthritis. Modern treatment and management of arthritis mean that we, and our cats, should be able to live comfortably in our golden years.

1b(ii) Feline progressive polyarthritis

As mentioned earlier feline progressive polyarthritis is the cat equivalent to rheumatoid arthritis in human beings. This type of arthritis causes the same type of damage to the joints as osteoarthritis and thus similar symptoms, i.e. lameness, but the cause of the inflammation and damage is very different. Osteoarthritis is caused by injury to one or more joints or long-term wear and tear on the joints. Feline progressive polyarthritis is inflammation in several joints caused by the immune system attacking the joints just as in the case of rheumatoid arthritis in human beings. This condition is called an autoimmune disorder and it means that the body's immune system is attacking its own cells for no apparent reason. It seems that the immune system simply fails to recognise that the joint cartilage cells covering the ends of the bones forming the joints are normal cells and it then attacks them as if they were invading bacteria. As the attack on the cells continues, they become damaged and unable to work efficiently and will eventually die. It is not understood why this process should happen for no apparent reason but unfortunately it does.

The vet will need to run several tests, including X-rays of the affected joints and analysis of the joint fluid in the inflamed joints. The only way to treat this condition is to try to stop the immune system attacking the joints by using medications that suppress the immune system. The most common medicines used to achieve this are cortisones (steroids). The dose of the cortisone is adjusted until it controls the inflammation in the joints and then the vet may try to reduce the dose gradually over a long period of time to find the lowest possible dose which controls the immune system and hence the pain and inflammation in the joints.

The above discussion is focused on the most common causes of lameness in cats but one should always be aware that other factors and conditions may cause sufficient pain in the leg to cause lameness so I would always advocate a thorough and systematic examination of the entire leg in every case of lameness.

2 Less common causes of lameness

When presented with a lame cat my thoughts and actions will proceed as follows.

Cats may limp on one or both of their front legs for many reasons. I examine lame cats by examining the entire leg starting from the paw and working my way up to the top of the leg.

I will discuss the problems that one might encounter as the cause of the lameness in this order. A very important part of the investigation of a lame cat is the information that you, the owner, are able to give the vet to describe the lameness. The questions the vet will ask may include the following:

- How long has the cat been lame?
- Did the lameness develop very suddenly or gradually?
- Has the lameness become more or less severe since it was first noticed or has it remained the same?
- Is the cat licking or biting at any part of the lame leg?
- Is the lameness most severe after exercise or after the cat has been resting/sleeping?
- Does the cat seem unwell in any other way besides the lameness?

These are very important questions and I ask my clients to answer them as accurately as possible. I ask that if they do not know the answer to any or all the questions to say so because if they are uncertain and merely take a guess or tell me what they think I want to hear, it may mislead me. There is no shame in not knowing the answer to any or all of these questions. Not being able to answer the questions does not imply that you are not concerned about your cat.

Many cat owners will have examined their cat themselves before consulting a vet and I encourage people to do so. The anatomy of the cat's leg has the same components as our own arms and hands and one should think about them as functioning in much the same way. The bones, joints, tendons, muscles and ligaments are virtually identical to our own. The two big differences are that cats do not have collarbones in the sense that we do and they walk on the tips of their toes, not on the palms of their hands as we do when we are on our hands and knees. A good tip is to compare what you think may be abnormal to the same area on the other front leg.

Examine the paw by looking at the claws, the toes, the pads and the spaces between the pads. What we are looking for are areas of inflammation, bleeding, swelling and bruising. The next step is to part the fur at the base of each claw and examine the claw beds. Each toe is then carefully felt to check for pain, swelling, heat or abnormal movement. Each toe consists of three bones (phalanges), just as our fingers do, and each individual joint must be checked for normal movement. The spaces between the pads should also be carefully felt to check for the same things. The same visual and manual examination is then continued up the bones (metacarpal bones) leading to the wrist (carpus).

2a The paw

The most common problems encountered when examining the paws are:

2a(i) - **Foot abscesses**. Abscesses may develop in the paws as a result of wounds from fighting with other cats. The abscess causes the paw to swell up very much larger than normal size and is very painful when touched. Please refer to the discussion on the diagnosis and treatment of cellulitis and abscesses earlier in this chapter.

2a(ii) - Broken or torn claws. Broken claws are treated by removing the broken part of the claw and the vet may prescribe antibiotics, painkillers and footbaths as necessary. If one or more of the claw tips are frayed then it is very likely that the cat has been hit by a car. Please refer to the above section on motor vehicle accidents for a discussion of this cause of lameness.

2a(iii) - Nailbed infections (paronychia). The nailbed is the groove between the nail and the skin and infections may arise in this groove. The infection is most commonly caused by bacteria or fungal infections. One would suspect an infection in the nailbed if the nail feels very loose or if there is a discharge from the nailbed. The discharge which may develop is either watery or looks like pus and may or may not have a foul odour. Once the vet has determined what kind of parasite has caused the infection they will prescribe appropriate treatment.

The important question to ask in cases of nailbed infections is "what has allowed the infection to develop?" The answer may be simply that a cut or graze in that area has become infected and the infection has moved into the nailbed. If a number of toes have the same infection we should ask ourselves why the body has not been able to fight off the infection. The explanation may be that the cat has diabetes and the high blood sugar levels have resulted in a high sugar content in the moisture in the nailbed and this has favoured the development of an infection. Other disease conditions which may compromise the body's ability to fight off infections are underlying Feline Leukaemia and Feline AIDS. These two underlying conditions are discussed in the chapter on weight loss.

2a(iv) - Tumours. Several types of tumours may develop in the nailbed. They are not usually immediately noticeable and the first sign of a problem in the nailbed is a secondary infection. If the vet suspects that the infection is the result of a tumour they will often investigate further by taking X-rays and biopsies from the affected toe. Most nailbed tumours are not cancerous and the vet will most commonly advise eliminating the infection first and then amputating the affected toe to remove the tumour. This seems a very extreme way of treating the problem but fortunately cats do not seem to miss the removed toe at all and function perfectly normally without it.

2a(v) - Cuts, grazes and puncture wounds. These may be treated by stitching and bandaging, plus antibiotics and painkillers as necessary.

2a(vi) - Swelling and bruising from sprains. These are treated with painkillers/anti-inflammatories, support bandages and rest from exercise as necessary.

2a(vii) - Swelling from pressure injuries like someone stepping on the paw or objects dropped onto the paw. These are treated with painkillers and rest from exercise as necessary.

2a(viii) - **Broken bones.** Severe painful swelling of one or more toes may suggest that one of the bones has been broken. Broken toe bones are most common in cats more than one year old. Broken bones and joint dislocations are uncommon in very young kittens as they have very flexible, soft bones which tend to bend rather than break when the paw is injured. X-rays are sometimes required to confirm that a bone has been broken. If any bones are broken then the fracture is treated either with casts and bandages or through surgical repair as necessary.

2b The wrist (carpus)

The wrist is also examined with your eyes and hands. The wrist is a complicated joint composed of the arm bones at the top and the metacarpal bones at the bottom. The wrist bones consist of seven individual bones arranged in two rows between the arm bones and the metacarpal bones. All of these bones are held together by many small ligaments and joint capsules. Start by looking at the wrist and comparing it to the wrist on the other leg. Look for swelling, bruising and wounds. When feeling the wrist one should bend (flex) and straighten (extend) the wrist to check for signs of pain. The wrist should also be bent gently to the left and right.
The most common problems encountered when examining the wrist are:

2b(i) - **Abscesses and cellulitis** in and around the joint which cause pain and swelling. These are treated with antibiotics and anti-inflammatories/painkillers. Please refer to the discussion on the diagnosis and treatment of cellulitis and abscesses earlier in this chapter.

2b(ii) - **Sprains and strains** which cause pain and swelling. These are treated with rest from exercise, support bandages and anti-inflammatories/painkillers as necessary.

2b(iii) - **Broken bones and dislocations.** Severe painful swelling of the wrist may suggest that one or more of the bones or ligaments of the joint have been broken or dislocated. Broken wrist bones and dislocation are most common in cats more than one year old. Broken hock bones and joint dislocations are uncommon in very young kittens as they have very flexible, soft bones which tend to bend rather than break when the wrist is injured. X-rays are generally required to confirm that a bone has been broken or ligaments have been ruptured. If any bones are broken then the fracture is treated either with casts and bandages or through surgical repair as necessary. If ligaments have been ruptured or parts of the wrist are dislocated then they are treated either with casts or surgical repair depending on which ligaments have been damaged and how severely they have been damaged.

2b(iv) - **Tumours.** Severe painful swelling of the wrist may very occasionally suggest tumours developing in the bones of the wrist. X-rays and biopsies are generally required to confirm the presence of tumours. Most tumours affecting this area are highly malignant cancers and the treatment options will often involve amputation of the leg and chemotherapy. Fortunately these tumours are the least common cause of pain and lameness in this area. Middle-aged and old cats are more commonly affected by tumours than young cats.

2b(v) - **Arthritis** may cause thickening of the whole joint or part of the joint. The thickened joint is usually firm to the touch and not painful when touched. The joint will seem thicker than the same joint on the other leg. The joint may be painful when you bend or straighten the joint and it may produce a "crunchy" sensation when it is bent and straightened. X-rays will usually be taken of the joint to confirm the diagnosis. Please refer to the paragraph earlier in this chapter for a discussion of arthritis and appropriate treatment.

2c The forearm

The forearm is also examined with your eyes and hands. The forearm has two long bones called the radius and ulna. These bones can be felt extending from the wrist to the elbow joint. One should check for pain and swelling when applying pressure to the bones and the surrounding muscles.

The most common problems encountered when examining the forearm are:

2c(i) - **Abscesses and cellulitis** in and around the muscles resulting in pain and swelling. These are treated with antibiotics and anti-inflammatories/painkillers as necessary. Please refer to the discussion on the diagnosis and treatment of cellulitis and abscesses earlier in this chapter.

2c(ii) - **Sprains and strains** which cause pain and swelling. These are treated with rest from exercise, and anti-inflammatories/painkillers as necessary.

2c(iii) - **Broken bones** in the forearm are uncommon in very young kittens as they have very flexible, soft bones which tend to bend rather than break when the wrist is injured. X-rays are often required to confirm that a bone has been broken. Most fractures that do occur in the long bones in young cats are found on X-ray to be "greenstick fractures". A "greenstick fracture" is exactly what the name implies. If you bend a dry stick or branch it tends to snap in half but if you bend a green stick or branch it tends to splinter only on one side and doesn't break into two pieces. The same thing happens in the bones of young growing cats because, like a green stick/branch, they are softer and more "bendy" than a dried stick which is more like a mature bone. If any bones are broken then the fracture is treated either with casts and bandages or through surgical repair as necessary.

2d The elbow

The anatomical design of the elbow joint in cats is the same as the human elbow. The basic structure of the elbow is a hinge joint. The bone of the upper arm (humerus) is at the top and the forearm bones (the radius and the ulna) are at the bottom. The joint between these bones is composed of the ends of these bones, the joint capsule and the collateral ligaments on either side.

On either side of the elbow we find ligaments called collateral ligaments. The ligament on the inner aspect of the joint is called the medial collateral ligament and the one on the outer aspect is called the lateral collateral ligament (refer to the diagram). These ligaments run from the humerus (the bone of the upper arm) to the radius and ulna (the bones of the forearm) and allow the elbow to bend in one plane only, i.e. the elbow can only bend (flex) or straighten (extend). Consider your own elbow, it can only bend and straighten. The reason that it cannot bend sideways so that the outer surface of the wrist touches the outer surface of the shoulder is that the collateral ligaments do not allow this movement. The elbow functions in only one plane in much the same way as a door hinge. These collateral ligaments are found on the outside surface of the joint capsule.

Because the elbow is a very tightly fitting and complicated joint, even "minor" problems that may cause little or no pain in a loose joint like the shoulder are liable to cause significant pain and lameness in the elbow joint.

The most common problems encountered when examining the elbow are:

2d(i) - **Abscesses and cellulitis** in the vicinity of the elbow may cause sufficient pain to cause lameness. Please refer to the discussion on the diagnosis and treatment of cellulitis and abscesses earlier in this chapter.

2d(ii) - **Sprains and strains** which cause pain and swelling. These are treated with rest from exercise, support bandages and anti-inflammatories/painkillers as necessary.

2d(iii) - **Dislocations** of the elbow are very uncommon because it is such a tightly fitting joint. If the elbow has been dislocated the cat will have to have a general anaesthetic to put the elbow back into its normal position. This is because it is very painful to relieve the dislocation but fortunately it can usually be done by manipulation only, without the need for surgery. However, surgery may be required if the elbow does not remain in position after the dislocation has been reduced. The object of this surgery will be to repair the torn ligaments which help to hold the bones in the correct position.

2d(iv) - **Fractures** of the bones forming the elbow are fortunately not very common. The repair may involve bone screws, pins and bone plates. After the surgery the cat must be rested for six weeks. During this period of rest the cats should have light, controlled exercise to keep the joint mobile and supple.

2d(v) - **Arthritis** may cause thickening of the whole joint or part of the joint. The thickened joint is usually firm to the touch and not painful when touched. The joint will seem thicker than the same joint on the other leg. The joint may be painful when you bend or straighten the joint and it may produce a "crunchy" sensation when it is bent and straightened. X-rays will usually be taken of the joint to confirm the diagnosis. Please refer to the paragraph earlier in this chapter for a discussion of arthritis and appropriate treatment.

2e The shoulder

The most common problems encountered when examining the shoulder are:

2e(i) - **Abscesses and cellulitis** in the vicinity of the shoulder may cause sufficient pain to cause lameness. Please refer to the discussion on the diagnosis and treatment of cellulitis and abscesses earlier in this chapter.

2e(ii) - **Sprains and strains** which cause pain and swelling. These are treated with rest from exercise and anti-inflammatories/painkillers as necessary.

2e(iii) - **Dislocations** of the shoulder are very uncommon. If the shoulder has been dislocated the cat will have to have a general anaesthetic to put the shoulder back into its normal position. This is because it is very painful to relieve the dislocation but fortunately it can usually be done by manipulation only, without the need for surgery. However, surgery may be required if the shoulder does not remain in position after the dislocation has been reduced. The object of this surgery will be to repair the torn ligaments which help to hold the bones in the correct position.

2e(iv) - **Arthritis** may cause thickening of the whole joint or part of the joint. The thickened joint is usually firm to the touch and not painful when touched. The joint will seem thicker than the same joint on the other leg. The joint may be painful when you bend or straighten the joint and it may produce a "crunchy" sensation when it is bent and straightened. X-rays will usually be taken of the joint to confirm the diagnosis. Please refer to the paragraph earlier in this chapter for a discussion on arthritis and appropriate treatment.

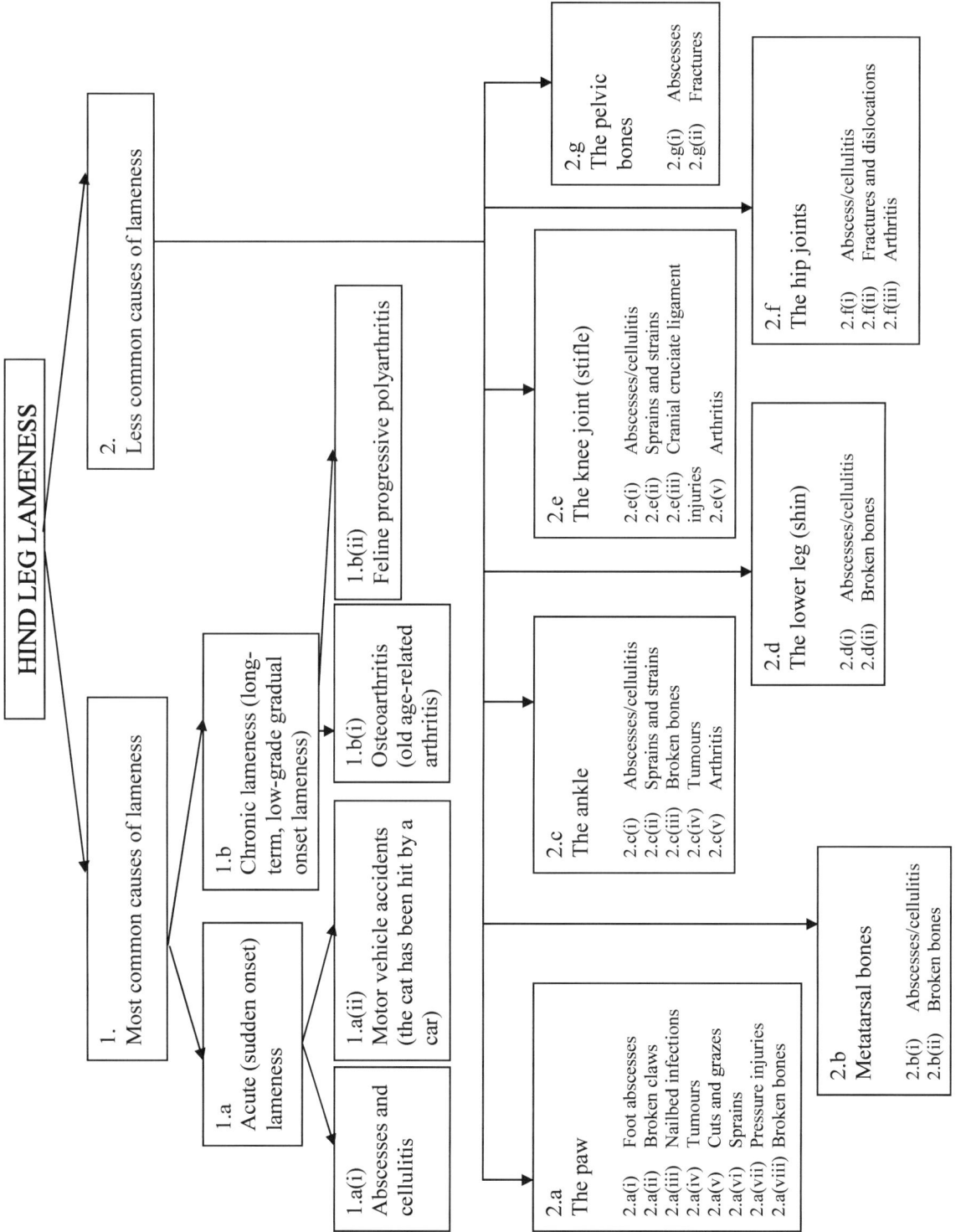

HIND LEG LAMENESS

1.
Most common causes of lameness

1.a
Acute (sudden onset) lameness

1.b
Chronic lameness (long-term, low-grade gradual onset lameness)

1.a(i)
Abscesses and cellulitis

1.a(ii)
Motor vehicle accidents (the cat has been hit by a car)

1.b(i)
Osteoarthritis (old age-related arthritis)

1.b(ii)
Feline progressive polyarthritis

2.
Less common causes of lameness

2.a
The paw

2.a(i)   Foot abscesses
2.a(ii)   Broken claws
2.a(iii)   Nailbed infections
2.a(iv)   Tumours
2.a(v)   Cuts and grazes
2.a(vi)   Sprains
2.a(vii)   Pressure injuries
2.a(viii) Broken bones

2.b
Metatarsal bones

2.b(i)   Abscesses/cellulitis
2.b(ii)   Broken bones

2.c
The ankle

2.c(i)   Abscesses/cellulitis
2.c(ii)   Sprains and strains
2.c(iii)   Broken bones
2.c(iv)   Tumours
2.c(v)   Arthritis

2.d
The lower leg (shin)

2.d(i)   Abscesses/cellulitis
2.d(ii)   Broken bones

2.e
The knee joint (stifle)

2.e(i)   Abscesses/cellulitis
2.e(ii)   Sprains and strains
2.e(iii)   Cranial cruciate ligament injuries
2.e(v)   Arthritis

2.f
The hip joints

2.f(i)   Abscess/cellulitis
2.f(ii)   Fractures and dislocations
2.f(iii)   Arthritis

2.g
The pelvic bones

2.g(i)   Abscesses
2.g(ii)   Fractures

9

HIND LEG LAMENESS (LIMPING)

Cats may limp on one or both of their back legs for many reasons. I examine lame cats by examining the entire leg starting from the paw and working my way up to the top of the leg. I will discuss the problems that one might encounter as the cause of the lameness in this order. A very important part of the investigation of a limping cat is the information that you, the owner, are able to give the vet to describe the lameness. The questions the vet will ask may include the following:

- How long has the cat been lame?
- Did the lameness develop very suddenly or gradually?
- Has the lameness become more or less severe since it was first noticed or has it remained the same?
- Is the cat licking or biting at any part of the lame leg?
- Is the lameness most severe after exercise or after the cat has been resting/sleeping?
- Does the cat seem unwell in any other way besides the lameness?

These are very important questions and I ask my clients to answer them as accurately as possible. I ask that if they do not know the answer to any or all of the questions to say so because if they are uncertain and merely take a guess or tell me what they think I want to hear, it may mislead me. There is no shame in not knowing the answer to any or all of these questions. Not being able to answer the questions does not imply that you are not concerned about your cat.

Many cat owners will have examined their cat themselves before consulting a vet and I encourage people to do so. The anatomy of the cat's hind leg has the same components as our own feet and legs and one should think about them as functioning in much the same way as our own. The bones, joints, tendons, muscles and ligaments are virtually identical to our own. The big difference is that cats walk on their toes, not on the palms of their hands as we do when we are on our hands and knees. When an owner finds that their cat is lame I encourage them to feel and examine the leg in the same way that you would examine your own leg if it were painful. I start from the toes and feel each bone and joint systematically as I progress toward the top of the leg. What you are looking for are signs of pain, heat and abnormal movement. A good tip when you examine a lame leg is to compare what you think may be abnormal to the same area on the other leg. As a general rule of thumb in the case of cats, assume the lameness is caused by an abscess or an emerging abscess until you have proved that it is due to some other cause.

1 Most common causes of lameness

The most common causes of lameness in one or both back legs can be divided into two categories:

- Sudden onset (acute) lameness
- Long-term, low-grade, gradual onset (chronic) lameness

Acute lameness means that the cat is suddenly lame, i.e. they were not lame yesterday but are lame today. Chronic lameness means that the cat has been becoming gradually lame over a long period of time.

1a Acute (sudden onset) lameness

Acute (sudden onset) lameness is usually the result of trauma or damage to the front leg. The most common cause of trauma to the front leg is a cat fight and the second most common cause is motor vehicle accidents.

1a(i) Abscesses or cellulitis as a cause of lameness

When your cat appears home and is suddenly lame, assume that they have an abscess or are developing an abscess as the most likely explanation for the lameness. The first thing to do is examine the leg with your hands rather than with your eyes. I will explain what I mean by this later in this section but first it is important that you understand what an abscess is and how it develops.

The world of cats is a very violent place. You may think you own your garden around your house but cats have no perception of property ownership in the way that we do. Any cat living near you will own their own piece of territory and our fences play no role in determining the boundaries of each cat's territory. Cats obtain and keep their territory by fighting other cats for possession of that territory. Your cat does not have automatic ownership of your garden just because they live in your house. They will have to stake their claim for ownership of your garden and they will have to defend it against other local cats trying to expand their territory. Your cat may, for example, own half of your garden and half of your neighbour's garden while the rest of your garden may be owned by another cat. When your cat strays into another cat's territory or vice versa there will very likely be a fight to defend the territory.

Cats fight differently from dogs. When dogs fight they rip large holes and gashes into each other. These wounds appear very dramatic and severe but they do offer one good feature, which is that the wound is large enough to allow natural drainage. Drainage from a wound is very important in that the wound can ooze just as your own cuts and grazes do. This oozing from wounds is the body's way of removing dirt and bacteria (infection) from a wound. Only when the body is satisfied that the dirt and bacteria have been removed will the wound heal. If a wound heals before all the bacteria have been removed there is a high risk that an abscess will develop under the skin. Cats, unlike dogs, have very small teeth and claws and when they fight they tend to pepper each other with small puncture wounds. The dirt and bacteria on the tips of the teeth and claws are thus pushed through the skin into the tissue beneath. The actual puncture wounds are very small and generally seal off very quickly. The result is that the dirt and bacteria deposited under the skin tend to develop into abscesses just as a thorn or splinter would do. The abscess will progressively enlarge until it bursts.

The initial stage in the development of an abscess is called cellulitis and this stage is very painful. Once the abscess has matured and is full of pus it will burst and once it has burst it is less painful. This process is similar to the process we have all experienced when developing a pimple on our face or nose. A pimple is simply a very small abscess. In the first stage of developing a pimple there may be nothing to see on the surface of the skin but the affected area is painful especially when touched; this stage is called cellulitis. Cellulitis means inflammation in the tissue under the skin and is painful because the inflammation causes the tissues in the area to stretch and this stretching effect is what hurts. During the cellulitis stage pus has not yet developed. If you then wait a few days one of two things may happen; either the painful area will simply stop being painful and the problem will disappear, or the painful area will develop into a ripe and yellow pimple full of pus. This stage is still painful because the accumulation of pus under the skin is still causing the surrounding tissues to be stretched but once the pimple is popped it is less painful. The pain subsides when the pimple is popped because this allows the pus to drain away, reducing stretching of the tissue in the area. An abscess behaves in exactly the same way but on a larger and more dramatic scale.

The most painful stage in the development of an abscess is the cellulitis stage and this is the most difficult time to diagnose the appearance of an abscess because the affected area is simply painful without any other obvious clues as to the cause of the pain. If the cellulitis develops into a full-blown abscess full of pus, the painful area is more easily identified as a painful swelling which is soft to the touch; the painful area feels like a balloon filled with water. As the pus accumulates under the skin the pus has the effect of "poisoning" the skin covering the abscess. This causes the hair follicles that anchor the fur in that area to lose their grip on the hairs they produce. In practice this means that if you suspect a painful swollen area under the skin is an abscess, simply tug the fur overlying the swelling. If a tuft of hair is very easily and painlessly pulled out then you know that the swelling you are feeling is indeed an abscess.

If the abscess is not lanced to drain out the pus, then the pus will continue poisoning the skin overlying it until a circular piece of skin dies off and a hole appears over the abscess to drain the pus out. Thus if we do not lance the abscess it will eventually "lance" itself. The reason that we always lance an abscess once we have identified it is that it immediately reduces the pain and starts the healing process because the body can only start healing a wound once the dirt and infection in the wound have drained away. The second reason for lancing the abscess is that, if it is left to lance itself by making a piece of skin die off and fall away, an unnecessarily large hole will be created and the wound will take longer to heal than if it is simply lanced with a small incision. The third reason we always lance an abscess is that it may sometimes take a long time to lance itself, thus allowing a very large amount of pus to accumulate for several days. A large amount of pus trapped in the body has a toxic effect on the body and makes the cat feel very unwell with a high fever. In severe cases of accumulations of large amounts of pus the toxic effect on the body may even be life-threatening.

In the cellulitis stage of the formation of an abscess there is no benefit in trying to lance the area because there is no pus yet to drain away. The problem at this stage is simply hard and painful swelling, i.e. the affected area feels very firm in contrast to the feel of an abscess which feels soft and "spongy" like a balloon filled with water. At this stage the immune system is fighting the infection and very often it will win the fight and the problem simply goes away without a proper abscess ever appearing.

A good indication that cellulitis has been caused by puncture wounds from teeth or claws is that there may be small scabs over the painful swollen area. I look for these scabs with my fingertips rather than with my eyes. I very gently feel the surface of the skin with my fingertips by moving up the leg against the direction of hair growth. This means my fingers lift the fur from the skin and my fingertips are moving under the hairs and feel the surface of the skin. If you run your finger over the leg in the direction of hair growth then you will feel only the surface of the fur coat and not the skin. Once you have found a small scab or even a tuft of fur matted with blood or ooze from the puncture wound, then you have found the site of the injury. You should remove a small amount of fur overlying the puncture wound by plucking the fur out or trimming it away with scissors. This is done so that you can monitor the puncture wound and keep it clean.

The vet will usually use painkillers and antibiotics to assist the immune system in the fight against the bacteria. If an abscess containing pus has been identified, then the vet will lance the abscess to drain it. The vet will once again prescribe painkillers and antibiotics to clear the infection and they will ask you to clean the incision they made to lance the abscess twice daily. They will stress to you that you must remove the scab trying to form at the incision twice a day otherwise the incision will simply seal off and the abscess will simply refill as the pus is no longer draining out. In practice the vet will usually advise dabbing the scab which forms at the incision site with wet cotton wool. Warm tap water is quite sufficient for the purpose because the intention is simply to dab the scab until it is so soggy that it falls off. In this way the opening into the abscess is kept open and the pus can keep draining out. You should do this twice daily for a week to prevent the incision sealing off and the abscess recurring.

1a(ii) Motor vehicle accidents (the cat has been hit by a car)

Cats are free spirits and their inquisitive nature means that they constantly roam and explore their environment. This inevitably means that your cat will cross roads in their search for adventure. Cats have no road sense and often run in front of cars travelling on the roads around your house. If they are struck directly by a car they are usually killed outright and we are presented with the trauma of finding our cats dead on the road often with horrific external injuries. If the cat is struck a glancing blow by a car then they may simply suffer painful bruising or broken bones. If your cat returns home after an adventure in the great outdoors and is obviously lame then you need to consider whether the lameness is due to the pain caused by fight wounds or being struck by a car. The first thing to consider is just how lame the cat is. If they are still walking and taking some weight on the affected leg despite the pain then it is unlikely that any bones have been broken. If the affected leg is not taking any weight and is either being carried up off the ground or is being dragged on the ground then there is quite possibly significant damage to the leg in terms of damage to bones and/or the nerve supply to the leg.

However, even if it seems that no leg bones have been broken this does not mean that the pelvic bones may not be broken. If cats fracture their pelvic bones they are often still able to walk on the back leg on the side of the fracture but they only gently touch the paw to the ground and only bear a minimal amount of weight because of the pain in the pelvis.

The first and most obvious thing to do is to examine the leg by feeling all parts of the leg with your hands. If the leg is floppy and swinging like a pendulum then there is almost certainly a broken bone so be very gentle when you feel the leg. I examine the leg by starting at the paw and working my way upwards toward the top of the leg. The first thing to examine is the claws; if the tips of the claws look ragged and frayed like miniature mopheads then it is very likely that the cat has been involved in a car accident. The reason the tips of the claws look ragged in these cases is that as the cat is shunted by the car, they slide and skid over the road and will extend their claws to try to get a grip and stop the slide. Obviously the tarmac is too hard for them to dig their claws into so the road surface acts like a massive piece of sandpaper and shreds the tips of the claws. If you find that the tips of the claws are ragged then you can assume that something, like a car, has shunted the cat across a rough surface. The ragged claw tips are not painful per se so we must continue examining the leg to find where the leg has been injured by the shunting impact.

Continue examining the leg by systematically examining every part with your hands. The anatomy of the cat's front and back legs is virtually identical to your own so simply imagine you are examining a human being's arm or leg. Feel each toe individually and then examine the bones leading up to the next joint which will be the ankle (the hock or tarsus).

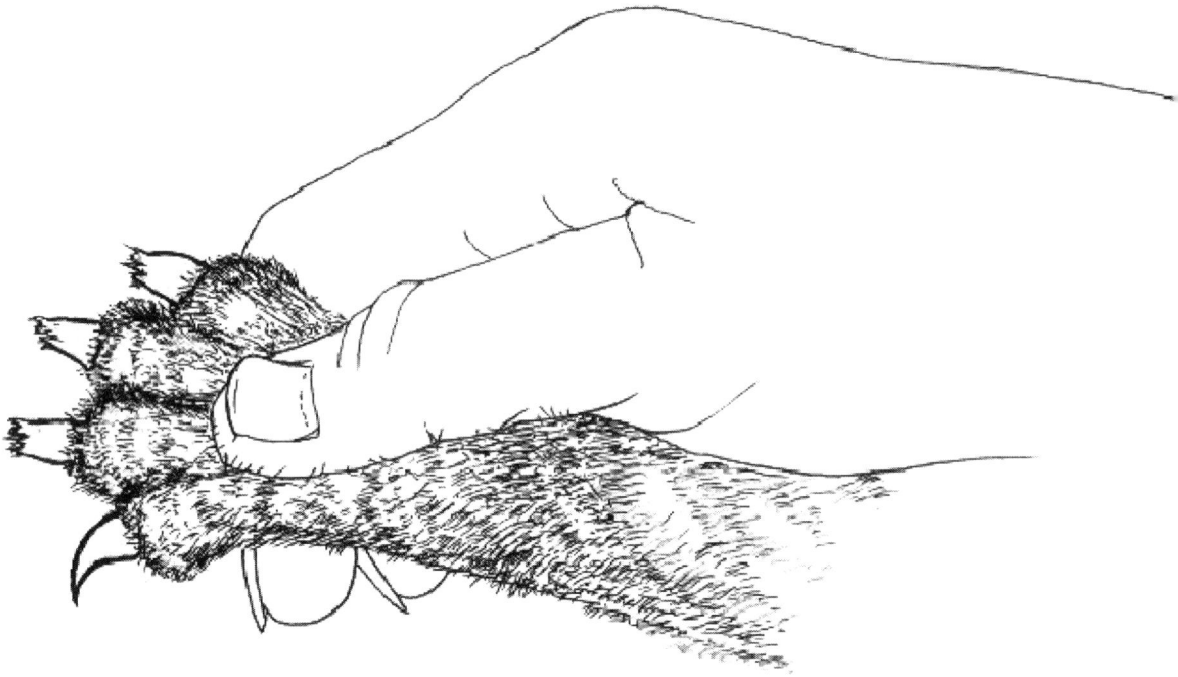

Fig 27. - Torn nails are usually an indication that a cat has been hit by a car or has had a very near miss

Continue upwards by feeling the bones in the lower leg (the tibia and fibula). Examine the knee (the stifle) by flexing and extending it and then continue upwards toward the hip joint along the thigh bone (the femur). Examine the hip by bending and flexing it and drawing the leg outwards away from the body and then feel the pelvic bones at the top of the leg. If the cat seems lame on both back legs and resents being touched over the pelvic bones and the base of the tail then there may be fractured pelvic bones. This will obviously affect both back legs because the pain is from the pelvis which is attached to both back legs. Be very gentle initially and be careful because when you find the painful part as the cat may hiss and spit and may lash out at you. When you examine the parts of the leg simply try to move all the joints in their natural type and range of movement and check that the bones between the joints are solid, i.e. the leg should not bend in between the joints. At the same time run your fingers against the direction of hair growth to feel the surface of the skin to check for superficial injuries like cuts and grazes or scabs caused by bite and fight wounds as discussed previously.

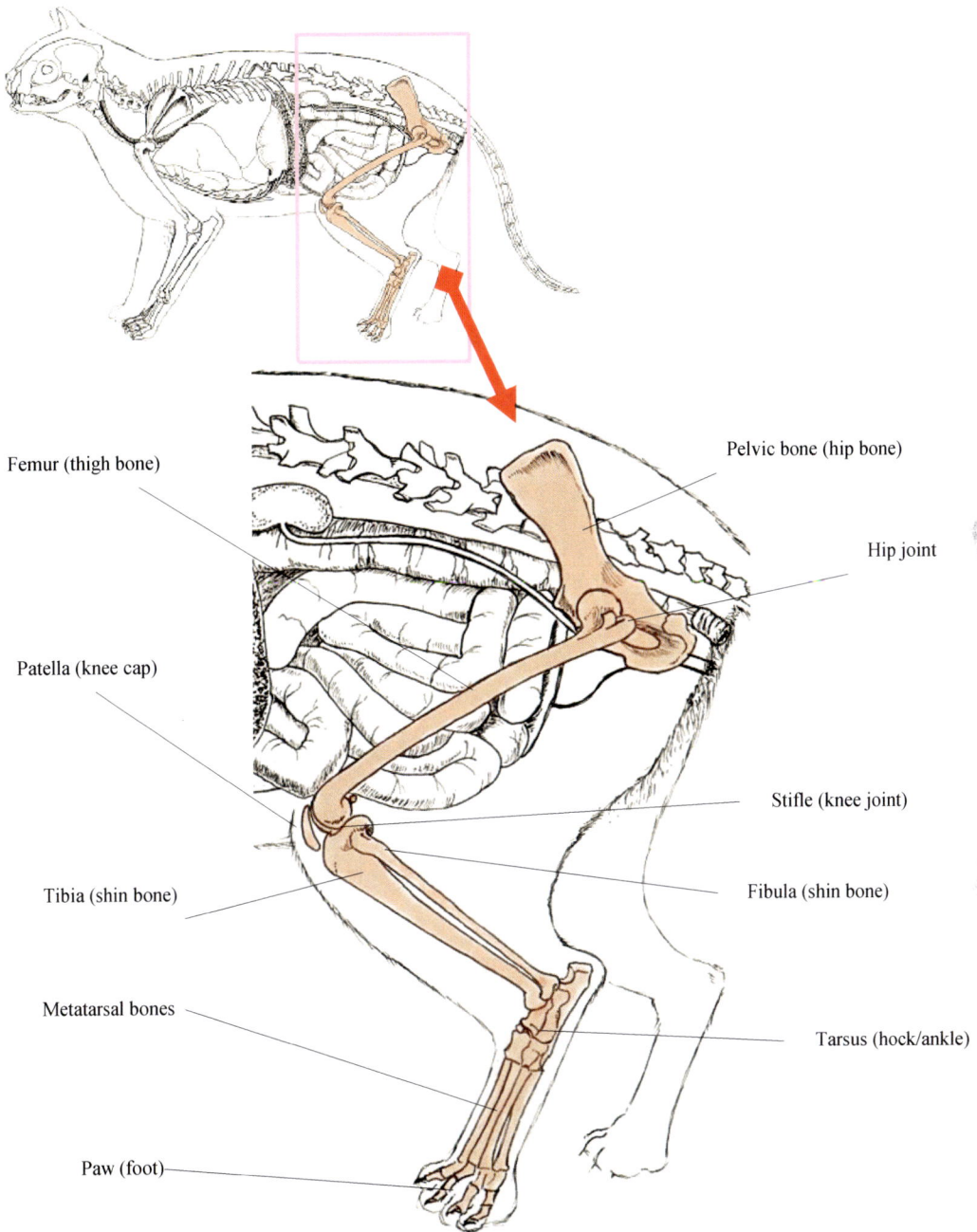

Femur (thigh bone)

Pelvic bone (hip bone)

Hip joint

Patella (knee cap)

Stifle (knee joint)

Tibia (shin bone)

Fibula (shin bone)

Metatarsal bones

Tarsus (hock/ankle)

Paw (foot)

Fig 28. – Anatomy of the hind leg

In conclusion, if you find that your cat is suddenly lame and has frayed claws then assume they have been struck by something that has shunted them across the road. The shunting injury may simply have caused deep and painful bruising or sprained a joint or it may have broken bones or more seriously damaged joints. If bones are broken the cat will be unable to stand on the leg and it will often swing like a floppy pendulum and the leg can be bent at points between the normal joints in the leg. If a joint has been damaged the leg won't swing like a pendulum but rather it is held off the ground and the joint is painful when you try to bend and straighten it. If the pelvis is damaged both back legs may appear lame. It would always be prudent to have your vet double-check the cat's lame leg and the rest of the cat's body when you identify frayed claws as these trauma cases may also involve damage to other body parts other than the obviously lame leg. The treatment for the damage will depend on the exact type of damage you and your vet identify and will be discussed later in this chapter.

1b Chronic lameness (long-term, low-grade, gradual onset lameness)

Chronic lameness (long-term, low-grade, gradual onset lameness) is usually caused by arthritis in one or more joints. When people talk about arthritis what they mean is long-term low-grade pain and inflammation in one or more joints usually associated with growing older. The word "chronic" means that the arthritis is a long-term problem. The classic example of this is the arthritis we develop in the joints of our fingers as we grow old. To be pedantic, the word arthritis is actually a very vague term meaning simply inflammation in a joint. The term arthritis does not explain why the joint is inflamed. Thus if you sprain your ankle it would be technically correct to say that your ankle has acute (sudden onset) arthritis because the sprain has caused inflammation. For the sake of simplicity I will use the word "arthritis" as it is used in common everyday speech to imply long-term low-grade inflammation in one or more joints.

There are two common types of arthritis in cats. The first type of arthritis is osteoarthritis which is the technical term for old age-related arthritis caused by the wear and tear on the joint as it is used throughout life. The joints will wear out in old age just as an old door hinge wears out over time. The second type of arthritis is feline progressive polyarthritis which is the cat equivalent of rheumatoid arthritis and may develop at any age, although it is most commonly seen in older cats. The name of this condition in cats sound complicated but is actually very simple when broken down: "feline" means relating to cats; "progressive" means literally that the condition is progressive and will gradually become worse over time; "poly" means more than one joint is affected; and "arthritis" means that the affected joint becomes inflamed and thus painful.

The effects and symptoms of both types of long-term arthritis in cats are very similar but the treatments are different so I will discuss each condition individually.

1b(i) Osteoarthritis (old age-related arthritis)

Factors that cause acute arthritis may develop into chronic arthritis. Arthritis may develop after a joint has been injured or infected. The types of injuries which may cause acute or chronic arthritis are sprains, fractures, dislocations, etc. Injuries to joints should thus be treated as quickly and efficiently as possible to try to prevent long-term permanent arthritis developing in that joint. We are all familiar with the concept of someone injuring a joint and then either having permanent low-grade discomfort in that joint, or the injury may have seemed to heal well but as we get older the joint may cause discomfort due to the delayed onset of arthritis. Arthritis may also develop in a joint which is not anatomically perfectly formed, i.e. it is dysplastic. Dysplasia is the technical description for a joint which is not perfectly formed. Most people are familiar with the term hip dysplasia, most commonly seen in certain breeds of dogs like German Shepherd dogs, which means that the hips are not properly formed, but any joint in any type of animal may suffer from dysplasia. If a joint is dysplastic then it will wear out faster than a normally formed joint. This process of wearing out causes arthritis. Most commonly, however, arthritis develops simply due to ordinary "wear and tear" in a normal joint due to old age.

The process of chronic osteoarthritis is often referred to as degenerative joint disease (DJD). Chronic arthritis causes thickening of the tissues around the joint, making the affected joint feel larger and thicker than normal. This thickening is caused by "scar tissue" forming around the joint. The bones forming the joint will develop irregular thickenings called osteophytes and the lining of the joint capsule will be permanently inflamed and thickened. These three changes represent the body's attempt to heal and strengthen the affected joint. These changes often make the arthritis worse as they will continue permanently and lead to the pain of the arthritis becoming progressively worse. The second effect of these three processes is that the joint will lose its full range of movement. This happens because the "scar tissue" laid down around the joint will make it less flexible, rendering the joint less able to perform its full range of movements.

The ends of the bones forming moving joints are covered with a layer of cartilage called articular or joint cartilage. This cartilage is very smooth and is essential for smooth movement of the joint. This joint cartilage has very few nerve cells supplying it and this relatively nerve-free layer is essential in covering the bone ends which have a good nerve supply. The best way to understand this concept is to consider the forces acting on the ends of the bones when they are bearing weight during walking or standing. When we walk or stand our entire body weight is pressing down on our joints. The reason this doesn't cause pain is the layer of numb cartilage covering the ends of the bones (the articular cartilage). If we didn't have this layer of articular cartilage then the ends of the bones wound be pressed together by our body weight and as the bone ends have a good nerve supply this would cause severe pain. Even limited areas of damage to this articular cartilage allow small areas of bone to be exposed and pressure on this exposed bone causes pain. The process of arthritis causes erosions in the articular cartilage and this contributes significantly to the pain in the affected joint.

The bone ends forming the joint are held together by the joint capsule which effectively forms a sealed bag around the bone ends. The purpose of the joint capsule is not only to hold the ends of the bones forming the joint together but also to produce joint fluid, which fills the joint. The joint fluid in turn serves two main purposes, namely to serve as lubrication for the joint in the same way that oil lubricates a door hinge and, secondly, to carry nutrients to feed and maintain the articular cartilages and other structures inside the joint. This joint fluid is called synovial fluid and is produced by the synovial membrane, which is the inside layer of the joint capsule. To my knowledge there are no man-made lubricants for machinery which are as efficient as synovial fluid in terms of lubricating moving parts. Many cats with arthritis do not produce enough joint fluid to feed and lubricate the affected joint and this leads to increased grinding of the joint cartilage which further contributes to the pain and progression of the arthritis.

Once the processes of chronic arthritis have been present for a few months or years the affected joint will feel thicker than the same joint on the other leg. When a joint with chronic arthritis is flexed and extended one will notice that it may not be able to bend or straighten as much as a healthy joint does. During bending and straightening one may also notice a "crunchy" sound or feeling in the joint. This "crunchy" sensation is called crepitus. Once the process of chronic arthritis has started, the changes in the joint are irreversible. The changes in fact will become more severe as time goes on. This process of arthritis is identical to the process of arthritis in human beings as we grow old.

When the vet is faced with an arthritic joint the treatment they apply will have three objectives, i.e.

- Relieve the pain and inflammation in the joint
- Slow down the ongoing changes which worsen the arthritis over time
- Improve the range of movement of the joint

The first step is to find a suitable long-term anti-inflammatory drug that will alleviate the pain in the joint. The second treatment I use is the category of agents called mobility supplements (chondroitin sulphate and/or glucosamine). These are agents that help the joint to produce synovial (joint) fluid to maintain its lubrication and to promote natural healing of the eroded articular cartilages covering the bone ends. This is an important component of the treatment as these erosions expose the nerve endings in the bone, causing a lot of the pain and if we can repair these areas the patient will obviously require a lower daily dose of anti-inflammatories.

A change in lifestyle also benefits these patients in that overweight individuals should lose weight to take the extra strain off the joints and gentle controlled exercise should be encouraged to maintain the size and strength of the muscles of the affected leg to help support the joints. This programme of sustained, controlled exercise is effectively the same as a physiotherapy programme for human beings. The objective of this programme of activity (physiotherapy) is to keep the joints as flexible as possible and improve their range of movement as this will make movement easier and less uncomfortable for the cat.

The individuals who show very little or no pain can often be successfully treated using only natural remedies like glucosamine and chondroitin sulphate or natural oils like cod liver oil and evening primrose oil, or homeopathic remedies like sulphur, arnica and rhus tox. These remedies work by relieving the pain and, in the case of glucosamine and chondroitin sulphate, also help the joint to lubricate itself and repair the damage to the joint cartilage caused by the grinding action of the unstable bone ends.

If these products are not sufficient to alleviate the pain then they can be combined with long-term anti-inflammatory and painkilling medications. A major problem faced by vets all over the world is that there are currently no anti-inflammatory or painkilling medications available for long-term use in cats. This is in stark contrast to the wide range of medicines available for human beings and dogs to treat the pain of long-term osteoarthritis. The main reason that there are no licensed medicines for long-term pain relief in cats is that they are very sensitive to adverse reactions to anti-inflammatory and painkilling medicines. For example even a tiny dose of paracetamol will kill your cat despite being very safe to use on your baby. Other human medicines like ibuprofen and aspirin can also cause severe damage to cats. The result is that vets have been forced to try some of the dog arthritis medications on cats. In some cases this has led to disastrous and fatal side effects and in other cases some of these medicines appear to be safe if used at very low doses. My advice would be to consult your vet about current unofficial (unlicensed) use of some of the dog medicines in cats if osteoarthritis is causing severe pain. There are some natural remedies available to try to alleviate the pain of osteoarthritis and these include green-lipped mussel extract and curcumins. These remedies are not as effective as conventional anti-inflammatory medicines but they are not dangerous. Once again, you should consult your vet about the state of current knowledge regarding the use of these remedies.

If one particular medication does not seem to help much then others should be tried until one is found that works for your individual cat. This trial and error period in which different medicines in different combinations are tried should be controlled and monitored by your vet, as there are many medicines that should not be used in combination with each other.

Most cats who have developed arthritis for whatever reason should be able to enjoy an active and happy life when the appropriate treatments are used. The process of developing arthritis is, just as in human beings, something one should expect in old age but one does not have to accept the pain or discomfort which may accompany the arthritis. Modern treatment and management of arthritis mean that we, and our cats, should be able to live comfortably in our golden years.

1b(ii) Feline progressive polyarthritis

As mentioned earlier feline progressive polyarthritis is the cat equivalent to rheumatoid arthritis in human beings. This type of arthritis causes the same type of damage to the joints as osteoarthritis and thus similar symptoms, i.e. lameness, but the cause of the inflammation and damage is very different. Osteoarthritis is caused by injury to one or more joints or long-term wear and tear on the joints. Feline progressive polyarthritis is inflammation in several joints caused by the immune system attacking the joints just as in the case of rheumatoid arthritis in human beings. This condition is called an autoimmune disorder and it means that the body's immune system is attacking its own cells for no apparent reason. It seems that the immune system simply fails to recognise that the joint cartilage cells covering the ends of the bones forming the joints are normal cells and it then attacks them as if they were invading bacteria. As the attack on the cells continues, they become damaged and unable to work efficiently and will eventually die. It is not understood why this process should happen for no apparent reason but unfortunately it does.

2 Less common causes of lameness

2a The paw

The most common problems encountered when examining the paws are:

2a(i) - **Foot abscesses**. Abscesses may develop in the paws as a result of wounds from fighting with other cats. The abscess causes the paw to swell up very much larger than normal size and is very painful when touched. Please refer to the discussion on the diagnosis and treatment of cellulitis and abscesses earlier in this chapter.

2a(ii) - **Broken or torn claws**. Broken claws are treated by removing the broken part of the claw and the vet may prescribe antibiotics, painkillers and footbaths as necessary. If one or more of the claw tips are frayed then it is very likely that the cat has been hit by a car. Please refer to the above section on motor vehicle accidents for a discussion of this cause of lameness.

2a(iii) - **Nailbed infections (paronychia)**. The nailbed is the groove between the nail and the skin and infections may arise in this groove. The infection is most commonly caused by bacteria or fungal infections. One would suspect an infection in the nailbed if the nail feels very loose or if there is a discharge from the nailbed. The discharge which may develop is either watery or looks like pus and may or may not have a foul odour. Once the vet has determined what kind of parasite has caused the infection they will prescribe appropriate treatment.

The important question to ask in cases of nailbed infections is "what has allowed the infection to develop?" The answer may be simply that a cut or graze in that area has become infected and the infection has moved into the nailbed. If a number of toes have the same infection we should ask ourselves why the body has not been able to fight off the infection. The explanation may be that the cat has diabetes and the high blood sugar levels have resulted in a high sugar content in the moisture in the nailbed and this has favoured the development of an infection. Other disease conditions which may compromise the body's ability to fight off infections are underlying Feline Leukaemia and Feline AIDS. These two underlying conditions are discussed in the chapter on weight loss.

2a(iv) - Tumours. Several types of tumours may develop in the nailbed. They are not usually immediately noticeable and the first sign of a problem in the nailbed is a secondary infection. If the vet suspects that the infection is the result of a tumour they will often investigate further by taking X-rays and biopsies from the affected toe. Most nailbed tumours are not cancerous and the vet will most commonly advise eliminating the infection first and then amputating the affected toe to remove the tumour. This seems a very extreme way of treating the problem but fortunately cats do not seem to miss the removed toe at all and function perfectly normally without it.

2a(v) - Cuts, grazes and puncture wounds. These may be treated by stitching and bandaging, plus antibiotics and painkillers as necessary.

2a(vi) - Swelling and bruising from sprains. These are treated with painkillers/anti-inflammatories, support bandages and rest from exercise as necessary.

2a(vii) - Swelling from pressure injuries like someone stepping on the paw or objects dropped onto the paw. These are treated with painkillers and rest from exercise as necessary.

2a(viii) - Broken bones. Severe painful swelling of one or more toes may suggest that one of the bones has been broken. Broken toe bones are most common in cats more than one year old. Broken bones and joint dislocations are uncommon in very young kittens as they have very flexible, soft bones which tend to bend rather than break when the paw is injured. X-rays are sometimes required to confirm that a bone has been broken. If any bones are broken then the fracture is treated either with casts and bandages or through surgical repair as necessary.

2b Metatarsal bones

The part of the leg leading from the toes to the next joint, called the hock (the ankle), is called the metatarsal region. This part of the leg contains four slender bones called the metatarsal bones. In human beings these are the bones leading from your toes to your heel and form your foot. Cats walk on the tips of their toes and they carry these bones off the ground, unlike human beings who walk on these bones.

The most common problems affecting the metatarsal area are:

2b(i) - Abscesses and cellulitis. Cellulitis and abscesses may develop in this area as a result of wounds from fighting with other cats. The infection initially causes a firm painful swelling which may ultimately develop into an abscess and burst. If this area is painful examine it carefully by looking for small scabs or holes or cuts which would suggest that the cat has been involved in a cat fight. Please refer to the discussion on the diagnosis and treatment of cellulitis and abscesses earlier in this chapter.

2b(ii) - Broken bones. Severe painful swelling in this area may very occasionally suggest that one or more of the metatarsal bones have been broken. X-rays are sometimes required to confirm that a bone has been broken. If any bones are broken then the fracture is treated either with casts and bandages or through surgical repair or simply rest as necessary.

2c The ankle

The ankle (hock) is also examined with your eyes and hands. The hock is a complicated joint composed of the shinbones at the top and the metatarsal bones at the bottom. The hock bones consist of seven individual bones arranged in two rows between the shinbones and the metatarsal bones. All of these bones are held together by many small ligaments and joint capsules. Start by looking at the hock and comparing it to the hock on the other leg. Look for swelling, bruising and wounds. When feeling the hock one should bend (flex) and straighten (extend) the joint to check for signs of pain. The hock should also be bent gently to the left and right.

The most common problems encountered when examining the hock are:

2c(i) - Abscesses and cellulitis. Cellulitis and abscesses may develop in this area as a result of wounds from fighting with other cats. The infection initially causes a firm painful swelling which may ultimately develop into an abscess and burst. If this area is painful examine it carefully by looking for small scabs or holes or cuts which would suggest that the cat has been involved in a cat fight. Please refer to the discussion on the diagnosis and treatment of cellulitis and abscesses earlier in this chapter.

2c(ii) - Sprains and strains which cause pain and swelling. These are treated with rest from exercise, support bandages and anti-inflammatories/painkillers as necessary.

2c(iii) - Broken bones. Severe painful swelling of the hock may suggest that one or more of the bones or ligaments of the joint have been broken or dislocated. Broken hock bones and dislocations are most common in cats more than one year old. Broken hock bones and joint dislocations are uncommon in very young kittens as they have very flexible, soft bones which tend to bend rather than break when the hock is injured. X-rays are generally required to confirm that a bone has been broken or ligaments ruptured. If any bones are broken then the fracture is treated either with casts and bandages or through surgical repair as necessary. If ligaments have been ruptured or parts of the hock are dislocated then they are treated either with casts or surgical repair depending on which ligaments have been damaged and how severely.

2c(iv) - Tumours. Severe painful swelling of the hock may also, very rarely, suggest tumours developing in the bones of the hock. X-rays and biopsies are generally required to confirm the presence of tumours. Most tumours affecting this area are highly malignant cancers and the treatment options will often involve amputation of the leg and chemotherapy. Fortunately these tumours are the least common cause of pain and lameness in this area. Middle-aged and old cats are more commonly affected by tumours than young cats.

2c(v) - Arthritis may cause thickening of the whole joint or part of the joint. The thickened joint is usually firm to the touch and not painful when touched. The joint will seem thicker than the same joint on the other leg. The joint may be painful when you bend or straighten the joint and it may produce a "crunchy" sensation when it is bent and straightened. X-rays will usually be taken of the joint to confirm the diagnosis. Please refer to the paragraph earlier in this chapter for a discussion of arthritis and appropriate treatment.

2d The lower leg (shin)

The lower leg (shin) is also examined with your eyes and hands. The lower leg has two long bones called the tibia and fibula. These bones can be felt extending from the hock to the knee joint. One should check for pain and swelling when applying pressure to the bones and the surrounding muscles.

The most common problems encountered when examining the lower leg are:

2d(i) - Abscesses and cellulitis. Cellulitis and abscesses may develop in this area as a result of wounds from fighting with other cats. The infection initially causes a firm painful swelling which may ultimately develop into an abscess and burst. If this area is painful examine it carefully by looking for small scabs or holes or cuts which would suggest that the cat has been involved in a cat fight. Please refer to the discussion on the diagnosis and treatment of cellulitis and abscesses earlier in this chapter.

2d(ii) - Broken bones. Severe painful swelling of the lower leg may suggest that one or more of the bones have been broken. Broken bones in the lower leg are uncommon in very young kittens as they have very flexible, soft bones which tend to bend rather than break when the leg is injured. The lower leg often seems "floppy" or swings like a pendulum when the bones are fractured and the cat is unable to walk on the affected leg. X-rays are required to confirm where the bones have been broken. Most fractures that do occur in the long bones in young cats are found on X-ray to be "greenstick fractures". A "greenstick fracture" is exactly what the name implies. If you bend a dry stick or branch it tends to snap in half but if you bend a green stick or branch it tends to splinter only on one side and doesn't break into two pieces. The same thing happens in the bones of young growing cats because, like a green stick/branch, they are softer and more "bendy" than a dried stick which is more like a mature bone. If any bones are broken then the fracture is treated either with casts and bandages or through surgical repair as necessary

2e The knee joint (the stifle)

The anatomical design of the knee joint in cats is the same as our own human knee. The veterinary term for the knee is the stifle. The basic structure of the stifle is a hinge joint.

The thigh bone (femur) is at the top and the shin bones (tibia and fibula) are at the bottom. The joint between these bones is composed of the joint capsule, the kneecap (patella) and its tendon, the collateral ligaments on either side, the two internal cruciate ligaments and two internal cartilage cushions called the menisci.

On either side of the stifle we find ligaments called collateral ligaments. The ligament on the inner aspect of the joint is called the medial collateral ligament and the one on the outer aspect is called the lateral collateral ligament (refer to the diagram). These ligaments run from the thigh bone to the shin bones and allow the knee to bend in one plane only, i.e. the knee can only bend (flex) or straighten (extend). Consider your own knee, it can only bend and straighten. The reason that it cannot bend sideways so that the ankle joint touches the hip joint is that the collateral ligaments do not allow this movement. The knee functions in only one plane in much the same way as a door hinge. These collateral ligaments are found on the outside surface of the joint capsule.

The kneecap or patella is a small bone in the tendon of the large thigh muscle on the front of the thighbone called the quadriceps femoris muscle. This muscle starts at the top of the thigh bone and attaches to the top of the shin bone at a point called the tibial crest. The tibial crest is the bulge of bone at the front edge of the top of the shinbone just below the knee joint. This is a very long muscle and the bottom edge of the muscle crosses the knee joint before attaching to the shin bone. The purpose of the kneecap is to serve as a guide to make sure the bottom part of this very long muscle doesn't slide off the side of the knee. The kneecap slides up and down in a groove at the bottom of the thigh bone called the trochlear groove. The reason for this is that the knee can only bend and straighten so the muscle which straightens the knee should only work from a position across the front of the knee. If the muscle were to slip off to the side, the effect of contracting the thigh muscle would be to try to bend the knee sideways, which would be prevented by the collateral ligaments. Thus, by developing a small guide bone in the bottom part of such a long muscle, and having a groove along the front end of the thigh bone for this bone to slide in, the body ensures that the muscle stays in a straight line and thus can only move the knee joint in one direction. The tendon which then runs from the knee cap to the shin bone is the one doctors tap with a small rubber hammer to check our knee reflexes. This tendon, together with the collateral ligaments and the joint capsule, helps to keep the knee joint tight and stable.

Inside the knee joint are two more ligaments called the cruciate ligaments. The word cruciate comes from the Latin word meaning "crossed". The cruciate ligaments are indeed two independent short ligaments inside the knee joint, which run across each other to look like the letter "x". The function of these two ligaments is to keep the ends of the bones forming the joint together. The cranial cruciate ligament stops the shinbone sliding forwards and the caudal cruciate ligament stops the shin bone sliding backwards.

The bones forming the knee joint do not fit together very well. Compare the knee joint to the hip joint which functions like a ball and socket joint, which fits together very well. To overcome this relatively poor fit the knee joint has two strips of cartilage wedged between the ends of the bones, one on the left side and the other on the right. This cartilage is called a meniscus; the plural of meniscus is menisci. These menisci function like two small lumps of putty in that they are compressed between the bones and conform themselves to the bone surfaces. Imagine clenching your fists and compressing a lump of putty between your fists, the putty will compress in the centre and squelch out at the edges thereby moulding itself to your fists and the space between them. The menisci function in exactly the same way and this gives the bones of the knee joint a much better fit.

The most common problems encountered when examining the knee (stifle) are:

2e(i) - Abscesses and cellulitis. Cellulitis and abscesses may develop in this area as a result of wounds from fighting with other cats. The infection initially causes a firm painful swelling which may ultimately develop into an abscess and burst. If this area is painful examine it carefully by looking for small scabs or holes or cuts which would suggest that the cat has been involved in a cat fight. Please refer to the discussion on the diagnosis and treatment of cellulitis and abscesses earlier in this chapter.

2e(ii) - Sprains and strains which cause pain and swelling. These are treated with rest from exercise, and anti-inflammatories/painkillers as necessary.

2e(iii) - Cranial cruciate ligament injuries. Cats with injuries to the cranial cruciate ligament present in one of two ways. The more common presentation is a sudden, total lameness of one of the hind legs. The leg is held in a bent position with the foot well clear of the ground. The other presentation is a cat that has a long-term (several weeks or months) lameness affecting one or both hind legs. These cats will walk on the affected leg but do so with an obvious limp and are reluctant to jump up onto beds and furniture. The diagnosis in these long-term cases is suggested by the presence of a thickening of the joint capsule and adjacent tissues over the inside (medial) surface of the knee (stifle). There may also be a crunching sensation felt inside the knee when it is flexed and extended. Occasionally, in these cases of long-standing injury, the examining vet will also be able to demonstrate what is called the anterior drawer sign. In the case of cats who have suffered a recent acute injury to the cranial cruciate ligament, the presence of the anterior drawer sign is what confirms the diagnosis. The anterior drawer sign is the test that isolates the cause of the lameness to the cranial cruciate ligament. The test involves grasping the thigh bone and shin bones above and below the knee and sliding the shin bone forwards while holding the thigh bone very still. The ability to demonstrate this forward sliding movement is called the anterior drawer sign. One will only be able to elicit this movement if the cranial cruciate is stretched or ruptured. The major obstacle to demonstrating the anterior drawer sign is that it may be painful to the patient and they will often flex all the muscles of the leg in response to the pain of the injury and the examination. The result is that the cat's tensed muscles will not allow the test to be carried out. The demonstration of the anterior drawer sign is vital to make the diagnosis. Thus if there is a sufficiently strong suspicion of a cranial cruciate ligament injury many cats will need to be anaesthetised to relax the muscles so that the anterior drawer test may be done on a completely relaxed leg.

In the case of a long-standing (chronic) injury to the cranial cruciate ligament one may not be able to demonstrate the anterior drawer sign even if the cat has been anaesthetised. This is because the thickening over the inside (medial) aspect of the knee is composed of scar tissue which has contracted and holds the shin bone too tightly to allow it to slide forwards. In these cases the diagnosis is based largely on the presence of this band of thickened tissue which can be felt and seen on X-rays of the knee. Other associated changes on X-rays will further support the diagnosis. These changes include displacement of the sesamoid bones associated with the knee joint and signs of arthritis affecting the knee.

Human beings, typically skiers and football players, occasionally suffer damage to their cruciate ligaments just as cats do. The injury in cats and human beings usually results as a consequence of twisting or hyper-extending the knee. Cats suffer the injury through sheer misfortune in that there is generally no underlying or predisposing factor causes them to injure the cruciate ligament. The situation in cats is far more complex and currently is not entirely understood.

There are a number of additional factors which may make the diagnosis and treatment of cranial cruciate ligament injury difficult in cats. The first is that the ligament may not rupture entirely. This is because it in fact consists of two components which act to support the knee under different stress situations in different knee positions. If only one portion of the ligament has ruptured then the patient will present with all the signs of cranial cruciate ligament injury but the vet will be unable to demonstrate an anterior drawer sign because the remaining, intact portion of the ligament will prevent the shin bone from being slid forward during the examination. The second factor is that the ligament may not have ruptured and the lameness which is seen is due to the ligament having only been stretched. If the ligament has been severely stretched an anterior drawer sign will be present and the diagnosis and treatment are the same as for a ruptured ligament. The difficult diagnosis to make is when the ligament has not stretched enough to result in an anterior drawer sign but has stretched enough to cause microinstability of the joint. In these cases the shin and thighbone are sliding across each other sufficiently to cause pain but not sufficiently to be appreciated on examination of the knee. These cases usually present as long-standing cases of hind leg lameness with thickening over the medial (inside) aspect of the knee. This thickening represents the body's attempt to stabilise the knee to eliminate the microinstability. This attempt by the body, however, is largely ineffective and arthritis will worsen rapidly in the affected knee. The third factor is that the effect of the bones sliding across each other after the ligament has ruptured may crush, pinch or tear the meniscal cartilages inside the knee. The presence of damaged cartilages as a component of the lameness in the knee is alluded to by a crunching sensation which may be heard or felt when the knee is flexed and extended. These three complicating factors will often need to be confirmed by examining the inside of the knee via arthroscopic examination (placing a small camera inside the knee joint) or more commonly by surgically opening the joint and direct visualization of all the structures within the joint.

A further complicating factor is that many different techniques are used to repair the damaged joint and this implies that there is not one particular technique which is superior to the others. Research has shown that all the different modern techniques deliver approximately the same success rate. This is a concern to me because the same research has also shown that all cats will have some degree of permanent arthritis in the affected knee within six months of the injury. This arthritis will develop despite the skill of the surgeon and the type of repair technique used. The arthritis will also worsen as time goes by. The obvious question to ask in the face of this research is why do we bother to repair the injury if arthritis will develop anyway? The answer is that the repair is done as a damage limitation exercise. The sooner the knee is operated on, the less severely and the less rapidly the arthritis will develop. The object of the surgery is to restrict the inevitable arthritis to the point where it is so limited that, although its presence can be demonstrated on X-rays, it will not be sufficient to cause lameness after the cat has recovered from the surgery.

Many factors will affect the success of the surgery. The first is the length of time that has elapsed from the moment of injury to the moment of repair. The sooner the knee is operated on the better the long-term prospects for the knee. As a general rule I would want to operate on the knee within three weeks of the injury occurring. The second factor is the presence of any other structures being injured in addition to the cranial cruciate ligament. The most common associated injury is damage to the menisci (cartilages) inside the joint. One or both menisci may be damaged as a result of the joint instability. The medial (inner aspect) meniscus is more commonly damaged. The damage to the meniscus varies from mild to severe and the extent of the damage correlates directly with the severity of the arthritis which will develop. If the meniscal damage is minor and can be repaired then the long-term prognosis is good. If the damage to the meniscus is more severe then the damaged portion must be removed and the amount removed correlates with the degree of arthritis which will ensue. The more meniscus which must be removed, the more severe the subsequent arthritis will be because a greater quantity of cushioning between the bone ends has been removed. Not removing the damaged meniscus would produce an even worse outcome.

Another structure which may be found to be damaged at the same time is the lateral collateral ligament. If this is the case this must also be repaired. It should be regarded as a significant injury in its own right and should be repaired individually.

The third factor is the personality of the patient. The more boisterous the cat, the less likely they are to rest the operated leg and, consequently, the greater the risk of them damaging the repair before the knee has healed.
The best course of action with all cruciate injuries is swift diagnosis and swift treatment. The current wisdom offered by specialists is that all cats should have this injury repaired. In my experience many cats do very well without surgery and my criteria for natural healing through enforced rest is a patient with no other injuries to the other components of the knee joint, only very slight instability of the knee, a calm disposition and a slight build. I would very often rest these patients for six to twelve weeks and only operate on those who did not show a full return to function.

The approach to patients with a long-standing injury is far more subjective. Many of these patients have developed a significant thickening of the tissues on the medial (inside) aspect of the knee as discussed earlier and have significant arthritis already established in the joint. I tend to assess these patients under anaesthetic, employing the anterior drawer sign. If there is no appreciable instability in the joint, no indication of meniscal damage, but evidence of advanced arthritic changes on X-rays of the joint, then I feel there is no benefit from surgery as the object of surgery is to achieve stability of the joint and to preserve the menisci. In these cases these two objectives will have been achieved by natural healing but at the cost of severe arthritis so I concentrate my efforts on treating the arthritis with long-term remedies as discussed in the earlier section on arthritis in this chapter. If, however, there is severe instability and/or suspicion of meniscal damage then the patient would benefit from surgery.

The goals of surgical repair of injured cranial cruciate ligaments are very simple. The primary goal is to stabilise the joint to eliminate the anterior drawer sign. The other essential component of the repair is to examine the inside of the joint and treat additional injuries, including damage to the menisci.

The most common method of surgical repair of this injury is often called the "modified de angelis" technique. This technique places a nylon band on the outside of the joint running in the same direction as the original cranial cruciate ligament. The problems encountered here are that the nylon or wire implant may rupture before the knee has healed in this supported position. The problem is not that the implant snapped but that it did so prematurely. The object, with this type of implant, is to pull it tight enough to eliminate the anterior drawer sign and thus restore stability to the joint by holding the bones in the correct alignment. The knee capsule will then thicken slightly around the joint and this, together with strong scar tissue which forms around the implant, will keep the knee stable in the future. All artificial implants will eventually snap through repeated use, as the artificial material will fatigue with repeated movement. Compare this to repeatedly bending a piece of wire at the same point until it snaps. This happens because the wire develops metal fatigue. The wire or nylon implant used will eventually snap approximately six to eight weeks after the surgery. This poses no problems because the implant has held the knee in the correct position while the joint capsule has grown thicker and stronger and a strong band of scar tissue has developed along the implant. So by the time the implant snaps the healing process has had a chance to guide the knee into the correct position. The ruptured ends of the implant rarely cause problems and are therefore not generally removed. But the problem that can arise with this technique is premature rupture of the implant before the necessary guided healing has taken place. The implant per se may have ruptured or it may have torn out of the tissue it has been stitched into which acts as an anchor. Either event will result in instability of the joint just as at the point of the original injury. If this happens the best course of action is usually to replace the implants. The decision to perform repeat surgery depends on the stability of the joint at the time the implant ruptures.

The recovery from this surgery, in terms of regaining full use of the leg, varies a lot from one individual to another. After the surgery all cats will hold the leg up with the foot well clear of the ground for one to several weeks before starting to use it again. I generally advise strict house rest on non-slip surfaces for six weeks, then a gradual return to full exercise.

The disappointing aspect of treating cranial cruciate injuries in cats is that the knee will develop some degree of arthritis at some point after the injury. The object of the surgery is to delay the onset of arthritis for as long as possible and minimise its severity. The long-term prospects for cats who suffer this injury are not as good as in human beings but all these cats can be expected to live out their lives comfortably and with sufficient pain-free mobility to do whatever they wish. There are many long-term, safe, effective arthritis treatments available today to control the arthritis which will ensue at some time in the cat's life. Please refer to the section on arthritis earlier in this chapter for a discussion of these.

2e(iv) - Arthritis may cause thickening of the whole joint or part of the joint. The thickened joint is usually firm to the touch and not painful when touched. The joint will seem thicker than the same joint on the other leg. The joint may be painful when you bend or straighten the joint and it may produce a "crunchy" sensation when it is bent and straightened. X-rays will usually be taken of the joint to confirm the diagnosis. Please refer to the paragraphs earlier in this chapter for a discussion on arthritis and appropriate treatments.

2f The hip joints

The anatomy of the pelvis and the hip joints in cats is exactly the same as our own. The hip joint is a ball and socket joint held together by a ligament inside the joint and a capsule around the outside of the joint. The joint capsule produces fluid which feeds and lubricates the joint. The muscles positioned around the outside of the joint also help to support the joint and keep the ball in position in the socket. The ball part of the joint is the rounded head of the thighbone (the femur) and the socket (the acetabulum) is a cave-like depression in the pelvic bone. This ball and socket joint is a tightly fitting joint which allows movement in almost any direction because of its spherical design.

The ends of the bones forming moving joints are covered with a layer of cartilage called articular or joint cartilage. This cartilage is very smooth and is essential for smooth movement of the joint. This joint cartilage has very few nerve cells supplying it and this relatively nerve-free layer is essential in covering the bone ends which have a good nerve supply. The best way to understand this concept is to consider the forces acting on the ends of the bones when they are bearing weight during walking or standing. When we walk or stand our entire body weight is pressing down on our joints. The reason this doesn't cause pain is the layer of numb cartilage covering the ends of the bones (the articular cartilage). If we didn't have this layer of articular cartilage then the ends of the bones wound be pressed together by our body weight and as the bone ends have a good nerve supply this would cause severe pain

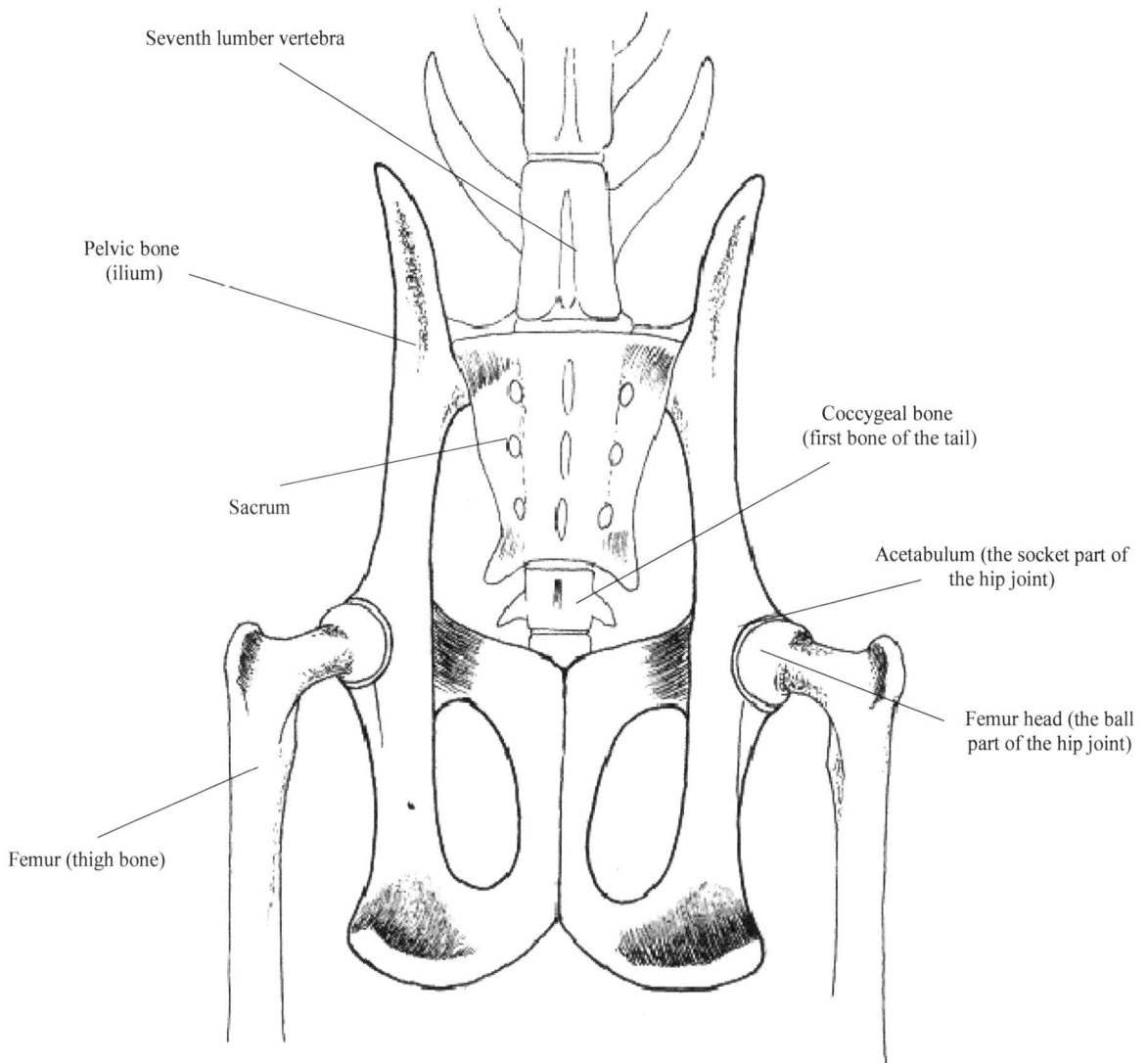

Fig 29. – Normal anatomy of a cat's pelvis and hip joints

Even limited areas of damage to this articular cartilage allow small areas of bone to be exposed and pressure on this exposed bone causes pain. The process of arthritis causes erosions in the articular cartilage and this contributes significantly to the pain in the affected joint.

The bone ends forming the joint are held together by the joint capsule which effectively forms a sealed bag around the bone ends. The purpose of the joint capsule is not only to hold the ends of the bones forming the joint together but also to produce joint fluid, which fills the joint. The joint fluid in turn serves two main purposes, namely to serve as lubrication for the joint in the same way that oil lubricates a door hinge and, secondly, to carry nutrients to feed and maintain the articular cartilages and other structures inside the joint. This joint fluid is called synovial fluid and is produced by the synovial membrane, which is the inside layer of the joint capsule. To my knowledge there are no man-made lubricants for machinery which are as efficient as synovial fluid in terms of lubricating moving parts. Many cats with arthritis do not produce enough joint fluid to feed and lubricate the affected joint and this leads to increased grinding of the joint cartilage which further contributes to the pain and progression of the arthritis.

The examination of the hip joints involves moving the thighbone forwards, backwards, inwards and outwards. If any of these movements causes pain then one should suspect that the hip is the cause of the lameness in the hind leg.

The most common problems affecting the hip joints are:

2f(i) - **Abscesses and cellulitis.** Cellulitis and abscesses may develop in this area as a result of wounds from fighting with other cats. The infection initially causes a firm painful swelling which may ultimately develop into an abscess and burst. If this area is painful examine it carefully by looking for small scabs or holes or cuts which would suggest that the cat has been involved in a cat fight. Please refer to the discussion on the diagnosis and treatment of cellulitis and abscesses earlier in this chapter.

2f(ii) - **Fractures and dislocations.** Severe painful swelling of the hip may suggest that one or more of the bones of the joint have been broken or ligaments have been torn, or that the hip joint has been dislocated. X-rays are generally required to confirm that a bone has been broken or that ligaments have been ruptured. If any bones are broken then the fracture is usually treated through surgical repair as necessary.

If the hip is dislocated the vet will have to administer a general anaesthetic to try to put the hip back into position. Most cases of hip dislocation can be treated in this way and after the hip is put back into position the vet may put the leg into a special type of sling called a Velpeau bandage. The object of this sling is to keep the hip joint in position for a few days to weeks to ensure that it does not dislocate again before it has had a chance to heal. In some cases the vet will be unable to put the hip back into position or it may keep dislocating. The reason for this is that a large blood clot may have formed in the socket part of the joint (the acetabulum), preventing the ball part of the joint moving back into the socket. In these cases the vet will have to operate to remove the blood clot and then put the hip joint back into position. In some severe cases the hip joint will keep dislocating and the vet may have to perform further surgery to keep the joint in position.

2f(iii) - **Arthritis** may cause thickening of the whole joint or part of the joint. The thickened joint is usually firm to the touch and not painful when touched. The joint will seem thicker than the same joint on the other leg. The joint may be painful when you bend or straighten the joint and it may produce a "crunchy" sensation when it is bent and straightened. X-rays will usually be taken of the joint to confirm the diagnosis. Please refer to the paragraphs earlier in this chapter for a discussion on arthritis and appropriate treatments.

2g The pelvic bones

The structure of the cat's pelvis is exactly the same as your own. The pelvis is effectively a "box" formed by two pelvic bones. The top of the "box" is formed by the sacrum which is the large flat bone at the base of the backbone. The large flat pelvic bones form the left and right sides of the "box" and the hip joints are situated in the left and right sides of this "box". The left and right pelvic bones are attached to the left and right sides of the sacrum respectively. The bottom of the "box" is formed where the left and right pelvic bones are fused together. The inside of the "box" (the pelvis) is often called the birth canal and this is where we find the last part of the intestines called the rectum and, below this, the urethra which is the tube leading from the bladder to the urethral opening in the penis or vagina. In female cats the vagina and cervix are situated between the rectum and the urethra.

The most common problems affecting the pelvis are:

2g(i) - **Abscesses and cellulitis.** Cellulitis and abscesses may develop in this area as a result of wounds from fighting with other cats. The infection initially causes a firm painful swelling which may ultimately develop into an abscess and burst. If this area is painful examine it carefully by looking for small scabs or holes or cuts which would suggest that the cat has been involved in a cat fight. Please refer to the discussion on the diagnosis and treatment of cellulitis and abscesses earlier in this chapter.

2g(ii) - **Fractures of the pelvis.** Cats who have been hit by a car often have fractured pelvic bones. When there is damage to the pelvis there are usually at least two fractures because the pelvis is effectively a box. Imagine a cardboard box – when you collapse or crush the box you have to collapse at least two sides of it. When the car hits the pelvis on one side and fractures it, another side of the "box" also has to collapse to disperse the force of the impact. Depending on the force and direction of the impact, the pelvis fractures may occur anywhere in the pelvis. If the bulk of the injury is on one side then the cat is often still able to walk, albeit painfully, on the leg on the other side. If the fracture causes the left and right pelvic bones to be ripped apart then the cat will appear to be lame in both back legs and will often only be able to walk short distances often with a crouched posture. When you or your vet touches the damaged pelvis the cat will let you know that you have found the source of the pain causing the lameness.

The vet will advise X-rays of the pelvis and lower back to assess the type and extent of the damage. In many cases the pelvic fractures and damage will heal by themselves provided the cat is kept inactive in a cage for six weeks. This confined healing is often called "cage rest" by vets. Natural healing with cage rest is only appropriate if the fractured ends of the pelvic bones have not moved very far from their correct position, are stable (i.e. the fractured ends of the bones do not move around), and the effect of the fractures has not narrowed the pelvic canal (the birth canal). This is important in male and female cats because if the pelvic canal heals in a narrowed position, the cat may have difficulty passing faeces (poo) in the future and as a result may end up having repeated bouts of constipation. If the fractured bones are unstable, displaced far from their normal position, or if the pelvic canal has been narrowed, then the vet will usually advise surgery to repair the damage, most commonly using steel plates and screws.

The broken pelvic bone has moved inwards. This effectively narrows the pelvic canal (birth canal). If the fracture is not repaired the pelvic canal will be permanently narrowed and the cat may have difficulty passing normal sized faeces (poo) through this narrowed space. This may lead to permanent constipation. Female cats will not be able to give birth to kittens because the kittens cannot pass through this narrowed space

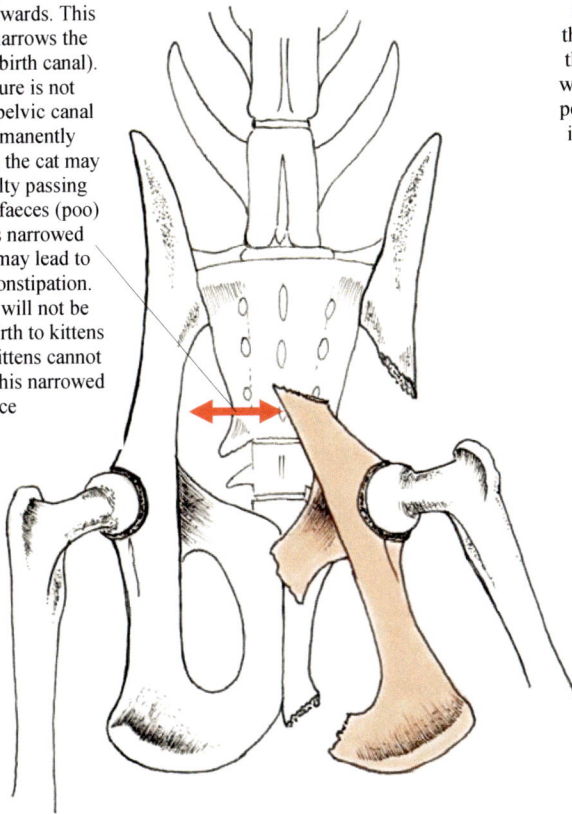

By repairing the fracture the normal width of the pelvic canal is restored

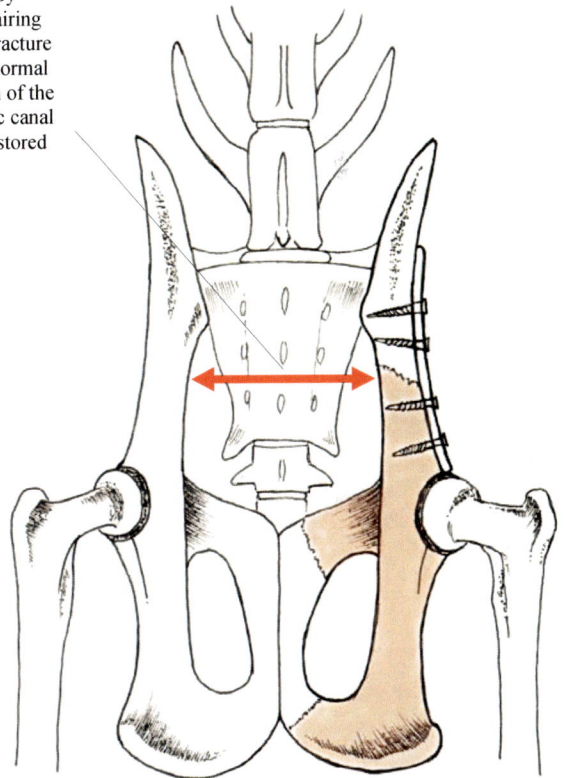

Fig 30a. – Fractured pelvis with broken bone displaced into pelvic canal

Fig 30b. – Fractured pelvis repaired with a plate and screws to restore the normal width of the pelvic canal (birth canal)

Another reason for taking X-rays is to check whether the lower part of the backbone has been injured because, if it has, the cat may also have spinal damage. The part of the lower spine lying over the top of the pelvis provides the nerve supply to the back legs, the bladder and the rectum. So if this part of the spine has been damaged then the cat may not be able to walk, or pass urine (pee) or faeces (poo). If the vet finds that the lower part of the back has been damaged then this will also require either surgical repair or natural healing through rest and confinement. Occasionally spinal damage will be permanent and then one will have to consider whether the individual cat is able to live with the disability or not. I would usually recommend waiting at least two to four weeks before deciding whether the spinal damage is permanent or not. If the cat is unable to pass urine or faeces during this time then the vet will have to empty the bladder and rectum manually every day while waiting for the spine to heal.

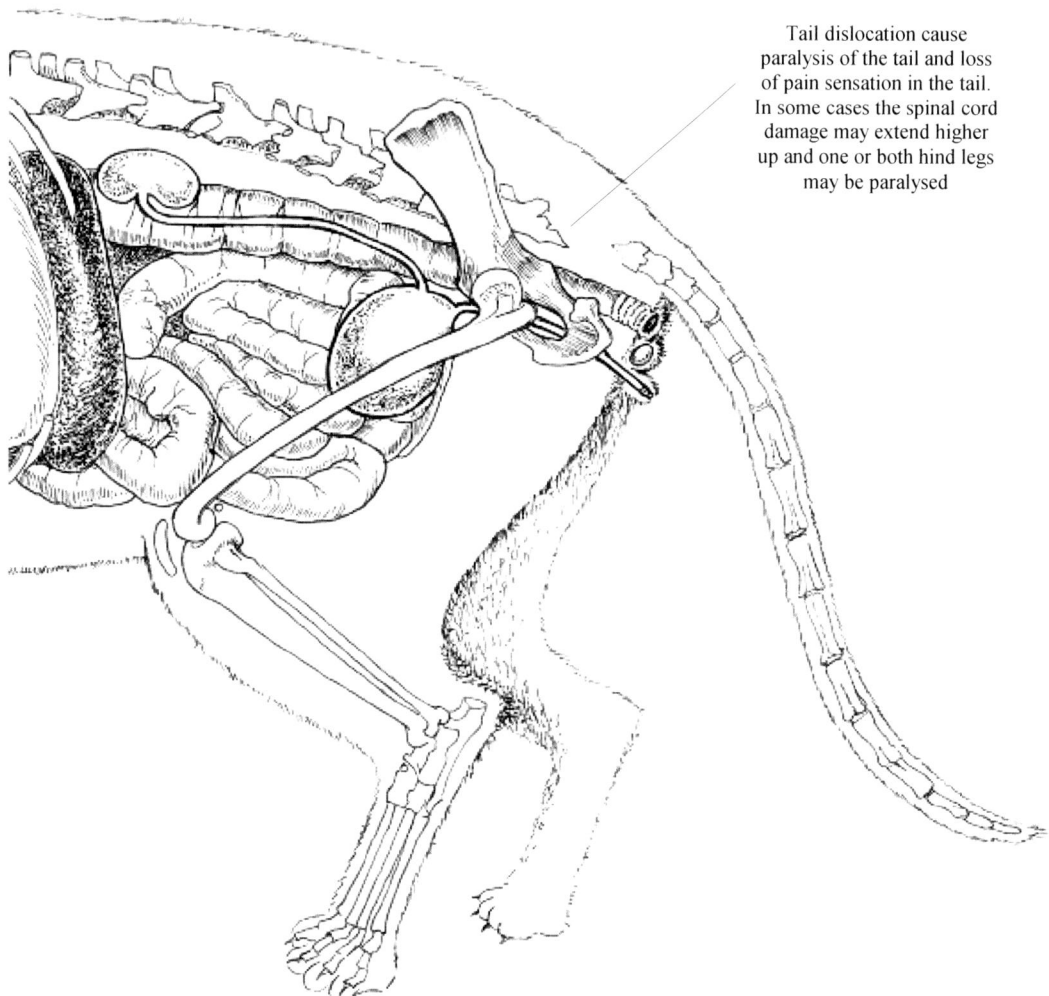

Tail dislocation cause paralysis of the tail and loss of pain sensation in the tail. In some cases the spinal cord damage may extend higher up and one or both hind legs may be paralysed

Fig. 31 – Sacro-coccygeal luxation (dislocation of

10

EAR PROBLEMS

The components of the cat's ear are the same as human ears. The "ear flap" is technically called the pinna, the plural being pinnae. The pinna is simply a flat piece of cartilage covered with skin. The base of the pinna is attached to several muscles that can move the pinna in a variety of directions. The ear canal consists of a hollow tube that leads from the eardrum in the skull to the outside word, and acts as a funnel, collecting sounds and leading them to the eardrum. The ear canal is simply a cone of cartilage that is lined by hairless skin and can be divided into two parts. The first part which we can see and look down is called the vertical ear canal because it literally runs vertically downwards from the base of the earflap (pinna). The vertical ear canal then takes a sharp turn inward towards the skull to form the horizontal ear canal which is attached to the eardrum. The eardrum is simply a thin membrane, much like the membrane of a drum. On the inside of the eardrum are the middle ear and inner ear. The middle ear is a hollow chamber in the skull bone which acts like the body of a drum, and the inner ear is a separate structure composed of rings full of fluid which act as our balance centre and have nothing to do with the process of hearing.

The first sign that may alert us to a problem affecting the ear of a cat is that they may twitch the ears more than normal. In more severe cases the cat may shake their head and scratch at one or both ears either by rubbing the head along the ground or furniture or by scratching the ear with their hind paws. In more advanced cases there may also be an unusual or foul smell coming from the ear canals. If one or both ears start bothering the cat, one should examine the ear flap, the ear canal and the skin around the ear.

The ear can be divided into three parts when one considers diseases and conditions that affect the ears. I will discuss conditions that affect the earflap (pinna), the ear canal and the skin around the ear.

1 The ear flap (pinna)

The most common abnormality that one may notice when examining the pinna is that a portion of the earflap or even the entire earflap may seem very thick and swollen. This swelling feels firm and sometimes warm when touched but is not usually painful.

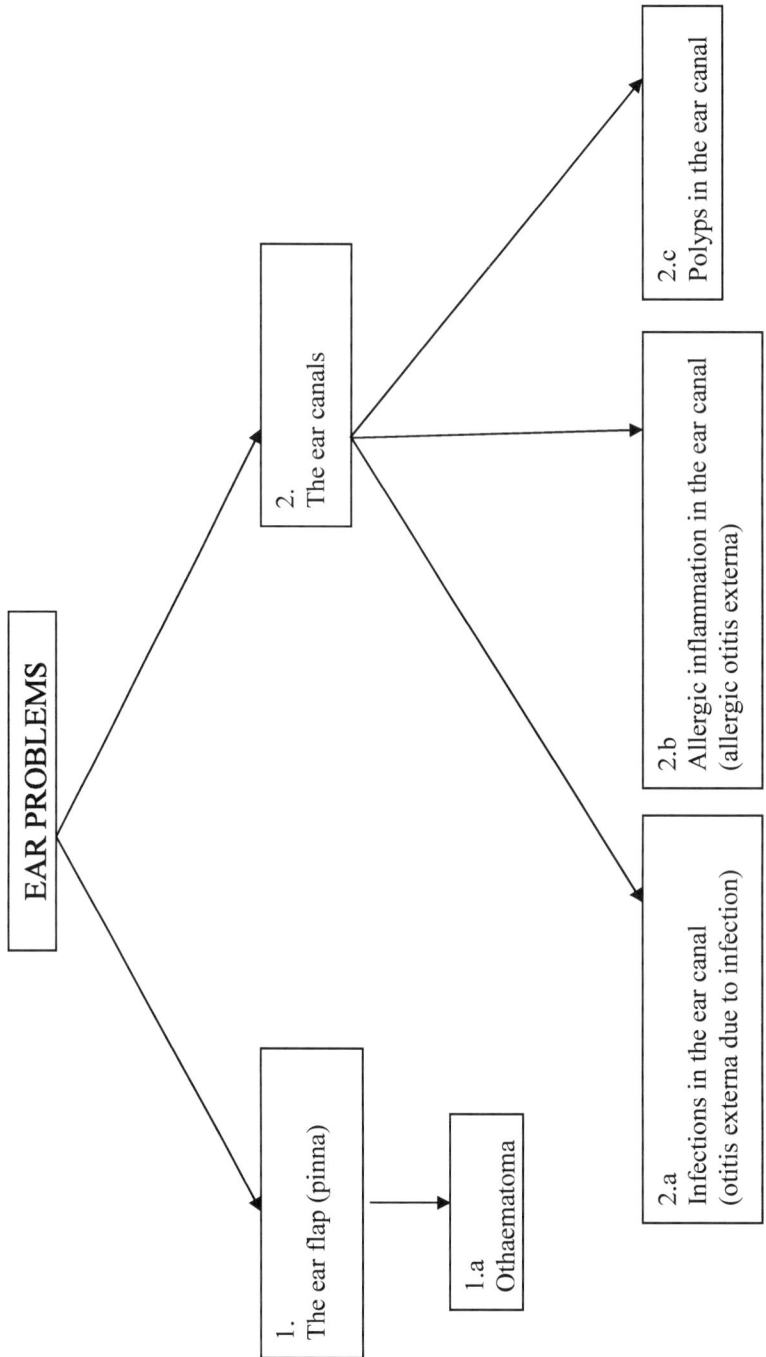

EAR PROBLEMS

1.
The ear flap (pinna)

2.
The ear canals

1.a
Othaematoma

2.a
Infections in the ear canal
(otitis externa due to infection)

2.b
Allergic inflammation in the ear canal
(allergic otitis externa)

2.c
Polyps in the ear canal

Many people think that the cat has developed an abscess in the earflap but the most common explanation for this swelling is a condition called an othaematoma.

1a Othaematoma

An othaematoma is effectively a large "blood blister" under the skin of the earflap. Most of us have heard of rugby players and boxers developing "cauliflower ears". These develop when the pinna has been damaged by a punch or a hard knock; small blood vessels may be damaged and bleeding may occur under the skin. Because the pinna is simply a flat piece of cartilage covered by skin, if bleeding occurs inside it the blood will accumulate in a pocket between the skin and the layer of cartilage, separating the two layers. The amount of bleeding that occurs will determine the size of the "blood blister". This pocket of blood will eventually contract just like scabs do on external wounds on the skin. As the blood in the othaematoma clots, the edges of the clot will stick to the skin and the cartilage layer. The next step in the natural healing process is that the blood clot, just like a scab on the skin, will start to contract and shrink and, as this happens, a lump of scar tissue will form, sticking the cartilage layer and the overlying skin together. This often results in the ear healing in a lumpy and ultimately malformed way and the final appearance is called a "cauliflower ear".

Othaematomas may develop in cats' ears in the same way that they develop in sportsmen. The cat may start with an infection or irritation in the ear canal which makes them shake their heads. If they shake their heads very violently the ear flaps may slap against the skull bones hard enough to damage blood vessels in the pinna and the bleeding between the cartilage layer and the skin layer causes a "blood blister" or othaematoma to develop. Thus, if one examines a cat's ear and finds an othaematoma, the first thing to do is to determine why the cat might have been shaking their head violently enough to cause this damage. The most common cause is pain, infection or irritation in the ear canal which will be discussed more fully in the section on problems of the ear canals. If one finds a problem in the ear canal then it is important to treat the ear canal problem as well as the othaematoma. There are, however, often cases where there is no evidence of any problems in the ear canal and the cat hasn't been shaking their head. These cases present simply as an othaematoma that suddenly and spontaneously appeared in the earflap. We do not fully understand why some othaematomas develop for no apparent reason but we suspect that it may be the result of an autoimmune disorder, when the body's own immune system starts attacking and damaging specific tissues in the body. There is often no explanation for this but the process may sometimes cause bleeding in the pinna and lead to an othaematoma.

There are a variety of ways to treat an othaematoma. The most common way is to drain the blood out of the othaematoma using a needle and syringe then, once it has been completely drained, inject a small amount of cortisone through the same needle into the remaining empty pocket between the ear skin and cartilage. This process will normally stimulate the ear to heal but sometimes the othaematoma will reform within a few days and the vet will have to re-drain the blood from the ear several times. The old method of treating this condition was to make an incision in the ear flap to drain the blood and then re-attach the cartilage and skin layers to each other with many large stitches through the ear flap. This procedure can be very painful and I would only use this technique if repeatedly draining the ear and instilling cortisone into the earflap failed to solve the problem.

An important point to make at this stage is that it is very important to treat any problems that may be present in the ear canal at the same time. The reason for this is that if the problem in the ear canal is not treated then the cat will continue shaking their head, continuing the damage to the pinna and preventing the othaematoma from healing.

Many people ask me what would happen if we did not treat the othaematoma. The answer to this is that it will eventually heal itself by clotting and contracting as discussed earlier. The reason for treating the ear is that if we leave it to heal naturally then the cat will end up with a cauliflower ear that will be permanently thickened and misshapen.

2 The ear canals

The most common symptoms encountered when examining the ear canal is that it may be inflamed, swollen, and painful and may have a discharge. The medical term for these symptoms is otitis externa. The most common explanations for these findings are that there may be an infection in the ear canal, there may be an allergic reaction in the ear canal, or there may be one or more polyps growing in the ear canal. I will discuss each of these three possibilities individually.

2a Infections in the ear canal (otitis externa due to infection)

Bacteria, yeasts, fungi and ear mites may cause infections in the ear canal. Many people refer to ear canal infections as canker. I do not like to use this word as I feel that it is too vague to mean anything. If there is an infection in the ear canal, the type of discharge may often give the vet an idea what type of infection it is. If the ear canal contains a thick, black, crusty discharge then ear mites are the most likely cause of the problem. Ear mites are most commonly encountered in kittens and young cats and are easily dealt with by using appropriate ear drops. If the ear canal contains pus then bacteria are the most likely cause of the infection. The pus may have a foul smell and the infection may be very painful. The treatment would involve the use of painkilling anti-inflammatory treatment and antibiotic drops and tablets. In more severe cases the vet may also suggest that the ear canal be flushed and cleaned under sedation or general anaesthesia. Yeast and fungal infections are often secondary infections that take advantage of an ear canal that is already inflamed or infected or obstructed by polyps in the ear canals. Most modern ear drops contain multiple ingredients to treat all possible infections and vets will often only use tests like bacterial cultures if the problem does not resolve quickly and easily.

2b Allergic inflammation in the ear canal (allergic otitis externa)

I have used the word "allergy" very loosely thus far and at this point it is worth discussing in more depth. Cats develop allergies just as people do. The allergies that they develop are often due to the same things that we develop allergies to. The most common causes of allergies in cats and people seem to be house dust and house dust mites, grasses and pollens, and various types of food. The way that we manifest our allergies is to develop hay fever, asthma or skin eczema. Cats with allergies will develop asthma, itchy skin and/or itchy ears. The substance that causes the allergy is called the allergen. The route by which the allergen is taken into the body does not necessarily affect where in the body the allergic effect will be produced. Consider people with an allergy to nuts or bee stings; if they are exposed to the nuts in their food or a sting in their skin they will often develop severe swelling in their airways which may cause suffocation. This demonstrates that the site of the allergic reaction does not necessarily have to be the same as the route of exposure to the allergen. The same concept applies to cats in that they generally manifest their allergies as inflammation and itching in the lungs, skin and ear canals. This applies to food allergies; inhaled allergies like pollens and house dust mites, and injected allergies like fleabites. The most severe sites of itching in response to allergic reactions may be the ears and face as discussed in the chapter on itchy skin.

Allergic inflammation in the ear canals will cause redness and discomfort. There is no discharge from the ear but the cat will frequently twitch their ears and/or shake their heads

Fig 32. – Allergic inflammation in the ear canal (allergic otitis externa)

Cats suffering from allergies very commonly present with itchy, inflamed ears or even infected ears. The cases where the cat's allergies have caused the inflammation and itching in the ears are called allergic otitis externa. The lining of the ear canal down to the level of the eardrum is the same type of skin that covers the rest of the body; thus inflammation due to allergic reactions extends all the way down the ear canals. The ear canal is basically a tube of cartilage lined with skin. When the skin layer becomes inflamed, the cartilage will not allow the skin layer to swell outwards, as cartilage is not pliable enough. The result is that the swelling of the skin lining is inwards and the ear canal becomes narrowed when it is inflamed. This makes the ear canal feel like it is blocked, in the same way that the congestion associated with hay fever makes people feel that their nose is blocked and they need to blow their nose. The cat will feel as though there is something blocking the ear canal and the symptoms may vary from increased twitching of the ears to obsessively rubbing and scratching the ears and shaking the head.

The inflammation that develops in one or both ear canals can be demonstrated by comparing the colour of the skin in the ear canal with a piece of skin elsewhere on the body. The skin at the opening of the ear canal is generally pinker that the skin elsewhere but it should only be very slightly pinker than the rest of the skin. If the ear canal skin is much pinker than the rest of the skin then we know that it is inflamed. If there is no discharge from the ear canal and the vet confirms that there is nothing in the ear canal right down to the level of the eardrum, then we can assume that the ear discomfort is caused by the inflammation and congestion associated with allergies.

The treatment for allergic otitis externa may involve the use of ear drops, antihistamines or cortisone, and antibiotics if secondary infections have developed. It is necessary to implement long-term treatment and management of allergies in order to avoid frequent recurrence of the problem. I have discussed the long-term treatment for allergic otitis externa in the allergy section in the chapter on itchy skin.

2c Polyps in the ear canal

Long-term, low-grade inflammation in the ear canal, usually as a result of a long-term allergic reaction, may cause polyps to grow from the lining of the ear canals. Polyps are benign growths, i.e. they are abnormal growths but they are not cancerous in the same way that warts are growths but are not cancerous. Cats who develop polyps in the ear canals may develop a variety of different types of polyps. The most common type of polyps are called ceruminous polyps. The word ceruminous is derived from the cerumen which means wax (as in ear wax). This implies that the polyps grow and develop from the wax-producing cells lining the ear canal. There may be anything from one polyp to several hundred, ranging in size from one millimetre to five millimetres. They usually have a bluish or purplish colour and are easy to see when you look down into the ear canal. The second most common type of polyp is called a pedunculated ear canal polyp. Pedunculated means that the polyp grows from a narrow stalk much like cauliflower or broccoli. These pedunculated growths usually develop from the bottom of the ear canal near the eardrum and can only be seen using an otoscope (auroscope), the instrument the vet uses to look down into the cat's ears. The net effect of both types of polyps is that they obstruct the normal air flow in the ear canal because they partially or completely obstruct it. The deeper parts of the ear canal then trap heat and moisture and are poorly ventilated, creating the ideal growth environment for opportunist yeasts and bacteria to grow in.

Thus when you notice that your cat has an infection in their ear it is important to determine whether it is a primary infection, i.e. an infection for no apparent reason, or whether the infection is secondary to the abnormal conditions created in the ear canal by polyps. If the infection is secondary to the polyps then one must address both problems, i.e. treat the polyps and the infection. The pedunculated polyps can be surgically removed but multiple small purple ceruminous polyps cannot be removed without causing a lot of damage to the ear canal. If one considers that the two different types of polyps usually develop as a consequence of long-term inflammation in the ear canal, it is obvious that one must treat this underlying inflammation to try to prevent more polyps from growing. This is also the case even after a pedunculated polyp has been succesfully removed because if the long-term inflammation is not controlled, another polyp is bound to develop. The underlying problem of long-term inflammation is usually due to allergic inflammation and we must treat that allergy. The treatment for allergic inflammation in the ear canals is the same as the treatment for itchy skin allergies and is discussed in the chapter on itchy skin.

Summary

When a cat develops an ear infection, we must not only treat the pain and infection in the first instance but also try to identify how and why the infection developed. More often than not the infection will have developed for no apparent reason, but we should always look to see if it developed secondarily to the narrowing of the ear canal due to inflammation caused by an allergic reaction. This is even more important in the case of recurring ear infections, as the long-term allergic inflammation and recurrent secondary infections will result in ongoing narrowing of the ear canal throughout the cat's life, meaning that secondary ear infections will occur more and more often as the cat grows older.

An important point to make here is that an inflamed ear canal containing abnormal matter is not necessarily an infected ear. One will get a very good idea of what secondary problem has affected the ear canal by looking at the abnormal matter accumulating in the ear canal. Pus would suggest a bacterial infection and/or fungal and yeast infections; a black tarry substance which may look like clotted blood may suggest ear mites; and a dark brown waxy substance suggests just an allergic reaction without secondary infections. The accumulation of this dark brown waxy substance is often misinterpreted as an infection as it may have a foul smell, but is generally just an overproduction of earwax. The reason this happens is once again best understood by comparing the allergic reaction manifesting in cats' ears to the allergic reaction manifesting in human beings' noses called hay fever.

In the case of human beings, hay fever produces inflammation in the lining of the nose, the nose doesn't know whether the inflammation is due to an allergic reaction or an infection starting in the nose, so it does the only thing it can to protect itself – it produces a protective layer of mucous. In the case of hay fever sufferers it effectively overdoes it and we develop a very watery, bunged-up snotty nose. The ear canal, when it is inflamed, also doesn't know whether the inflammation is due to allergy or infection and it also does the only thing it can to protect itself which is to produce more wax to build up a defensive barrier. The wax production is, however, also often overdone, leading to a dark brown waxy accumulation of "muck" in the ear canal. The long-term inflammation may also result in the growth of ear canal polyps and this will further predispose the cat to secondary infections until the polyp and/or the allergic inflammation are dealt with. If your cat suffers from repeated ear problems you should consider all the symptoms and identify which are the cause and which are the effect of the problem and only once you have addressed all the factors involved will you solve the problem. Ear inflammation and infections are very painful so it is morally imperative that we leave no stone unturned in our efforts to spare cats from either continuous or relapsing long-term ear canal problems.

11

MY CAT IS HAVING
SEIZURES/CONVULSIONS

Most people think of epilepsy when they think of seizures. The classic image of an epileptic fit (seizure) is of a person who suddenly falls to the ground unconscious and has violent muscle spasms. This is called a grand mal seizure. A common misconception is that one should try to help someone who is having a seizure by pulling their tongue forwards to prevent them from "swallowing their tongue". This is not the correct thing to do because the individual having the seizure may clamp their jaw tightly shut during a muscle spasm. If you have your fingers in their mouth when they clamp their jaws shut, they may very severely damage your fingers. With cats, there is not only this danger but also the risk of serious infection from a deep bite. Moreover, cats often lash out with their claws during a seizure so it is best to not even try to restrain them during a seizure as you may be seriously hurt. Wait until the seizure has ended before handling the cat even though it is very difficult to just stand there and watch and do nothing while the seizure is happening.

One can think of the brain as being a computer, and computers may occasionally "jam" or "crash" for no apparent reason. When the computer crashes it may scramble the information contained within it and the way to remedy this is to re-boot the computer. When it then comes back online, most computers will unscramble themselves and function normally again until the next time they "jam" or "crash", if they ever do. The computer may also crash if, for example, someone accidentally unplugs it while you are working on it and the computer may scramble or lose the document you were working on at the time. When you then plug it back in, the computer will re-boot and unscramble itself. Thus a computer may "crash" because of a problem inside the computer or it may "crash" because of external problems affecting it, e.g. if the power cable is accidentally knocked out.

The brain is very much like a computer in that it controls and processes all the information in the body. When an individual has a seizure it is very similar to a computer "crashing". The brain, like the computer, may seizure (crash) either because of a problem in the brain, or because of external problems affecting the ability of the brain to function normally. Once a seizure has happened, the brain may correct the fault within a few minutes but, if the brain is unable to correct the fault, then the seizure may continue for several hours.

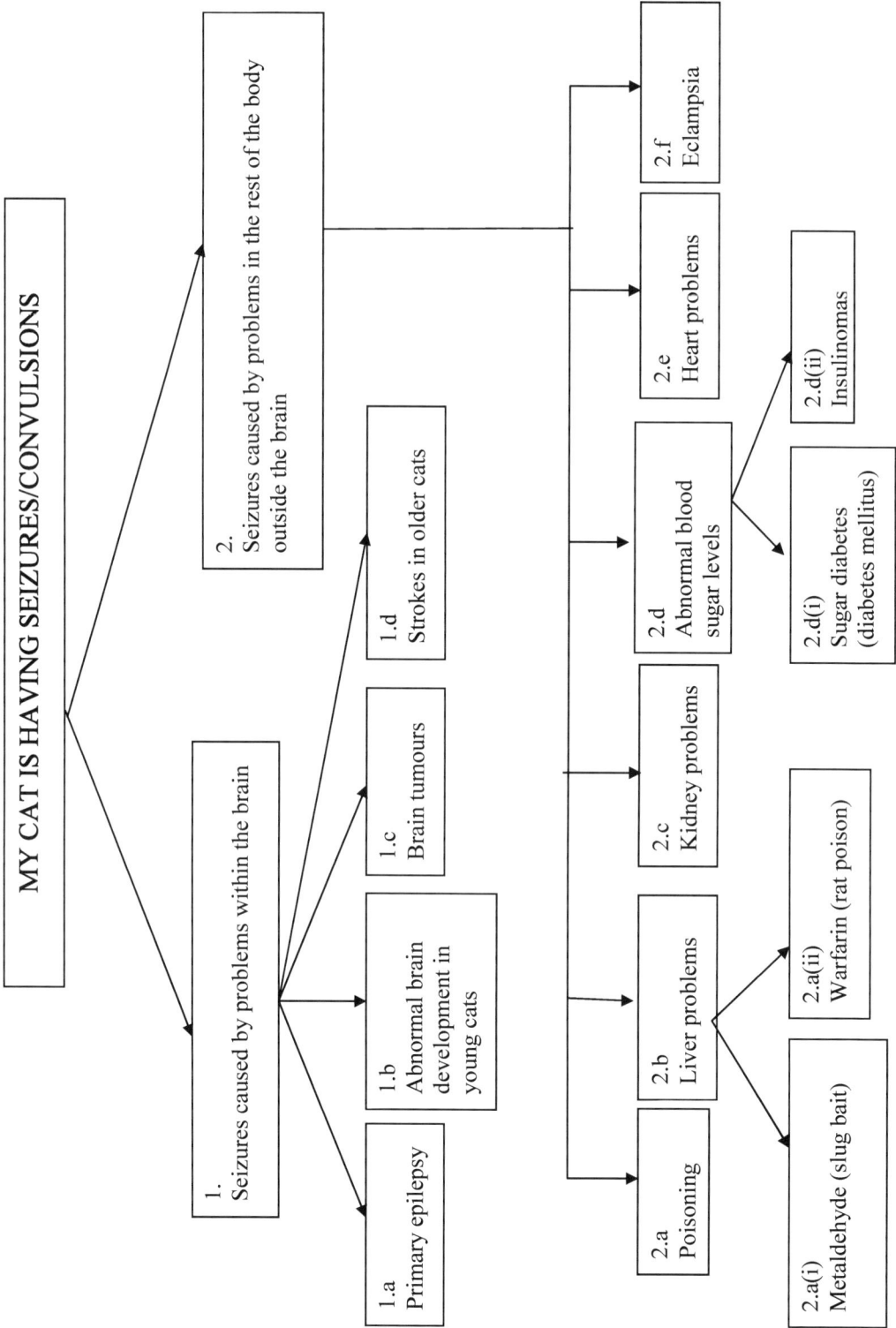

MY CAT IS HAVING SEIZURES/CONVULSIONS

1.
Seizures caused by problems within the brain

2.
Seizures caused by problems in the rest of the body outside the brain

1.a
Primary epilepsy

1.b
Abnormal brain development in young cats

1.c
Brain tumours

1.d
Strokes in older cats

2.a
Poisoning

2.b
Liver problems

2.c
Kidney problems

2.d
Abnormal blood sugar levels

2.e
Heart problems

2.f
Eclampsia

2.a(i)
Metaldehyde (slug bait)

2.a(ii)
Warfarin (rat poison)

2.d(i)
Sugar diabetes (diabetes mellitus)

2.d(ii)
Insulinomas

If the seizure is very short then the brain will usually "re-boot" itself but if the seizure continues for more than ten minutes then the brain may need to be "re-booted" by a vet or doctor. The vet will do this by using medications which stop the seizures and "knock the cat out" for one or several hours. When they wake up, the brain will have been "re-booted". A grand mal seizure is the equivalent of a computer "crashing" and a petit mal seizure is the equivalent of a computer "jamming".

Grand mal seizures are the classic seizures most people think about when I discuss seizures or convulsions. When a grand mal seizure happens it usually strikes very suddenly and the cat will fall to the ground, either on their chest or their side. They may miaow or cry out as the seizure strikes them. Their eyes may seem to be "rolling in the eye sockets" and they may drool and salivate. They may then have muscle twitching or violent spasms affecting any or all of the muscles of the body. They may pee and poo onto themselves or the floor. During the seizure the cat may or may not seem unconscious. Even if they seem conscious during the seizure, they usually do not seem to be aware of other people or things around them. The muscle twitching or spasms will continue for anything from a few seconds to a few hours. When the seizure ends you will notice that they may seem confused or disorientated. They will then either return back to normal within a few minutes or hours, or another seizure may strike within a few minutes or hours. As mentioned before, do not try to handle your cat during the seizure as they may seriously injure you. Wait for the seizure to end and wait until the cat is aware of who you are and where they are.

Petit mal seizures have also been called "fly-gazing" or "star-gazing". Petit mal seizures do not involve most of the symptoms of a grand mal seizure, i.e. there are usually no muscle spasms and the cat usually does not fall over. The only symptom that the cat is having a mild seizure is that they seem to watching an invisible fly flying around their head or gazing at invisible stars over their heads. This vacant staring may go on for a few seconds to a few minutes. When it stops, the cat may seem a bit confused for a few minutes but then usually they seem completely normal again.

Thus grand mal and petit mal seizures appear very different but both reflect abnormal brain activity. The time before the seizure is called the pro-drome and the time after the seizure is the recovery phase. The pro-drome is a very important concept. During the pro-drome many cats will seem anxious and unsettled. These cats will often produce a very distressing yowling sound that you will never have heard them make before as they seem to realise that something is about to happen to them. The pro-drome may last for a few minutes or even a few hours. If we learn to recognise the symptoms of the pro-drome it gives us the opportunity to try to stop the impending seizure from happening by either giving medication and/or stimulating the cat to distract them. This stimulation simply takes the form of talking to them and focusing their attention on yourself while reassuring them. This process of distracting the patient and focusing their attention on something will often prevent the seizure from happening. This is a concept employed by some doctors. We have all heard of guide dogs for blind people but few of us have heard of seizure dogs for people with epilepsy. These are dogs who are able to recognise when a person is about to have a seizure, i.e. they know when a person is in the pro-drome even though the person doesn't realise it themselves. No one knows how some dogs can do this, but if they can, then they can be used to warn an epileptic person that they are about to have a seizure. This gives that person the opportunity to quickly take their medication and possibly also to try to activate and focus their minds with an activity to try to prevent the seizure from happening.

The recovery phase is the time after the seizure has stopped. Some cats will recover within a few minutes and then continue as if nothing had happened. Other cats may seem disorientated and shaken by the experience and they may take several hours to "get over it" and return to normal.

Once you have witnessed a seizure, take careful note of the time of day and all the symptoms associated with the seizure. There is nothing you can do at home to stop the seizure once it has started. Do not try to pick the cat up or cuddle them to comfort them even though your natural instincts tell you to do this. You definitely should not reach into their mouth to pull their tongue forwards because they may accidentally severely injure you and you might even lose your fingers. The only thing you can do during the seizure is to watch all the stages carefully so that you can answer the vet's questions about it later. If possible, get someone to phone the vet for advice while you watch the cat. Once the seizure is over you should reassure the cat and then it would be wise to phone the vet for advice.

Emergency treatment for grand mal seizures

If the grand mal seizure does not stop within a couple of minutes you should phone your vet for advice. The vet will almost certainly want to examine the cat immediately. The most suitable place to examine a cat that is having a seizure or has just stopped fitting is at the veterinary clinic because the vet may not be able to bring all the equipment they need to your house. If the seizure has not stopped naturally within five minutes the vet will probably advise that they have to use medication to stop the seizure. If the seizure does not stop and you have to transport your cat to the vet while they are still fitting then you must protect yourself from possible injury. The safest way to handle them during a seizure is to wrap them in a thick blanket to protect you from their teeth and claws. Be very aware of your face as the cat may lash out and injure your face or your eyes.

The vet may use two or more types of medication to stop a continuous seizure. The first thing the vet will do is to check the blood glucose levels. If these are not normal they may need to be corrected before doing anything else. Once the vet knows what the blood glucose levels are they may need to sedate the cat with an injection. If one or more sedative injections do not stop the convulsions then the vet will have to administer a full general anaesthetic. Once the cat is under the general anaesthetic the vet will need to keep them asleep for as much as several hours. While they are sleeping under the general anaesthetic the vet may also start anticonvulsive treatment. This is because, although the general anaesthetic stops the muscle spasms, the seizure in the brain may continue without any obvious outward signs. The anticonvulsive treatment thus stops the abnormal activity in the brain and the anaesthetic stops the muscle spasms. While the cat is under the anaesthetic and asleep, these treatments will "re-boot" the brain just like a computer. Once the vet has administered the treatment and has stopped the seizure they will ask you several questions and may start running some tests. The questions and tests are discussed in the next few paragraphs.

When the vet is presented with a cat who has had one or more seizures, they will initially try to determine whether the cause of the problem is inside the brain or whether it is due to external factors affecting the brain. The vet will ask you a wide variety of questions. Some of the questions will relate directly to the seizure and others will be directed to other symptoms that may have been developing before the seizure occurred. Your answers to the questions are very important and it is important not to try to guess the answer. It is better to answer a question with "I don't know" rather than to guess, as the information that you give the vet will very often give them enough information to make the diagnosis without expensive tests. The questions will include some or all of the following.

- What time did the seizure occur?
- What was the cat doing when the seizure occurred?
- Did the cat realise that something was wrong before having the seizure (was there a pro-drome)?
- When the seizure occurred, did the cat fall over and if they did, did they fall onto their chest or onto their side?
- Did the cat lose consciousness during the seizure?
- How long did the seizure last?
- How long after the seizure did it take the cat to seem normal again (how long was the recovery period)?
- Has the cat had seizures before?
- How old is the cat?
- Does the cat have a previous history of diabetes and are they currently on insulin treatment?
- Have you used any pesticides, e.g. snail or slug poison in or around your house and garden?
- In the days or weeks before the seizure, was the cat's appetite increased, decreased or normal?
- In the days or weeks before the seizure, was the cat drinking more, less or the same amount of water as normal?
- In the weeks before the seizure was the cat breathing normally and maintaining a normal level of activity or have they been less active and sleeping more ?

The purpose of these questions is to guide the vet's thinking which will go something like this:

- If the seizures happen in a very young cat (less than one year old) one might suspect a birth defect in the brain or elsewhere in the body.
- If the seizures happen soon after the cat has eaten a meal then one might suspect that a liver problem is affecting the brain.

- If the seizures happen during exercise then one might suspect that a heart condition or a blood glucose disorder is affecting the brain.
- If the seizures happen when the cat is resting or sleeping then one might suspect primary epilepsy.
- If the cat had an altered thirst or appetite in the days or weeks prior to the seizure then one might suspect that a problem elsewhere in the body is affecting the brain.
- If the cat is very old one might suspect that they have had a stroke.
- If there was a clear pro-drome period then one might suspect primary epilepsy.
- If pesticides have recently been used at home the cat may have eaten some and poison may be affecting the brain.
- If the cat is on daily insulin injections for diabetes they may have been given too much insulin.

Once the vet has thoroughly examined your cat and asked you some or all of the above questions, they may be able to make a specific diagnosis but in most cases they would need to run some tests to be sure of the diagnosis. The tests would include some or all of the following: blood tests, X-rays, ECG heart monitor, ultrasound scans, brain scans. The vet uses all this information to determine whether the seizures are caused by a problem within the brain or a problem in another part of the body which is affecting the brain.

If the problem is within the brain, the most common diagnoses are primary epilepsy (young or middle-aged cats) or abnormal brain development (young cats) or brain tumours (middle-aged or older cats) or "strokes" (older cats).

If the seizures are caused by problems outside the brain, the most common diagnoses are poisoning or problems with other organs in the body (liver, kidneys, pancreas or heart) or the diabetic cat has been given an overdose of insulin.

1 Seizures caused by problems within the brain

1a Primary epilepsy

Epilepsy is most commonly first noticed when the cat is between six months and three years old but it may develop at any age. The symptoms are usually grand mal seizures which occur when the cat is resting or sleeping. There is often a distinct pro-drome and a fast and full recovery after the seizure has ended. The seizures may occur as a single episode or several seizures may happen in a row. There are no other abnormalities besides the seizures, i.e. the seizures occur occasionally but at all other times the cat appears absolutely normal in every respect. Not all cats with epilepsy will have grand mal seizures. Cats with mild epilepsy may have "fly-gazing" as the only symptom.

There is not a specific test for epilepsy in cats. Epilepsy means that the brain suffers seizures for no apparent reason the same way that some computers will frequently crash for no apparent reason. This is the same as epilepsy in human beings. Because there is no specific test for epilepsy, the vet can only make this diagnosis by running enough tests to prove that none of the other causes of seizures exist in that individual. This is called making a diagnosis by exclusion, i.e. the vet will exclude all of the other possible causes of seizures and thus the only remaining diagnosis is epilepsy.

If the cat is presented to the vet during a grand mal seizure, the vet may have to use sedative injections or a general anaesthetic to stop the muscle spasms. They will usually start anticonvulsive treatment at the same time. The emergency treatment for a grand mal seizure is discussed at the beginning of this chapter.

Once the diagnosis has been made, the vet may use tablets to prevent future seizures. Not all cases of epilepsy need to be treated. If the cat only suffers two or three very short seizures a year with a rapid full recovery within a few minutes of each seizure, then the vet may suggest that no treatment is required. This is because most epilepsy treatments will strain the liver so one must decide which is the least damaging to the cat – the added strain on the liver or an occasional non-life-threatening seizure which does not significantly affect the cat before or after. I would usually only start treatment for epilepsy if the individual had more than one seizure a month or if each seizure lasted more that two minutes.

The decision to treat or not to treat the condition should be discussed with your vet on an individual case basis. If the decision is that treatment is required, the treatment consists of tablets that the cat will probably need to take for the rest of his or her life. The most common treatment used to control epilepsy in cats is called phenobarbitone. Phenobarbitone works on the brain by "lowering the seizure threshold". This effectively means that the treatment calms and stabilises the cells in the brain so that the cells are unlikely to function abnormally. Abnormally functioning brain cells cause seizures by causing a "short circuit in the wiring of the brain", similar to a computer where a short circuit in the electronics causes the computer to crash. The treatment usually does put some strain on the liver but usually we have no signs of this other than the fact that blood tests will reveal that the liver becomes slightly inflamed when this treatment is used. There is no specific dose of treatment which suits all cats so the vet will start the treatment at an average dose and then adjust the dose accordingly. The decision to increase or decrease the dose will be determined by how effectively the treatment is preventing the seizures and by using blood tests to measure the level of the drug in the blood. This treatment is intended to prevent all seizures without producing side effects. Thus, although blood tests may show that the treatment strains the liver, the patients should show no signs or symptoms of side effects from the treatment. Most epileptic cats can be expected to live long, happy, normal lives once the diagnosis has been made and treatment has been started.

1b Abnormal brain development in young cats

The most common brain abnormality that a kitten may be born with is called hydrocephalus. This is a very severe abnormality and most kittens will show obvious symptoms of abnormal brain function within a few months of being born. One of the symptoms may be grand mal seizures. Many other symptoms will also be present, i.e. the affected kitten seems dull and lethargic, is smaller than the other kittens in the litter and may not be able to walk, eat and play normally. There are currently no effective treatments for these patients and most of them will die. The vet will often make the diagnosis based on the age, the symptoms and the size and shape of the kitten's skull. The diagnosis can be confirmed by taking skull X-rays and brain scans. The vet may, if you request, try to treat the condition for as long as possible by using phenobarbitone to prevent seizures if they are occurring in the affected individual. The use of phenobarbitone is discussed in the paragraph on epilepsy.

Another very rare brain birth defect is called mucopolysaccharidosis. Kittens with this condition may have any or all of the symptoms seen with hydrocephalus with the difference that the skull may seem shorter than normal rather than larger than normal. There is once again no effective treatment for this condition and the best we can do is to use phenobarbitone therapy to control seizures if they happen in the affected kitten.

1c Brain tumours

Brain tumours are very rare in cats and usually occur in old cats. The symptoms caused by the brain tumour depend on which part of the brain is affected. If the tumour causes seizures then they are usually grand mal seizures. The diagnosis of a brain tumour can only be made by performing a brain scan. Some brain tumours may respond to radiation therapy while others are untreatable. This also applies to brain tumours in human beings. Any treatment for brain tumours should only be undertaken by an oncologist (tumour specialist).

1d Strokes in older cats

Cats may suffer a stroke just as people do. Strokes usually only occur in old cats and fortunately most cats will recover completely within a week of having the stroke. The word "stroke" means that a blood vessel in the brain has burst or become blocked. Once this happens a small piece of the brain that relies on blood from that blood vessel will die off. The stroke does not usually cause seizures but I have included it in this section because the affected cat will often not be able to stand or walk after a stroke and when they try to do so they have very jerky movements and often fall over. They usually have their head tilted to one side and their eyes may twitch from side to side or up and down. This twitching eye movement is called nystagmus. The cat may appear very disorientated or they may be fully aware of their surroundings. With severe strokes the affected cat may not be able to walk for one to three days. In the case of a mild stroke the cat may be able to walk immediately after the stroke but will be unsteady on their feet to varying degrees, i.e. some will repeatedly fall over and others might just seem a bit "wobbly". Once they are able to walk they will often tend to walk in circles either to the left or to the right. These cats will usually recover completely within seven days of the stroke.

The vet will often be able to make the diagnosis of a stroke based just on the above symptoms. To confirm the diagnosis the vet will have to take a brain scan. There is no treatment to "fix" a stroke. The various treatments that vets may use are intended to help the brain repair itself. The brain is similar to a computer and it will repair itself by "re-wiring" itself around the damaged part of the brain. Cats are able to do this "re-wiring" much more effectively than human beings and thus most cats will recover much better from a stroke than people do. The stroke may happen for no apparent reason or it may be the result of excessively high blood pressure, just as with human beings. The most common conditions causing high blood pressure are diabetes mellitus, hyperthyroidism and some heart diseases. These conditions will be discussed in the next part of this chapter.

2 Seizures caused by problems in the rest of the body outside the brain

The brain is a very sensitive structure and can be severely affected by lack of oxygen or various different types of chemicals. A good example of the effect of chemicals on the brain is alcohol. If one drinks alcohol it will affect brain function, e.g. slurred speech, loss of balance and staggering. In severe cases excessive alcohol will cause unconsciousness and possibly death. Lack of oxygen will also affect brain function, e.g. if a person stands still for long periods of time they may not pump enough blood and oxygen to the brain and so may faint. A lack of energy (food) may also affect brain function. If you haven't eaten for a long time you may start to feel faint. This happens because there is not enough glucose in your blood to feed your brain so you might pass out (faint). These are just everyday examples of how a lack of oxygen or blood glucose or excessive amounts of specific types of chemicals can affect brain function. I have used these everyday examples to illustrate that abnormal brain function does not necessarily mean that there is a problem with the brain and that abnormal brain activity may be caused by factors (problems) in the rest of the body outside the brain. These factors (problems) can cause a normal brain to function abnormally and thus result in seizures in an individual whose brain is actually completely healthy.

2a Poisoning as a chemical cause of seizures

The most common poisons which may be eaten by cats and cause seizures are metaldehyde and warfarin.

2a(i) Metaldehyde (slug bait)

Metaldehyde is a common poison used in gardens to kill snails and slugs. Dogs are more likely to willingly eat slug bait than cats. Most adults cats are very unlikely to eat slug bait but inquisitive kittens may well eat some of it while exploring your garden.

The initial symptoms of metaldehyde poisoning are drooling and muscle twitching. The muscle twitching may become more severe and severe muscle spasms and seizures may develop after a short time. The treatment for these patients is to make them vomit to get rid of the poison from their stomach. If you cannot make them vomit then they should have their stomach pumped out by a vet. If the cat has progressed to the point where they are having grand mal seizures then they will require sedatives and/or a full general anaesthetic and anti-seizure treatment. The emergency treatment for a grand mal seizure is discussed earlier in this chapter. Most cats will survive metaldehyde poisoning if they are treated quickly but cats can and do die from this chemical if they have eaten large amounts of it or if they do not get medical attention soon enough.

2a(ii) Warfarin (rat poison)

Warfarin is the most common rat poison. Once a mouse or rat has eaten the poison they will die and if your cat then eats that rodent then the cat may also be poisoned. Rat poison works by interfering with the normal blood clotting process, causing the poisoned individual to spontaneously start bleeding anywhere in their body. The most commonly seen areas of bleeding are the eyes and gums where there may be just bruising or actual bleeding. There is often also evidence of bleeding under the skin, demonstrated by bruising on the skin, which may range from many small bruises to only a few large bruises. If the affected cat bleeds from the brain then the pressure in the skull will rise and the cat may suffer seizures. If the bleeding does not stop the cat may die before the vet has time to make the diagnosis and/or start treatment. The treatment for rat poisoning is vitamin K injections and tablets for several weeks after the poisoning.

2b Liver problems as a cause of seizures (hepatic encephalopathy)

If a cat has a liver problem which damages the liver or interferes with its ability to function normally, one of the symptoms that may develop is seizures. This is because the liver has lost its ability to remove dangerous chemicals from the bloodstream. The liver has many functions, one of which is to remove harmful chemicals from the body. Most of these harmful chemicals are normal waste products produced by other organs in the body and the liver normally filters out and detoxifies these naturally occurring chemicals. Provided the liver is working normally, these chemicals are only ever present in the body in very small amounts because the liver is constantly detoxifying them but if the liver is malfunctioning then these naturally occurring chemicals will start to accumulate in the body. Once too high a level of these chemicals has accumulated in the bloodstream they will start to affect the brain in much the same way that alcohol does. If the blood levels continue to accumulate, these chemicals may cause the brain to have seizures because they effectively start to "poison" the brain. The treatment in these cases is thus to fix the liver problem and the seizures will stop once the liver again starts efficiently removing the waste chemicals from the body. The liver will be identified as the problem when the vet performs the tests mentioned earlier, i.e. blood tests, X-rays and ultrasound scans. The most common liver problem in young cats that may cause seizures is an abnormally developed liver, which may cause an abnormality called a hepatoportal or vena azygos shunt. Once this has been diagnosed, the vet will treat the problem either by operating on the liver or using medication and switching the cat onto a special diet. The most common liver problems causing seizures in middle-aged and older cats are tumours in the liver and cirrhosis of the liver. These are serious conditions and the vet may not be able to significantly help the cat. However, each case must always be considered individually and some cases will respond well to various treatments.

2c Kidney problems as a cause of seizures (renal encephalopathy)

The kidneys, like the liver, remove naturally occurring chemicals from the bloodstream but if the kidneys lose their ability to function properly then these chemicals will start to accumulate in the body. Once too high a level of these chemicals has accumulated in the bloodstream they will start to affect the brain in much the same way that alcohol does. If the blood levels continue to accumulate, these chemicals may cause the brain to have seizures because they effectively start to "poison" the brain. The treatment in these cases is thus to fix the kidney problem and the seizures will stop once the kidneys again start efficiently removing the waste chemicals from the body. Please refer to the chapter on weight loss for a full discussion on different types of kidney problems and how to treat them.

2d Abnormal blood sugar levels as a cause of seizures

2d(i) Sugar diabetes (diabetes mellitus)

Diabetes mellitus (sugar diabetes) may cause seizures. Please refer to the chapter on weight loss for a full discussion on diabetes and how to treat it. A common cause of low blood sugar is the diabetic cat being treated with insulin. If the cat is given more insulin than they need, then their blood sugar levels may drop so low that they have seizures. If this has happened the vet will quickly confirm this on a blood test and the cat will recover within minutes of being put on a glucose saline drip. The vet will then reassess the cat's diabetes and adjust the insulin dose accordingly. Some cats may actually recover from their diabetes by regaining the ability to produce their own natural insulin. This may happen without our knowledge and we continue treating the diabetic cat. Because the cat is producing their own insulin at the same time as being given artificial insulin their blood sugar levels drop below normal so they start fitting. Once the vet has established that the cat has regained the ability to produce their own insulin, they will advise either stopping all insulin injections or significantly reducing the insulin dose, depending on how much insulin the cat is able to produce naturally.

2d(ii) Insulinomas

Very low blood sugar levels may be caused by a very rare condition called insulinoma. This condition is caused by a tumour in the pancreas gland where insulin is produced. The diagnosis is made when the vet runs blood tests as discussed at the beginning of the chapter. The tumour must be removed to cure this very rare condition.

2e Heart problems as a cause of seizures

Heart problems that affect the cat's blood pressure, or the ability of the heart to pump blood containing oxygen to the brain, may cause abnormal brain activity. This happens because, if the brain cells are not receiving enough oxygen, the brain cannot function normally. The result of insufficient oxygen supply to the brain is usually that the individual will faint (pass out) rather than have a seizure, but I have included it in this section because fainting may look like a seizure.

The technical term for fainting is syncope. When an individual faints they fall to the ground unconscious and may show mild muscle twitching movements. The individual usually recovers within a few moments and may then seem dazed or disorientated for a short time. This may make it difficult for a pet owner to determine whether the cat has fainted or has had a true seizure. The primary difference between fainting and epileptic seizures is that fainting usually occurs during exercise or exertion and epileptic seizures usually happen during sleep or rest. The vet will, however, investigate the possibility of a heart problem when they examine the cat. This is done during the routine testing for a cat who has possibly had a seizure. The vet will then be able to determine whether the incident was a seizure or a faint and will be able to prescribe the appropriate treatment. If the heart condition causes high blood pressure then the cat may suffer a "stroke" similar to those seen in human beings with high blood pressure. If this is the case then the vet will start appropriate treatment to help restore normal heart function and reduce the blood pressure.

2f Seizures in cats who have recently had kittens (eclampsia)

Cats may, within three days of giving birth, develop mild or severe muscle twitching which may resemble a seizure. The muscle twitching or muscle spasms are caused by low calcium levels in the mother's bloodstream. Calcium has many functions in the body, one of which is to assist in the function of the nerve cells in the body. If there is insufficient calcium for this then the nerves may become unstable and abnormal signs are seen as the nerves discharge impulses spontaneously. This is the situation faced by women and animals when conditions like eclampsia (milk fever) cause low blood calcium levels.

Eclampsia (milk fever) may happen shortly after a mother has given birth when she diverts a lot of her own calcium to her milk for her kittens to help them grow strong teeth and bones. If her own blood levels drop too low, then her nerve cells become unstable and may fire impulses spontaneously, especially to the muscles. So the initial clinical symptoms of low blood calcium levels are twitching and muscle tremors, which may progress to full seizures, convulsions, and possible death if treatment is not started quickly. Treatment of low blood calcium is simple and highly effective, being simply a matter of injecting calcium into a vein, and the patient recovers within minutes.

Once the mother has recovered, the vet will suggest that you should add a calcium supplement to her diet and also possibly hand feed the kittens for a few days. There are many specially formulated artificial mild substitutes for kittens and hand feeding them is easy. The reason that the vet may suggest hand feeding the kittens for a few days is that, if they are not drinking milk from the mother, the milk in the mammary glands will accumulate and it will be reabsorbed back into her bloodstream. The second reason is that, because the kittens are not suckling from the mum for a few days, there is no ongoing loss of calcium via the milk. The kittens usually only need to be hand fed for one to three days and then the mum can continue suckling them. So one sees muscle tremors or seizure-like symptoms in a cat who has recently given birth, the diagnosis will almost certainly be eclampsia (low blood calcium levels caused by the production of a lot of milk).

12

MY CAT IS LOSING WEIGHT

Cats are often brought to my clinic because they are losing weight. The common question I am asked is, "My cat has lost weight recently. Do you think he just needs deworming?" It may indeed be that that the cat has worms but this is rarely the cause of significant weight loss.

The most common causes of weight loss in adult and geriatric cats are:

- Kidney and liver problems
- An overactive thyroid gland
- Sugar diabetes (diabetes mellitus)
- Cat AIDS, cat leukaemia or cancer

The vet will probably ask if the cat has been eating more, less or much the same amount as normal. The answer to this question will direct the vet's thoughts as follows:

If they are eating more than normal, then diabetes or an overactive thyroid is most likely.

If they are eating less than normal then the next question would be, "Do you think he doesn't want to eat or do you think he wants to eat but can't for some reason?"

If he simply doesn't want to eat, i.e. he has lost his appetite, then liver problems, kidney problems, AIDS, cancer or leukaemia are more likely.

If it appears that your cat wants to eat but isn't able to eat, there may be something wrong inside their mouth. If your cat wants to eat but can't, or starts eating then shies away from the food bowl, then a look in his mouth is warranted.

1 My cat wants to eat but doesn't seem able to lap, lick chew or swallow

Pain in the mouth may interfere with the cat's willingness to eat and thus cause weight loss. The most common conditions that will cause sufficient pain in the mouth to make a cat eat less than normal are tooth problems (like severely infected teeth) and/or severe mouth ulcers.

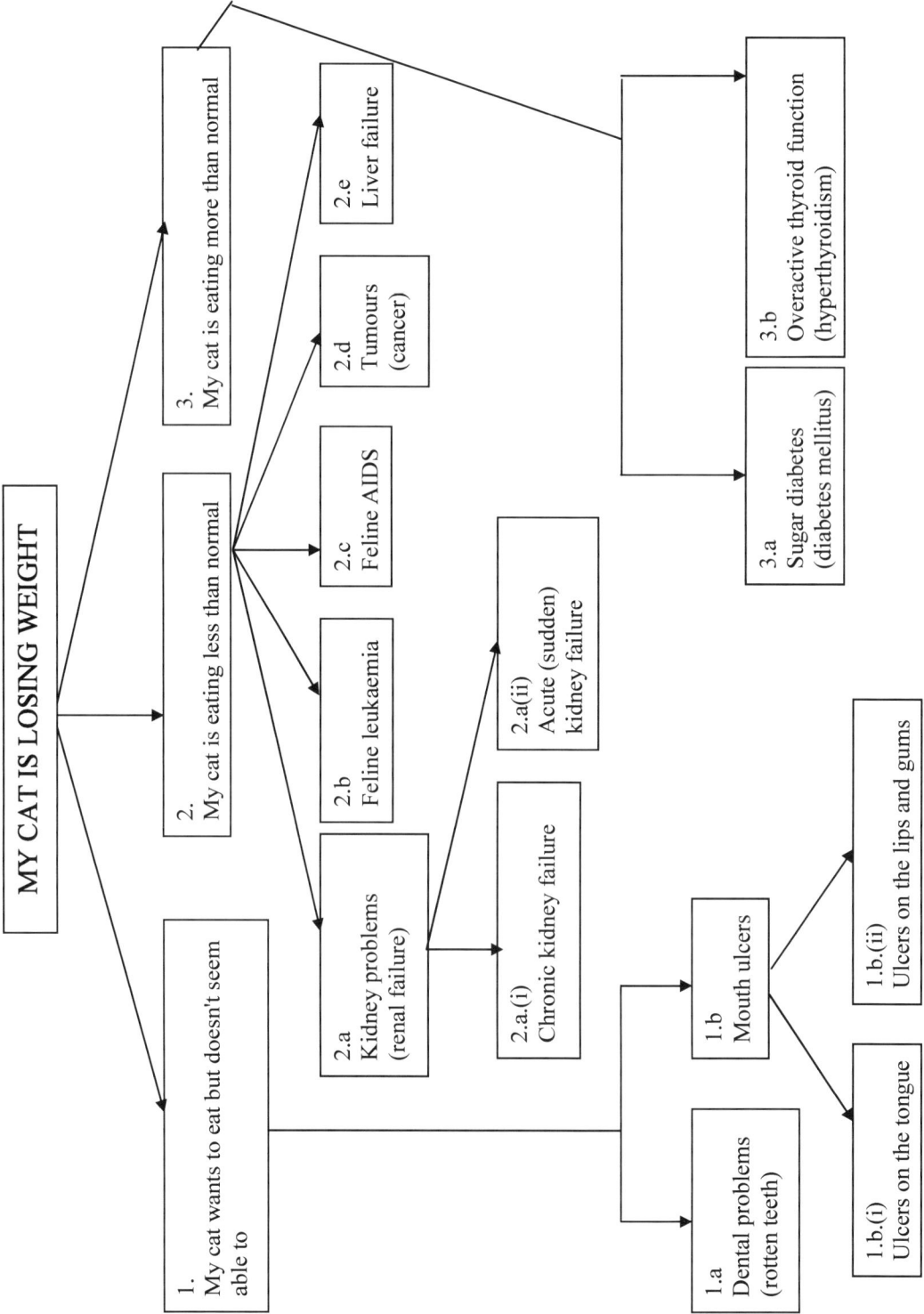

MY CAT IS LOSING WEIGHT

1.
My cat wants to eat but doesn't seem able to

2.
My cat is eating less than normal

3.
My cat is eating more than normal

1.a
Dental problems (rotten teeth)

1.b
Mouth ulcers

1.b.(i)
Ulcers on the tongue

1.b.(ii)
Ulcers on the lips and gums

2.a
Kidney problems (renal failure)

2.b
Feline leukaemia

2.c
Feline AIDS

2.d
Tumours (cancer)

2.e
Liver failure

2.a.(i)
Chronic kidney failure

2.a(ii)
Acute (sudden) kidney failure

3.a
Sugar diabetes (diabetes mellitus)

3.b
Overactive thyroid function (hyperthyroidism)

If a cat's mouth is so painful that they can eat only very little or no food, then, before we go any further, we must ask ourselves "Why is the mouth so bad?" The possibility is that your cat, like some people, simply has bad teeth, and good dental treatment might be enough to solve the problem. Alternatively, it could be that the body's normal defence mechanisms in the mouth are just not able to cope with the normal bacteria that all of us are fighting in our own mouths all the time. This scenario may suggest that the immune system has been compromised by conditions like cat AIDS or leukaemia, which may affect cats in the same way that AIDS affects us as human beings.

In cats suffering from Aids or leukaemia, minor infections may become major infections simply because the immune system has been damaged and is no longer able to cope with normal levels of common bacteria in the mouth. These bacteria involved are common bacteria found in everyone's mouth and a healthy immune system should easily be able to fight them off. If an individual develops a severe mouth infection then we must question whether their immune system is functioning properly and, if not, then we must establish why not. In the cat world this would imply testing for the underlying presence of cat AIDS or leukaemia.

Once we have determined that the cat with a painful mouth does not have feline AIDS or leukaemia then we will continue our investigation and treatment of mouth problems as follows:

1a Dental problems (rotten teeth)

Damaged or "rotten" teeth may occur in cats for much the same reasons that human beings may develop dental problems. I have found that it takes very severe dental problems to stop a cat eating so just a few broken or "rotten" teeth would rarely be enough to explain weight loss in these patients. It would take a great many damaged or "rotten" teeth, or severely inflamed and painful gums, to cause a cat to lose weight simply because it is too painful for them to eat enough food. If we can demonstrate significantly painful "rotten" teeth, and tests show that the cat has not got AIDS or leukaemia, then removing the bad teeth will solve the problem and the cat will gain weight again.

1b Mouth ulcers

Painful ulcers in the mouth may make a cat stop eating food. Mouth ulcers in cats are most commonly caused by one of two conditions: If a cat has painful ulcers on the upper surface of their tongue, the most likely cause is a viral infection in the mouth. If ulcers appear primarily on the lips and gums, then old age kidney failure is the most likely cause.

1b(i) Ulcers on the tongue

Cats may refuse to eat or drink if they have painful ulcers in their mouths. Ulcers on the tongue are usually less than five millimetres in diameter and are dark pink or purple. These ulcers are usually caused by a herpes virus or a calici virus. The ulcers may be so painful that the tongue hangs out of the mouth and it is simply too painful to eat or drink anything. The viruses that cause the ulcers may also cause a fever and this will contribute to the cat's loss of appetite. Conjunctivitis, sneezing and a nasal discharge are other frequent symptoms associated with herpes and calici viruses and these symptoms will be discussed under the section on sneezing cats.

Fig. 33 – Ulcers on the tongue

An important point to make here is that herpes viruses do not necessarily imply venereal disease. Although herpes is associated with sexually transmitted diseases in humans, the herpes virus family is huge and different animals are affected by various herpes viruses that may cause vastly different diseases. Let's consider the most common type in human beings, Herpes simplex B. This herpes virus causes cold sores in human mouths and we all know that the problem comes and goes. The reason for this is that once someone has the virus they often have it for life.

Whenever they feel tired, stressed or just run down, cold sores tend to develop in their mouths. The reason for this is that the virus is never completely eliminated by the immune system and lies dormant in the body until the body is run down and the immune system is functioning less efficiently. When this happens the virus is able to reappear and affect the body in the form of cold sores in the same way that these are the times we are likely to contract other viruses like colds and flu. As the body recovers, the immune function improves and the virus is beaten off to retreat and lie dormant once again. The cat version of herpes viruses behave in much the same way, reappearing and disappearing depending on how healthy the individual is feeling.

It would be reasonable to ask whether viral tongue ulcers imply that the cat should also be tested for the possibility of underlying AIDS or leukaemia viruses as these compromise the immune system and may thereby allow the herpes virus to flare up. In practice, however, this is generally not the case just as, in human medicine, most people who have cold sores do not have AIDS.

The treatment for a cat who is not eating because of the pain of viral tongue ulcers is largely supportive. Treatment consists of painkillers and antibiotics to prevent secondary bacterial infections in the ulcers while waiting for the immune system to beat off the virus. Young kittens may be in so much pain that they can't even lap water and so they may become dehydrated. In these cases the cat or kitten must be hospitalized and put on a drip to treat the dehydration in addition to treatment with painkillers and antibiotics.

1b(ii)   Ulcers on the lips and gums

Ulcers on the inner surface of the lips and on the gums have a greyish-yellow appearance and cause pain and discomfort. These ulcers are usually the result of chronic kidney failure. The reason that kidney failure can cause painful mouth ulcers is that one of the functions of the kidneys is to eliminate a waste product called urea.

If the kidneys are failing, the level of urea rises in the bloodstream and the body tries to eliminate the problem by other routes, such as via the digestive system or via the lungs. The process via the lungs involves releasing the urea into the air in the lungs thereby allowing its elimination when air is breathed out of the body. The problem with this route is that the exhaled urea is caustic and burns the lining of the mouth thereby causing ulcers, which are very painful, and stop the cat eating. The other alternative route of urea elimination, via the stomach and intestines, causes much the same problem. The urea released into the stomach and intestines may burn the lining of these organs and cause sufficient pain there to cause the cat to stop eating and, in more severe cases, the cat may also vomit and develop diarrhoea. In both of these instances the affected cat tends to appear lethargic and depressed as he will be feeling very unwell in addition to suffering obvious pain and discomfort.

This brings us back to the beginning of the consultation where I asked "Is he eating more, less, or much the same as normal?"

2 My cat is losing weight and is eating less than normal

If the cat is eating less or nothing at all in the absence of mouth pain, the most likely possibilities are:

- Kidney problems (renal failure)
- Feline leukaemia
- Feline AIDS
- Tumours (cancer)
- Liver problems

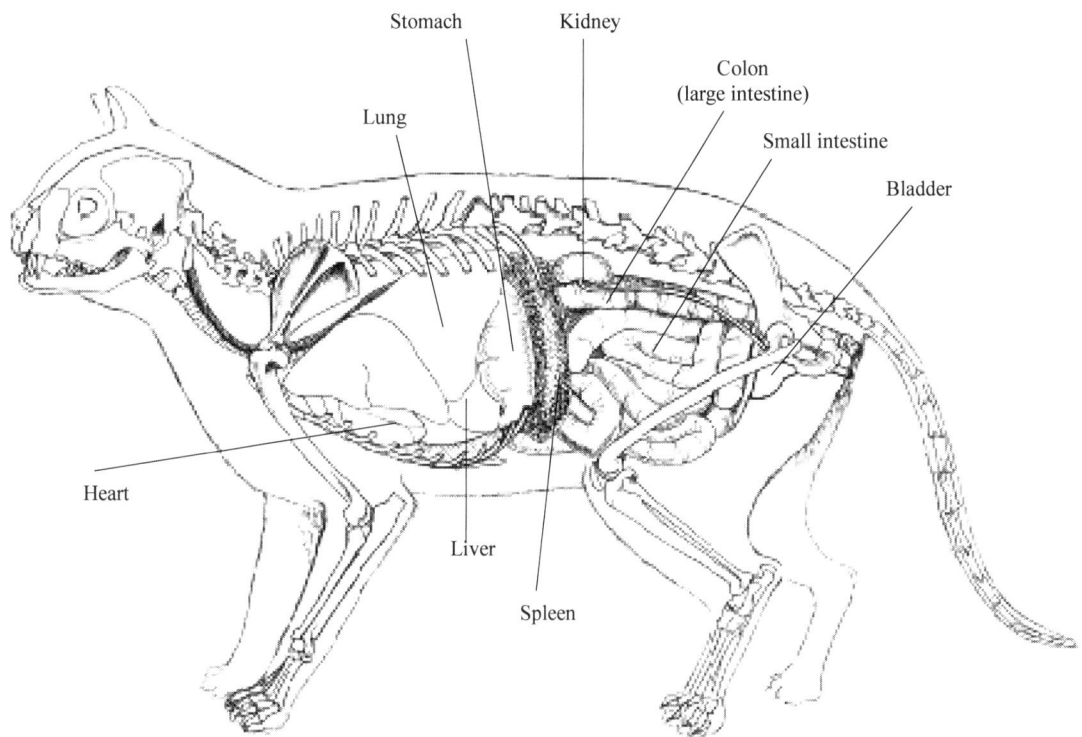

Fig. 34 – Side view of a cat showing the normal size and position of the major organs

2a Kidney problems (renal failure)

The kidneys have three primary functions in the body.

The first function is that they act as filters removing waste products from the blood supply which are then eliminated from the body in the urine.

The second function is to regulate the amount of water in the body. The amount of water which is eliminated by the kidneys will directly affect the concentration of the urine which is assessed as the specific gravity (SG) of the urine. The concentration of the urine varies from day to day depending on the overall amount of water in the body. To understand this concept consider your own urine – sometimes it is more concentrated (more yellow) and other times it is more dilute (less yellow). This is because the kidneys are constantly adjusting the amount of fluid in our bodies. When the urine is more concentrated the kidneys are actively reabsorbing water in the process of producing urine and when the urine is less concentrated the kidneys are actively allowing more water to be passed from the body in the urine.

The third primary function of the kidneys is the production of a chemical called erythropoetin. The function of erythropoetin is to stimulate the bone marrow to produce red blood cells.

When age or illness cause kidney failure, one or more of these functions may be affected to varying degrees. As each particular kidney function is diminished or lost, it will produce specific clinical signs which the cat owner or the vet will notice. The most commonly observed clinical sign is that the cat will lose their appetite and they will lose weight.

Kidney failure may be acute (develops very suddenly) or chronic (develops over a long period of time).

2a(i) Chronic (slow/gradual/long-term) kidney failure

Chronic renal failure (long-term/gradual kidney failure) is far more common than acute kidney failure.

The most common cause of chronic kidney failure is simply old age. Ultimately the reason we all die is because one or more organs fail. The reason for this is simply that our organs are only able to function for a fixed period of time. At the end of our life span our organs will fail due to long-term wear and tear just as various parts of our cars will start to break down after years of use.

The second most common cause of gradual renal failure is a condition called polycystic kidney disease (PKD). This is a condition seen most commonly in Persian cats and in Persian cats crossed with any other breed of cat. The affected individual develops fluid-filled cysts in the kidneys. They may develop only a few cysts or a great many. These cysts gradually enlarge and as they do so they crush and destroy the normal kidney tissue. This condition is confirmed by ultrasound scanning of the kidneys which allows us to actually see the cysts in the kidneys. It is a genetic condition and is usually diagnosed in young cats who show the same progression of symptoms that one would expect to see in a very old cat whose kidneys are failing due to old age.

Chronic renal failure is a slow, gradual process and often starts long before we see any indication that this process is underway. This is because the body will activate many compensatory mechanisms to overcome the reduced efficiency of the kidneys. I would loosely categorise chronic kidney failure as having three phases: mild (early) kidney failure, moderate kidney failure and severe end-stage kidney failure. Each of these phases can be further defined as being compensated or uncompensated. If the stage is compensated, few or no clinical signs will be present because the body's other systems are compensating for the reduced or lost kidney functions. In uncompensated kidney failure, clinical signs will be present. The most common clinical signs in uncompensated kidney failure are weeing and drinking more, lethargy, poor or no appetite and pale mucous membranes.

Kidney problems don't always cause the painful mouth ulcers mentioned earlier in this chapter. If the cat is eating less or nothing at all and there is no sign of painful ulcers on the lips and gums then kidney failure is still a possibility. Chronic renal failure may cause weight loss and loss of appetite just by making cats feel unwell due to the accumulation of urea and other waste products in the bloodstream. To make sense of this, think of the kidneys simply as filters for the body even though they fulfil a great many other functions. If the filters are not removing waste products from the blood then the waste products will accumulate despite the body's attempts to reroute some of them, like urea, to other organ systems for elimination. These waste products, like any other waste products in your car or swimming pool for example, will damage the system if they are not removed. Other kidney functions will also be lost, for example the kidneys' ability to produce a chemical called erythropoetin. Think of erythropoetin as a chemical messenger normally produced by the kidneys to tell the bone marrow to produce red blood cells. If this function is lost or reduced there will be fewer red blood cells in the blood supply and the affected cat will appear pale in addition to the other possible symptoms of kidney failure as discussed above. The technical term for appearing pale is "anaemia", which implies a reduced number of red blood cells in the circulation. The way the vet will initially assess whether your cat is pale is by looking at your cat's mucous membranes, typically in the mouth and eyes. The general rule of thumb is to check the colour of the cat's eye and mouth mucous membranes and compare them to your own.

A common and obvious clinical sign of chronic kidney failure is the "drinking and weeing more" syndrome. This happens because the ability of the kidneys to reabsorb water is reduced or lost. The initial sign is weeing more and once the body has realised that an excessive amount of water is being lost, then the individual will start drinking more to replace this lost water.

The presumptive diagnosis of kidney failure, based on the clinical signs described above, is confirmed by performing blood and urine tests. These tests include testing the level of urea and creatinine and phosphorus accumulating in the bloodstream as the kidneys slowly fail to filter them out.

The term kidney failure does not imply total loss of kidney function. Broadly one can categorise old-age kidney failure as mild, moderate or severe. Think about this in terms of our own ageing process. Once older than about seventy, we can expect to have to get out of bed once or several times during the night to have a pee. This is because we have lost some of our kidneys' ability to conserve and reabsorb water. I would categorise this state as mild compensated kidney failure. The reason I call it compensated kidney failure is that the body will compensate for the other kidney functions which are impaired, and we show no other symptoms than producing more urine and drinking more water to replace this loss. The loss of kidney function (kidney failure) happens because all our organs have a limited lifespan and start to deteriorate in old age as we approach the end of our lives. As the kidneys continue to deteriorate and function less efficiently, the body's compensatory mechanisms cannot cope and other symptoms of kidney failure will appear and we will move into moderate compensated kidney failure. We still do not necessarily feel unwell because the compensatory mechanisms will reduce the overall impact on the rest of the body. We will, however, start to lose weight and so become frail in old age. This is because the kidneys start to lose their ability to reabsorb proteins and we lose a lot of protein in our urine. Ultimately we will enter into severe kidney failure and the compensatory mechanisms will be unable to cope and we enter the phase of severe decompensated kidney failure. At this point the impact of the severe loss of kidney functions includes the loss of the chemical erythropoetin as discussed earlier with resultant pale mucous membranes. The accumulation of urea in the bloodstream makes us feel unwell because of its "toxic" effect and as a result of the body's attempts to eliminate it via the alternative pathways of the lungs and intestines as discussed earlier. The deterioration from this point tends to be rapid and ultimately we die of "old age".

As mentioned earlier, young Persian cats with polycystic kidney disease (PKD) will go through all the stages and show the same symptoms as seen in old cats with old-age kidney failure as I have just discussed.

Cats follow the same process of gradual kidney failure as we do and what we can do to help them depends on the stage at which they are presented to the vet. In the initial compensated stages, treatment is aimed at trying to maintain body weight by using anabolic agents and trying to reduce the kidneys' workload by feeding specially formulated diets. At this point, just as in human beings, the cats will feel fine in themselves but will lose weight despite apparently normal appetites and may show increased thirst as evidenced by drinking more water. Feeding specially prepared commercially available cat food designed for cats with kidney failure will significantly extend the cat's lifespan and, equally importantly, will yield a good quality of life during the gradual process of kidney failure. Many vets will also use a category of medication called ACE-inhibitors. This is administered in the form of daily tablets and the effect is to improve blood supply to the kidneys and to reduce the high blood pressure which may be induced by kidney failure. Once cats have entered the severe decompensated stage of kidney failure, the treatment is much the same but predictably the benefits are much diminished.

Occasionally cats may be prematurely pushed into the next phase of their progressing kidney failure by the strain of other illnesses and they may be pulled back to the earlier phase of their kidney failure by the use of a saline drip. The effect of the drip is to flush out the accumulating waste chemicals, like urea, which make us feel unwell. Consider the scenario of a cat who is actually only in moderate kidney failure but as a result of, for example, a respiratory infection refuses food and water for a few days. This cat is urinating more because of the pre-existing kidney failure and if they fail to replace this loss of water by drinking more they will rapidly dehydrate. The dehydration causes chemicals such as urea in the bloodstream to become more concentrated and thus blood tests will suggest that the cat is in more advanced and more severe kidney failure than they actually are. By replacing the lost fluid with a drip the true situation is reinstated and effectively the cat is pulled back into compensated kidney failure and should feel much better as the symptoms of severe kidney failure are reduced or resolved. Cats who are genuinely in severe advanced kidney failure will also be improved while on a drip line because the "toxic" chemicals in the blood are being diluted, but they will relapse when the drip is disconnected. It is obviously not a practical or feasible option to consider maintaining a drip line permanently in a cat but as a short-term treatment it will often significantly improve the cat's condition. At this stage, just as in human beings, the only thing that will save the individual is a kidney transplant and our best efforts in the absence of a kidney transplant will only serve to delay the process of decline. I feel that we should continue all feasible treatment for as long as the cat is able to live a happy, functional, comfortable life at home. Realistically this implies that when the cat reaches the point where the treatment is ineffective and they refuse to eat we have no option but to consider humanely putting him or her to sleep.

2a(ii) Acute (sudden) kidney failure

Acute kidney failure means that the kidneys' ability to function normally is lost very suddenly and abruptly. Acute kidney failure is very uncommon in cats.

Acute kidney failure may develop due to one of three causes i.e. toxic chemicals taken in by the cat, conditions which cause a sudden drop in blood pressure, or kidney infections.

Toxic chemicals causing acute kidney damage:

Various common chemicals in and around the home may be taken in by cats and have a toxic effect on the kidneys, damaging the kidneys and affecting their ability to function normally. The most common chemical which may cause this is ethylene glycol, found in car engine coolant, and which may have been spilt or leaked onto the floor. Ethylene glycol has a sweet taste and many cats will lap it up because of this sweet taste. The ethylene glycol, once in the body, may have a toxic effect on the kidneys and induce sudden (acute) renal failure. This initially manifests as a reduced production of urine as the kidney is so swollen that no urine can be produced and later, as the swelling subsides, an excessive amount of urine is produced because some of the ability to reabsorb water has been lost. Fortunately, most cats will recover from this poisoning effect if treated promptly and the kidneys will repair themselves adequately to return to normal function. The treatment for these cases is largely supportive care. This, in real terms, means using intravenous fluids via drip lines to flush the toxins out of the kidneys. The potential for recovery depends on the amount of toxin drunk by the cat; if very large amounts have been taken in, the cat's kidneys may be permanently and irreversibly damaged and some cats may die despite our efforts to save them.

Conditions which cause a sudden drop in blood pressure:

A drop in blood pressure in cats is unusual but if it happens it is most likely due to severe dehydration or, less commonly, congestive heart failure. In these cases, treating the cause of the sudden drop in blood pressure will also treat the acute kidney failure.
 A possible cause of sudden and severe dehydration is a cat which has been missing for a few days after accidentally getting locked in someone's garden shed or garage and being deprived of food and water. In severe cases they may require slow rehydration with a drip and intravenous fluids. Most cases will, however, respond to food and oral fluids.

Congestive heart failure is an uncommon condition in cats. If a cat develops congestive heart failure they may develop secondary kidney failure. The treatment for the heart failure will usually also improve the kidney failure caused by the heart failure. The specific treatments for heart failure will be discussed later in the chapter on breathing difficulties.

The reason that these two conditions may cause kidney failure is that both will cause a drop in blood pressure. This drop in blood pressure means that less blood is reaching all the tissues and organs in the body. The kidneys are very greedy organs and require a very good blood supply to function. Twenty five percent (one quarter) of the blood pumped by each heartbeat goes to the kidneys. The remaining three-quarters of the blood pumped by each heartbeat are shared by all the cells of the rest of the body. Thus, the kidneys have a very high requirement in terms of blood supply and are the first organs to fail when the blood supply to the body's tissues is reduced. The most common causes of reduced blood supply to the body's tissues are conditions which cause low blood pressure.

Kidney infections:

In addition to dehydration and heart failure, an infection in the kidneys will also cause acute kidney failure. This is the least common cause of kidney failure in cats and treatment consists of intravenous fluids and antibiotics.

2b Feline leukaemia

Losing weight, a loss of appetite and pale mucous membranes don't always indicate chronic kidney failure. Feline leukaemia may cause very similar symptoms. Feline leukaemia is a highly contagious, very nasty viral infection in cats. The virus is spread directly from cat to cat and is potentially spread from any secretions and excretions. This implies that the cat's urine and faeces are potential sources of infection but in practice the saliva seems to be the most common way the virus is spread. The implication of this is that if your cat meets an infected cat and they hiss, spit and swear at each other in the way that cats do, then your cat may become infected. If the infected cat fights with your cat or raids their food bowl then the risk is even higher. The virus, once in your cat's body, will produce one of two effects. The first possibility is that it may destroy the immune system producing a situation where the immune system is unable to deal with even very minor infections. This allows infections that would normally be dealt with so quickly and efficiently as to go unnoticed, to develop into severe and potentially life-threatening conditions. Gum infections, as discussed above, are a good example of this scenario. The other possible effect of the cat leukaemia virus is to produce a very aggressive cancer, which may spread very quickly throughout the body before the cat shows any symptoms at all. The most common site to find these tumours on a routine clinical examination is in the intestines, especially at the ileocaecal valve, the point where the large and small intestines meet. The vet will often detect an irregular or lumpy mass at this point in the intestines when they feel your cat's abdomen. I find that most cases of cancer at this point develop in the absence of the leukaemia virus in older cats. That is to say that the cancer develops for no discernible reason in older cats but, in young cats who test positive for the leukaemia virus, cancers of this type have been caused by the leukaemia.

2c Feline AIDS

Losing weight, a loss of appetite and pale mucous membranes may be a symptom of cat AIDS. The feline AIDS virus may cause very similar symptoms to feline leukaemia and is spread in much the same way as the leukaemia virus.

Cat AIDS usually behaves in much the same way as the human AIDS virus. It compromises the immune system to the extent that it is unable to deal with even very minor infections like gum infections. These minor infections in the gums or anywhere else in the body may then develop into serious and often fatal conditions.

This would be a good time to make three very important points about feline AIDS.

Firstly there is no connection between the cat AIDS virus and the human AIDS virus, so you cannot get AIDS from your cat and human beings cannot infect their cats with the human AIDS virus. The two viruses share the same name but affect completely different species. There is no risk to human beings from cats with cat AIDS. The other point is that, although both cat AIDS and leukaemia can compromise the function of the immune system, some cats may carry the AIDS virus without it affecting their own health. These cats are called carriers, and the risk they pose is that they may spread the virus to other cats without being affected by it themselves for a significant length of time. A similar situation is present in the human world where there is a difference between someone being HIV-positive and having full-blown AIDS. This means that one may be infected by the virus without it causing any obvious trouble for a variable period of time but during this time the individual may be spreading the virus without knowing it. If it progresses to full-blown AIDS, then the affected person will often develop serious and often fatal infections when attacked by infectious that virus-free individuals would easily recover from. The third point is that cat AIDS and leukaemia may often present with nothing more than the vague symptoms of weight loss and decreasing appetite.

Treatment options for cats with AIDS or leukaemia:

The diagnosis of feline AIDS or leukaemia will necessitate a great deal of discussion and soul-searching to decide on the most appropriate course of action. The first point to consider after the diagnosis has been made is the welfare of not just the affected cat but also all other cats that have been in contact with it. The best recommendation is to test all the other cats in the household. If all the cats in the household are affected then they can all be managed together as a group. The issues are their welfare and the welfare of all other cats in the household. The recommendation would be to avoid contact with any other cats. This implies keeping the cats indoors at all times unless they can be let out into a secure area outside of the home where they cannot make contact with other cats. This is likely to be very difficult in the case of cats that have always had free access to the outdoors but their activities must be controlled to prevent them from spreading the virus. Many people feel that this is impossible but I would counter their protests with the question, "How would you feel if your cat contracted the virus from your neighbour's cat, and found out later that your neighbour was aware of their cat's condition but made no attempt to prevent them from spreading the disease?" I would be highly offended to discover that my cat had contracted the disease because of someone else's failure to act.

The next issue is to attend to the wellbeing of the affected cats. There is, as yet, no cure for the condition and treatment is aimed at alleviating the symptoms as they present themselves. If specific infections arise, such as infections in the cat's mouth, then these are treated accordingly. This usually implies antibiotic and anti-inflammatory treatments and nursing care as required. If the symptoms are simply vague symptoms of malaise then supportive care in terms of maintaining physical condition and making the cats feel better should be instituted. I find that this often also boils down to antibiotic and anti-inflammatory treatments and I often include anabolic agents to help maintain body weight. A potentially contentious issue is the inclusion of "alternative" medicine for these cats. This usually implies herbal and homeopathic agents designed to boost the immune system. Echinacea is an appropriate example. Many people would dismiss these "alternative" remedies as a lot of hocus-pocus but I would counter this attitude with the notion that although they may not always help they will certainly never harm. In short, they are always worth trying. If a point is reached when all your and your vet's efforts have failed to give the cat a comfortable, contented, good-quality life then one would consider the option of humanely putting him or her to sleep.

The most common scenario in a multicat household is unfortunately the situation whereby, after testing all the cats in the household, one finds that some of them are not infected with the virus. This requires a number of actions. Firstly the unaffected cats must have no contact with the affected cats. This generally means that either the affected or the unaffected cats need to be re-homed unless they live in a very large house which would allow the two groups to be kept apart. One problem posed here is that if the unaffected cats are re-homed they should also be isolated from other cats for two to three months until they have been retested and confirmed as being free of the disease. The reason for this is that in the very early stages of these diseases the cat may test negative for the virus when in fact they are infected by it. Further problems are that if the infected cats are re-homed then they must be re-homed to a secure environment to avoid contact with other cats and their new owners must be fully informed about the conditions of feline AIDS and leukaemia. A major issue also to be considered here is the psychological impact of separation on the cats and the people in the household. There is no solution to the trauma of friends being wrenched apart but morally we have a duty to protect the unaffected cats from a killer virus. The most common outcome of this situation in a multicat household is that none of the cats can be re-homed. This situation forces us to act to protect the unaffected cats by humanely putting the infected cats to sleep. This is the hardest decision to make but is often the only humane one possible.

2d Tumours (cancer)

Tumours or cancers may develop in young or old cats without causing any specific symptoms other than weight loss and reduced appetite and often pale mucous membranes. The most common type of cancer in cats is called lymphoma. It usually develops in the intestines, especially the ileo-caecal valve, where the small intestine and the large intestine meet. In human beings this is the point at which our appendix is found. The intestines have associated lymph nodes along their length and these lymph nodes may also be affected by lymphoma either as the primary site of the cancer or as a result of spread from the intestine. Cats with lymphoma affecting their intestines are often found sitting at their food or water bowls without taking any food or water.

They appear to want to eat but fail to do so. When these cats are examined by the vet, the presence of pale mucous membranes will prompt the vet to consider the possibility of cancer and a thorough abdominal examination is always warranted. The vet will often identify the tumour as a lump in the abdomen and cats often resent the lump being touched by the vet. Once a mass has been identified in the abdomen treatment options will be considered. I tend to suggest that the first step is to test for the presence of AIDS or leukaemia, as this would affect decisions about whether to subject the cat to the rigours of cancer treatment. If the blood tests for the viruses are negative then the options to consider are medication, surgery, or a combination of both.

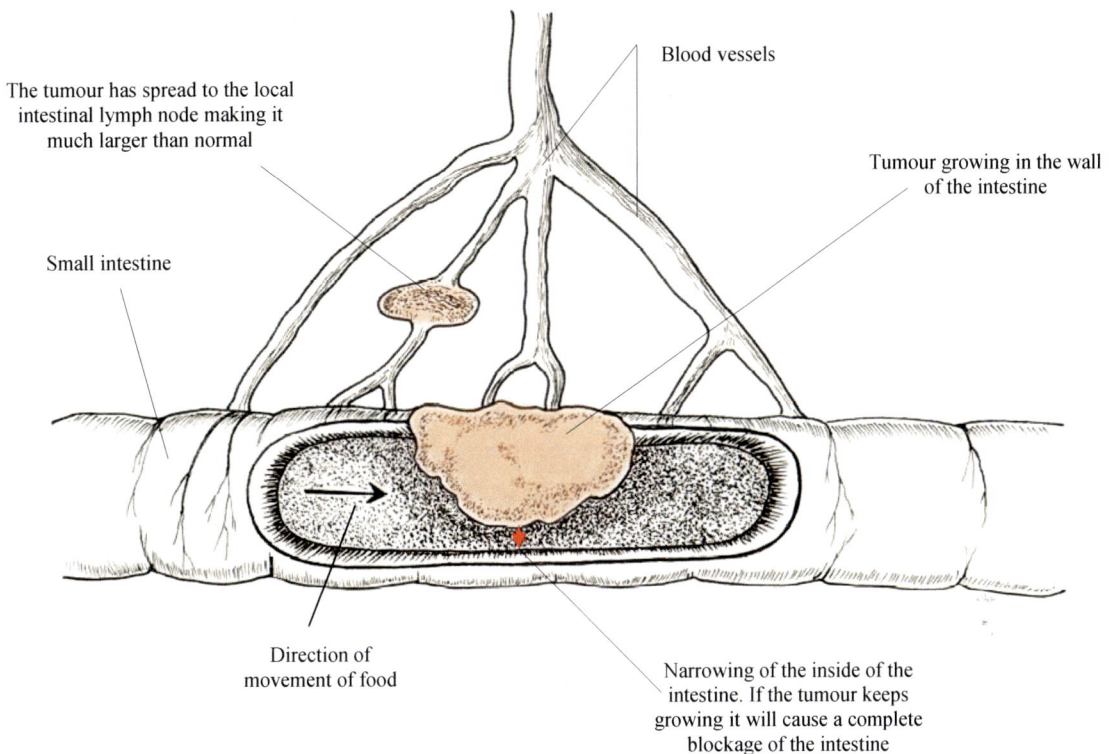

The tumour has spread to the local intestinal lymph node making it much larger than normal

Blood vessels

Tumour growing in the wall of the intestine

Small intestine

Direction of movement of food

Narrowing of the inside of the intestine. If the tumour keeps growing it will cause a complete blockage of the intestine

Fig. 35 – Cross-section of a tumour growing in the small intestine.
The tumour obstructs the normal movement of food.

I feel that if there is only one tumour present and there is no sign of any spread to other points, surgery to remove the mass would be considered. The way to check for spread to other sites is by X-rays, ultrasound scanning and blood testing. If it can be confirmed that there has been no identifiable spread of the cancer then surgery may proceed. This involves entering the abdomen and removing the mass. It is vital to remove not just the mass itself but also a margin of normal healthy tissue in every direction to try to ensure that no cancer cells are left behind. Furthermore, the mass can only be removed if vital blood vessels and nerves supplying other tissues and organs in the area can be left intact. A very frustrating situation arises when the surgeon finds that although the mass can be removed in its entirety, to do so would involve sacrificing the blood supply to other vital areas, perhaps because the bloody supply and nerves to other organs are trapped in the tumour mass and cannot be freed from it. This means that the mass cannot be removed because it would cause the death of the cat. In these cases the only remaining option is to try to eliminate the mass by radiation therapy and/or chemotherapy. Many surgeons would want to at least attempt to debulk the mass prior to proceeding with radiation or chemotherapy. This would involve removing as much tumour tissue as possible without damaging any vital structures trapped in the mass. In many cases, even if the surgeon is able to remove the mass, it might be advisable to follow up on the surgery with radiation and/or chemotherapy to ensure that no tumour cells, which may have spread on a microscopic level to other tissues, are able to grow into a new tumour. There are many different types and ways of using radiation and chemotherapy and the most appropriate protocol will be chosen after a specialist histopathologist has examined the tumour. For this reason some vets would want to perform surgery in cases where there is more than one tumour mass present or where there is clear evidence of tumour spread to other parts of the body. The object of the surgery in these cases would be to obtain a biopsy of the tumour for analysis by a histopathologist so that the best radiation and/or chemotherapy strategy can be formulated.

Many of my clients may not want to go through all the above steps and ask if we could just treat the cat to help them feel better without going down the route of chemotherapy or radiation therapy. This would often imply one of two strategies. One would be to treat the symptoms of pain and loss of appetite for as long as possible and, when the treatment fails to alleviate the cat's suffering, then humanely put him or her to sleep. The most effective way of trying to achieve this is with a category of medication called glucocorticoids. These chemicals are the same as those used to treat asthma in human beings but used at larger doses to treat the cat with cancer. In addition to this I would often use anabolic treatments to help the cat gain weight. The treatment would involve tablets or injections for the remainder of the cat's life. The treatment is intended only to alleviate the cat's pain and suffering and give them as much good quality, pain-free, happy life as possible. The second option is to remove the tumours that are found during the clinical examination and follow up the surgery with the lifelong glucocorticoid therapy as described above. The glucocorticoid therapy is only started when the cat has recovered from the surgery as otherwise it may slow down the healing of the operated site. While this is not a scientific approach to the problem, many people either do not have the financial resources to do more than this or may just not want to subject the cat to any more than this. The overriding consideration must always be the welfare of the cat and if this unscientific approach delivers results in terms of alleviating symptoms then I have no moral problem with it.

Many people feel strongly about cancer in respect of the "futility" of any treatment, or feel that they would want the option of humane euthanasia for themselves in the event of a diagnosis of terminal cancer. Many people feel that it is not humane to ask their pets to accept the discomfort, pain or suffering that may be caused by some types of cancer. Others want to treat only the symptoms of the cancer; most importantly any pain or discomfort. Many will request euthanasia when the treatment is no longer able to eliminate pain and discomfort or when they feel that the quality of life has deteriorated despite symptomatic treatment. People have often watched friends or family members lose the battle against cancer. These people will often request humane euthanasia for their pets with cancer and I feel that this is a reasonable request in the face of a diagnosis with a terminal prognosis. I personally would not deny the request for euthanasia of a cancer patient because we are not all able to cope with the emotional strain of caring for a pet with a terminal condition. Many people, living with this "sword of Damocles" over their heads, succumb to stress and anxiety and this will often adversely affect the pets living with them. There is never a good time to say goodbye to a pet but sometimes, if they are on a downhill slide, it is better to let them go before they hit rock bottom.

2e Liver failure

The last potential cause of the symptoms of weight loss and loss of appetite may be liver failure due to old-age liver failure or any other liver disease. The presence of this problem may be alluded to by the presence of icterus or jaundice. These terms imply a yellow discolouration of the mucous membranes which may be noticed by the vet when examining the eyes and mouth. This is the least common cause of this syndrome and the jaundice is often only apparent in the advanced stages of the condition. Blood tests, x-rays, ultrasound scans and liver biopsies are usually required to make an accurate diagnosis of why the liver has failed. Treatment options are very limited and often response to treatment will be disappointing.

The first question your vet will have asked you at the beginning of this consultation was, "Is your cat eating more, less or much the same as normal?" If your cat is losing weight despite an increased appetite then the vet's thoughts will proceed as follows:

3 My cat is losing weight and is eating more than normal

If your cat is losing weight and you have noticed an increase in their appetite or thirst levels then the two possibilities to consider are:

- Diabetes mellitus (sugar diabetes)
- Hyperthyroidism (overactive thyroid function)

3a Sugar diabetes (diabetes mellitus)

There are two types of diabetes – diabetes mellitus and diabetes insipidus. Here we are considering diabetes mellitus, or sugar diabetes, as it is sometimes called.

The most common symptoms of diabetes mellitus are a sudden increase in thirst and weeing with increased appetite and possibly also weight loss. There are two types of diabetes mellitus in human beings: insulin-dependent and non-insulin-dependent diabetes. Cats with diabetes mellitus have insulin dependant diabetes. To discuss this we first need to understand what diabetes mellitus is. Insulin is produced in a gland called the pancreas, which is situated along the first part of the small intestine. The pancreas has two functions. One is to produce a number of digestive enzymes which are led along ducts into the intestine where they digest food. The second function of the pancreas is to produce insulin, which is released into the bloodstream.

Insulin circulates in the bloodstream and its function is to move glucose from the blood into the body's cells. Think of insulin as a man stoking a furnace. The man is the insulin, the furnace represents the body's tissues and the wood being thrown into the furnace is the glucose. If the pancreas fails to produce insulin, then the man in this analogy is eliminated from the equation and the result is that although there is sufficient wood (glucose) to stoke the furnace (the body's tissues), none of this wood is being thrown into the furnace, which will then be unable to function. The additional effect is that as more wood is being transported to the site, the amount of wood (glucose) accumulates in the transporting mechanism (the bloodstream) which is why diabetics have high blood glucose levels.

The effect on the body is that the tissues (furnace) are being deprived of their food/energy source and call out for more glucose (wood). The body responds by eating more to raise the blood glucose levels but because the glucose is not being thrown into the cells by the insulin, the blood glucose level increases and the cells' ability to function is compromised because, like the furnace, they are not being fed. The clinical effect is a cat who is hungry and eating more to try to feed their hungry cells but, because there is no boilerman (insulin) to move the wood (glucose) into the furnace (the cells), the cat will lose weight despite the increased appetite. An important point to make here is that, in advanced cases of diabetes, the period of increased appetite may not have been noticed. In these long-term or more severe cases, the presenting sign may be weight loss in the face of a loss of appetite. These cats may feel too unwell to eat because of prolonged starvation of their body tissues and because of a condition called diabetic ketoacidosis whereby toxic chemicals called ketones accumulate in their bodies.

The basic principle in treating a diabetic cat is to inject insulin every day to move glucose from the bloodstream into the cells of the body. There are many different kinds of insulin available and they are classified as ultra-short-acting, short-acting, intermediate-acting and long-acting insulin. This classification is based on how long a single insulin injection will be effective for. The ultra-short-acting insulin may only work for eight hours and thus it needs to be injected three times daily, while the long-acting insulin works for about 24 hours and thus needs to be injected once a day. The most effective and thus the most commonly used insulin in cats is the short-acting insulin which works for about twelve hours and so needs to be injected twice daily. This is more inconvenient than using a once daily type of insulin but the once daily insulin usually does not control the blood sugar levels well enough for the cat to live a comfortable normal life.

A very important point is that the treatment for diabetes is aimed at "controlling" the diabetes. This means that the insulin does not cure the diabetes in the true sense of the word because if the diabetes could be "cured" then there would be no need for ongoing treatment. The principle of the treatment is to artificially (by injection) give the body insulin which it is unable to produce for itself. Thus, by injecting insulin, we are artificially controlling the glucose levels in the blood by moving the blood glucose into the body's cells to feed them so that they can function normally. This process is referred to as controlling the diabetic and implies controlling the movement of glucose from the blood into the cells. The amount of glucose required by each cell in the body is different every day and every hour. This is because our level of activity is always changing and we eat different types of food, each of which provides a different level of glucose (energy) for our bodies to use. Think about the day you are having today as compared to yesterday. You may have been at work yesterday and have the day off today doing different things. Thus the amount of glucose (energy) your body needs today is different from yesterday and every other day of your life. The food you have eaten today is different from what you ate yesterday and thus provides your body with a different level of glucose (energy). This is why people with diabetes need to check their blood glucose levels by pricking their fingers and testing the drop of blood to decide how much insulin they need to inject themselves with throughout the day. They can also check their glucose levels by testing their urine.

People with diabetes do not just rely on the test results from the drop of blood or urine but also on how they feel. If, for example, they feel tired and know that they have not eaten much that day, they will be fairly sure that they need to eat something high in energy to boost their blood sugar levels. By the same token, if they are tired but feel that they have eaten enough that day, then they will know that they probably just need a bit more insulin to help move the blood glucose into their body's cells. These people will test a drop of their blood or urine just to be sure that their assumption is correct and will either eat something or inject a bit of insulin or both so that they feel fine again. The amount of insulin they need to inject, or the amount of food they need to eat, will vary according to the kind of day they are having. Thus human diabetics are constantly fine-tuning their blood glucose levels and the amount of glucose being moved into their cells, based on how they are feeling at the time.

Cats are unable to speak and thus cannot tell us when they need to eat a bit more or when they need more or less insulin at any particular time on any particular day. Thus we treat them according to their blood and urine glucose levels at the time that we think they need another insulin injection.

In practical terms we would inject the diabetic cat with insulin twice daily. Just like every human diabetic, every cat diabetic will need a different kind of insulin and a different dosage. When a cat is first diagnosed as having diabetes mellitus, the first stage of their treatment is called the "stabilisation" phase. This is the phase where we need to determine which insulin they need, how much insulin they need and how often they need it. The starting dose of insulin that I use is two units of short-acting insulin given twice daily. Insulin is measured and dosed as units rather than as millimetres and insulin syringes are thus calibrated as units. The next point to consider during the stabilisation phase is that we need to control how much food the cat eats and when they eat it. This is because we need to know how much energy (glucose) they will have moving from their stomach and intestines into their blood supply. This is important because we need to know that a specific amount of glucose will move into their bloodstream and thus we know how much insulin we need to give them to move that amount of glucose into their cells.

The most common protocol used during the stabilisation phase is to calculate how much food the individual will eat in one day. We then divide that food into two portions. The first portion is fed in the morning and the second portion is fed eight hours later. The insulin dose is injected about thirty minutes after they have eaten their food. This is because we must first see them eat so that when we inject the insulin we know that there will be glucose in the bloodstream for the insulin to work on. The traditional approach during the stabilisation phase is to follow this protocol and then measure the blood glucose levels every two hours over a 24-hour period. The blood glucose levels are measured as nmol/l. This is just a measurement similar to measuring distance in yards or weight in kilograms.

These blood glucose levels are then plotted on a graph and we can then check that the amount of food and the amount of insulin used is able to maintain the cat at normal blood glucose levels all day every day. If the levels are too high then the insulin dose must be increased or if the levels are too low the insulin dose must be reduced. We will also be able to see from the graph how long each insulin injection lasts for and this will tell us whether we should change the dose or the type of insulin.

When the blood glucose graph (the glucose curve) has been drawn up we ideally want all the points on the graph to be between 3 and 9 nmol per litre. When the level of blood glucose goes above 9 nmol/l then glucose starts to move into the urine. The glucose moving into the urine pulls a lot of water with it and this is why diabetics will wee more than normal. If urine is tested and we find glucose in it then we know that the blood glucose is above the normal level of 9 nmol/l. We can approximate from the amount of glucose in the urine just how high above 9 nmol/l the blood glucose is likely to be. Thus a person or a cat with diabetes can monitor their condition by regularly testing their urine but this is not as accurate as blood testing. The further problem with monitoring according to urine glucose levels is that if there is no glucose in the urine we can say that the blood glucose level is below 9 nmol/l but we cannot say how far below 9 nmol/l the level is. This is important because if the blood level drops below 3 nmol/l then the diabetic person or cat has had too much insulin and this can be life-threatening.

Once we have determined the type and amount of insulin the patient needs by drawing up a normal glucose curve for that patient, they are then called a "stabilised" diabetic. Further monitoring and further adjustments can be made over the rest of their lives by once- or twice-weekly urine or blood tests. We should find that, when the diabetic cat has been "stabilised", their thirst, appetite and weeing should return to normal. Any future increases in thirst, appetite or weeing will alert us that their diabetes is no longer controlled and that we need to redetermine the dose and type of insulin that they require. A significant problem encountered when monitoring a cat's blood glucose levels is that the stress of transporting the cat to the vet and the stress of taking the blood sample causes the blood glucose levels to rise. It is common to find high blood glucose levels in cats in a veterinary clinic even if the cat is not diabetic. This means that it can be misleading to assume that the blood glucose level in a diabetic cat is accurate when the blood sample is taken from the stressed-out cat in a clinic. Thus if the blood glucose level is high when the sample is taken, it may simply be high because the cat is stressed and not because of the diabetes which may, in fact, be well controlled day-by-day when the cat is at home. A solution to this may be for the vet to travel to your home to do the blood test there but the stress of taking the blood sample may still artificially increase the blood glucose level. The best solution to this problem is to do a different type of blood test called a fructosamine test. This test measures a different chemical from blood glucose but it has the advantage of giving us a fructosamine blood level averaged out over the three weeks prior to the blood sample being taken. Thus, because it is an hour-by-hour average of the blood levels over the preceding three weeks, the increase caused by the stress of blood sampling does not affect the measurement. I prefer to monitor diabetic cats using the fructosamine test but the problem with this test is that it takes longer to determine the required insulin dose because the test is done after one to three weeks of therapy and only then can the insulin dose be adjusted.

Traditional thinking is that the best food for a diabetic is a high-fibre food. There are many commercially produced diets available specifically for diabetic cats. These diets make the diabetes much easier to control and often mean that a lower dose of insulin will be able to stabilise and control the diabetes over the long term. These foods ensure a slower release of glucose from food after the cat has eaten and thus the blood glucose levels do not rise and fall as rapidly during and after eating. This slower rise and fall of blood glucose makes it easier for the injected insulin to move the glucose into the cells throughout each day. An important point regarding feeding is that the two portions of food are the same amount and are given at the same time of day every day. This is so that we always know how much food is being digested and therefore that the same amount of insulin will be required at the same time every day to ensure that the blood glucose levels are constantly and predictably 3–9 nmol/l at any time. No other food or treats should be fed during or between meals as this will result in variations in the daily blood glucose levels which may not be controlled by the previously calculated insulin dose. The dose of insulin would have been calculated to manage only the normal meals fed at regular times and if additional food or treats are fed at different times then the blood glucose levels may become erratic, elevated and uncontrolled.

This conventional protocol for stabilising the diabetic cat has several potential flaws. The problems we may encounter are that the cat may refuse to eat the special food, and many people are unable to feed the second meal eight hours after the first due to other commitments. In addition, the cat will have been stabilised under hospitalisation conditions at the veterinary clinic, where it is likely to be more stressed than at home and so have higher glucose (energy) requirements. This may mean that the dose of insulin required to control their diabetes is different when they are at home and feeling more relaxed.

These potential flaws with the traditional approach to stabilising a diabetic cat have led me to take a slightly less rigid approach to treating diabetic cats. The main reason that I am prepared to take this less regimented approach to diabetic cats is that we can never control their diabetes as well as a human being could control their own diabetes. This is because human diabetics are constantly able to fine-tune their blood glucose levels by assessing how they feel at any moment in time and by testing themselves at any time of the day. They can make very subtle and accurate adjustments by increasing or decreasing the next insulin dose, by eating more or less or something different at any moment to adjust their blood glucose levels, and they can also adjust the number of insulin doses they require in any twenty-four-hour period. Cats cannot speak to let us know that they may need any of these subtle adjustments and thus we dose them according to test results from their blood and/or urine levels and according to their symptoms. So if we see that a diabetic cat starts to drink and pee more we know that we need to increase their insulin but the human diabetic would have made the adjustment before these symptoms appeared. When we retest a diabetic cat's blood and urine and find that we need to adjust the insulin dose, the human diabetic would have made the adjustment long before the glucose or fructosamine level had altered to the same extent as the cat's levels may have. This does not imply that diabetic cats suffer as a result of less tightly controlled blood glucose levels. It merely demonstrates that human beings control their blood sugar levels more quickly and more efficiently.

The approach that I take with my diabetic patients is that the object of treatment is to have a happy cat living a normal life despite being a diabetic. The way I decide whether their diabetes is controlled is that they should not show any symptoms of being diabetic. The object of my approach is to have a happy and energetic cat who has a normal appetite, who will drink and wee normal amounts and who has a normal and stable body weight. I find that I can achieve this despite bending a number of the rules of treatment as described earlier.

The first rule that I bend is the interval between meals and insulin injections. I find that most of my clients are working people who cannot be home to feed the second meal eight hours after the first. I suggest to these people that they feed half the cat's daily food in the morning when they get up for work and inject the insulin dose when the cat has started eating or as soon as they have finished eating. The second half of the daily food is then fed twelve hours after the first and the second insulin dose is also given when the cat is eating or when he has finished his meal. I also tell them that if they are out for a meal or at a movie when the second meal and insulin dose is due, that they do not have to rush home to do this. No harm will come from the second meal and insulin dose being a few hours late or early. The next rule I bend is that I suggest feeding the special diabetic food but if the cat refuses to eat it then try mixing the diabetic food with the usual food. If the cat still refuses to eat the special food then simply continue feeding the normal cat food. The third rule I bend is that some cats will refuse to eat two set meals a day as they prefer to have several small snacks throughout the day. If a cat refuses to eat two structured meals a day then I relent and leave food down all the time for them to eat small amounts as and when they want to. This obviously means that the blood glucose levels are not as stable as I would want but if the symptoms are adequately controlled then we have to accept that the cat refuses to play by the rules. As we all know, it is almost impossible to force a cat to do what we want them to do instead of what they want to do and how they want to live their lives. The fourth rule I bend is that I rely mostly on the symptoms rather than on blood and urine tests to control the diabetes. I try to stabilise these patients at home and adjust the levels of insulin according to how well the symptoms of increased appetite, thirst and urination are resolving. Once these symptoms have resolved I accept that we have found the correct insulin dose for that individual and suggest doing a fructosamine test every three months. I accept that this approach is less scientific than it should be but I find that is the only approach that many people can accommodate in their lives and the results are as good as the more regimented approach I described earlier as documented in most textbooks. If this more relaxed approach does not resolve all the symptoms then I will suggest to my clients that we revert to the more academic system of blood and urine tests to draw up a glucose curve to identify why the diabetes is not being controlled.

Once the diabetic cat has been stabilised and the symptoms of diabetes have resolved then we will have determined the dose and frequency of insulin required by that individual. The cat will be maintained on this dose permanently. This is called the maintenance phase. There may, however, be a need to adjust the dosages at various times in the cat's life for various reasons. My advice to people is to monitor their cat's symptoms and retest fructosamine levels every three months. If the symptoms of diabetes re-appear in the interim then we would retest fructosamine levels sooner to make adjustments to the insulin dose. It takes time for people with a diabetic cat to become confident in their own assessment of their cat's overall condition and initially adjustments will often only be made after a conversation with their vet to confirm their observations and proposed insulin dose adjustments.

The primary indication for reducing the dose of insulin is if the diabetic cat suddenly seems unwell in any way. They may appear unwell either because they have picked up another unrelated condition or infection or they may have been given too much insulin. They may have been given too much insulin because of an accidental overdose or their diabetes may have altered meaning that they simply need less insulin. If they have been given more insulin than they need they initially appear drunk, seeming weak, uncoordinated and unsteady or wobbly on their feet. This is due to the insulin dose dropping the blood glucose levels too low and thus the treatment in this situation is to get glucose (energy) into them immediately. When human diabetics experience this they will simply just eat chocolate to boost their glucose levels until they feel better. I advise people to use syrup or honey in this situation. This is easily done by smearing the syrup or honey into the cat's mouth until the signs of "drunkenness" disappear, which they should do within an hour. If the signs do not disappear then one should consult a vet to consider further intervention. The vet will often use a glucose drip to correct low blood glucose levels if this is required. The effects of too much insulin are far more serious than the effects of too little insulin and are potentially life-threatening so, if the cat suddenly seems drunk, immediate action in the form of high-energy foods like syrup is warranted. If one is unsure whether the cat has had too much or too little insulin and they appear drunk, it is better to assume that too much insulin has been given and to use syrup or honey to try to resolve the problem because too much insulin is the more serious possibility.

The golden rule regarding adjustments of the insulin level is to increase or decrease the dose by no more than one or two units per dose based on the results of blood tests. Once this adjustment has been made it will take about five days for the cat to adjust to this new dose so one must wait five days before adjusting the dose again. These minor adjustments can be made by the owner at home without first consulting the vet but if the adjustment fails to control the symptoms then it is wise to consult the vet regarding any further dose adjustments. The second golden rule in the maintenance phase of diabetes is never to stop the insulin. If the cat is ill and loses their appetite or if they simply do not want to eat a meal at any time for whatever reason the insulin dose should still be given but at half the normal dose. The vet should then be consulted to determine why the cat is ill or has lost their appetite. If they have simply picked up an unrelated illness like a chest infection or an upset stomach then this should be treated and half the insulin dose should be given until the illness has been cured by the appropriate treatment and the appetite has returned to normal. The third golden rule is that it is better to give too little insulin than to give too much. Thus if one is uncertain as to whether to increase or decrease the insulin dose if is safer to decrease the dose until a vet has been consulted. The basic principle is to increase the insulin dose if the cat starts to eat, drink or wee more and to reduce the dose if the cat appears to feel unwell.

Most cats with diabetes will stabilise within about two weeks of starting treatment and the insulin dose remains fairly constant once they are in the maintenance phase. Occasionally, however, we encounter the "problem diabetic". These are cats who are difficult to stabilise or maintain despite all the appropriate steps and treatments described earlier. These cats will require more intensive investigation and treatment of their condition to find out why they are not performing as expected. It may be a simple matter of determining their individual response to various types or doses of insulin or they may be experiencing insulin resistance or insulin antagonism. Insulin resistance means that the body's cells are unable to receive glucose from the blood supply despite adequate levels of insulin. This may happen for a variety of reasons which need to be identified and treated by your vet. Insulin antagonism means that the body is producing substances which interfere with insulin, preventing it from moving glucose from the blood into the cells. Insulin antagonism is much rarer and is the result of the body producing antibodies against insulin. These antibodies function just like antibodies that fight against disease and have the effect of attacking and inactivating the insulin. Thus these patients will not stabilise because even if high doses of insulin are injected, the body's antibodies simply inactivate the insulin. This condition is diagnosed with special blood tests and is very rare.

3b Overactive thyroid function (hyperthyroidism)

The second condition that results in weight loss despite an increased appetite, is overactive thyroid function. Cats have thyroid glands just like we do. The thyroids are two glands normally situated on either side of the windpipe (trachea) just below the voice box (larynx). Normal thyroid glands in the cat are too small to feel so the first step towards this diagnosis is to feel the area where the thyroid glands lie and, if one or both thyroid glands can easily be felt, then there is something wrong with them. The thyroids may be found anywhere along the length of the trachea so it is important to feel along the entire length of both the left and right jugular grooves. The jugular grooves are the same grooves we have in our necks on either side of the trachea. The groove is found between the trachea and the muscles of the neck adjacent to it. The jugular vein is one of the important structures lying in this groove. If the vet's fingers can feel the thyroid glands, the next step is to check the heart rate. The normal cat's heart rate in the consulting room, even when the cat is stressed by their visit to the vet, is rarely above 160 per minute. Cats with overactive thyroids (hyperthyroidism) generally have heart rates above 200 beats per minute. These cats are often agitated by the clinical examination and, although they rarely try to bite or scratch, will wriggle and try to shrug off the vet's hands. The owner of the cat will often confirm this agitated behaviour as one of the changes in the cat's home behaviour which they often think is simply the cantankerous behaviour of an old cat. Another common symptom noticed at home is that some cats with this condition may vomit and/or develop diarrhoea, either only occasionally or every day. This happens because the overactive thyroid glands have the effect of irritating the stomach and intestines.

To understand the symptoms I have briefly touched on, we have to understand what the thyroid glands do. The thyroid glands in cats, just like in human beings, control the basic metabolic rate of an individual. There is quite a big range in what is considered normal thyroid function, something which we have all noticed when out to dinner with friends. Some people eat mountains of food without gaining any weight and others gain weight very easily even though they may eat comparatively little. Think about these slim people we all know who eat as much as they like and remain slim. They probably have very active thyroid function which, although it is still in the normal range, will be at the high end of the scale. Other people we know may struggle to keep weight off despite eating very little because their thyroid function is probably at the low end of the normal range.

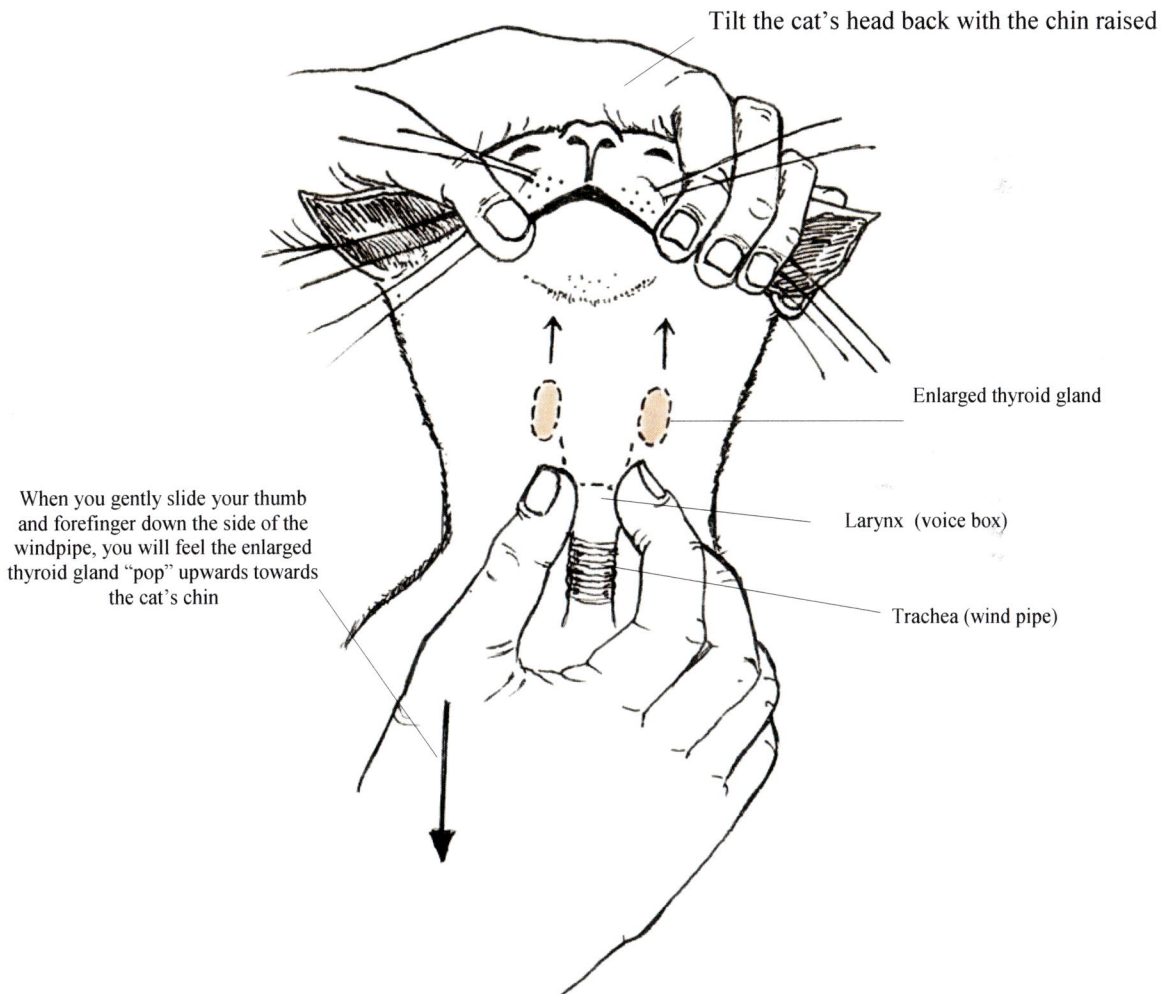

Tilt the cat's head back with the chin raised

Enlarged thyroid gland

When you gently slide your thumb and forefinger down the side of the windpipe, you will feel the enlarged thyroid gland "pop" upwards towards the cat's chin

Larynx (voice box)

Trachea (wind pipe)

Fig. 36 – Feeling the enlarged thyroid glands in a cat with hyperthyroidism (overactive thyroid glands)

The thyroid hormone controls the basic rate that every cell is functioning at, so the cells of a cat with an overactive thyroid function are much more active than those of a normal cat. This means that even when the cat is just sitting around it will be using more energy than normal to supply the cells and will need to eat more to provide this extra energy. Even so, the cat will generally lose weight despite the increased appetite because the cells are burning off energy at a much higher rate. The obvious clinical effects are that the heart must pump more rapidly to meet the extra demand so these cats have higher heart rates, often in excess of 260 beats per minute. The effect of this is that the heart is being overworked and the heart muscle will eventually be damaged. Once the heart muscle is damaged there is the risk that it will lose its efficiency in pumping blood around the body and other organs will start to fail as they are not receiving sufficient blood to function efficiently. The kidneys are often the first to be affected. It is because of this knock-on effect that we must do something before these cats literally waste away or suffer heart or kidney failure. The full extent of the damage to the heart muscle will not be reversed but it will recover to some extent and further damage will be prevented. The most obvious effects are that the cat will gain weight again, the vomiting and/or diarrhoea will stop, and the appetite and behaviour will revert to normal. The most common comment I hear after treatment is, "I've got my old cat back."

Treatment for these cats is either medical or surgical. After the diagnosis of hyperthyroidism as been made, either on the strength of the clinical symptoms and the presence of enlarged thyroid glands or by blood testing, the treatment options can be discussed. Medical treatment generally boils down to tablets being given once or twice daily. The tablets contain either 2.5 mg or 5 mg of neomercazole or felimazole and the dosage may need to be adjusted according to the assessment of response to treatment either by resolution of the symptoms or by assessing the level of thyroid hormone present in the bloodstream. Most cat owners find it difficult to administer a tablet twice daily for the rest of the cat's life and the patient's response to this treatment is often not as good as the response to surgical treatment, so my treatment preference for these patients is surgical.

Surgery will remove the enlarged glands. Only enlarged glands are removed so if only one side is affected then the other, normal, gland is not removed. If both glands are enlarged then both are removed. This raises the obvious question of how the cat can cope with no thyroid glands at all. Cats, in contrast to people who have had both thyroid glands removed, need no thyroid supplementation at all and all my patients thrive after having had both thyroids removed. If only one gland is enlarged and removed there is the possibility that the other gland may, at some time in the future, also enlarge and the condition will recur. Studies are variable in predicting the likelihood of this happening and the probability ranges from 40–80%. There is also the possibility that the gland or glands which were removed may re-grow if any thyroid cells remain after surgery. In my experience this is exceedingly rare if the surgery is performed carefully. Many people are concerned about the degree of risk involved in administering a general anaesthetic to an old cat with a compromised heart. This seems to be unfounded as all the cases I have dealt with cope with and recover from the anaesthetic as well as any young cat would. This would suggest that the anaesthetic risk is not significantly greater than for a young healthy cat. The most common age at which I find myself performing this surgery is between thirteen and sixteen years old and presently all these patients have fared very well.

The surgery itself is not technically difficult compared to many other operations vets perform. The operation consists of separating the muscles overlying the trachea to expose the thyroid gland/s. The thyroid gland is encased in an incredibly thin capsule or membrane with an abundant blood supply. There is a main blood supply leading to the front end and another blood supply leading to the back of the gland. The capsule encasing the gland is thinner than cling film and very tightly wrapped around the gland, which means that initially it cannot even be seen. I pick at the surface of the gland until I hook the membrane and once it is pulled away from the surface of the gland it is visible as a thin, almost transparent membrane. The next step is to make a small incision in the membrane and then carefully shell the gland out of its capsule. There is an important structure contained in the front end of the membrane called the parathyroid gland and this must be preserved. The blood vessels supplying the parathyroid gland are contained in the incredibly thin capsule and are so small that most cannot even be seen by the naked eye. It is important not to even touch the parathyroid gland, which is a small white structure a little smaller than a pinhead. Even the process of freeing the thyroid from this membrane may damage the blood vessels in the membrane, possibly robbing the parathyroid of its blood supply and causing it to die off. The problem here is that sometimes the membrane is very tightly adhered to the thyroid gland and the membrane must be stripped off the gland, taking every care not to bruise it in the region of the parathyroid gland. The additional problem is that, as the blood vessels in the membrane are too small to see, it is impossible to know whether they have been damaged in the process. The body only needs one parathyroid gland to function normally. If the operation is being performed on only one gland, there is no concern if the parathyroid is lost. However, one must take into account that at some point in the future, if the other thyroid also needs to be removed, then there is additional pressure on the surgeon to preserve the second parathyroid. For this reason, I make every effort to preserve every parathyroid gland. Forfeiting it during an operation to remove only one thyroid runs the risk that problems may be encountered if the other thyroid gland subsequently also needs to be removed, and its associated parathyroid gland is so tightly stuck to it that it is damaged when the membrane is stripped off. If one is confident that the other parathyroid gland was preserved during the first surgery then there is little concern. The same problems are encountered when both thyroid glands need to be removed at the same time. I personally am confident to remove both and am confident that I will be able to preserve the parathyroid gland but many surgeons prefer to remove only one side at a time and wait several weeks before removing the other side. The reason for this is that if the blood vessels to the parathyroid have been damaged, even though this damage may not be visible to the naked eye, they may recover within a few weeks after surgery and thus there is less risk of seeing the symptoms associated with the loss of the parathyroid function.

The function of the parathyroid is to control calcium levels in the body and if this function is lost then one sees the symptoms associated with low blood calcium levels. Calcium has many functions, one of which is to assist in the function of the nerve cells in the body. If there is insufficient calcium then the nerves may become unstable and abnormal signs are seen as the nerves discharge impulses spontaneously. This is the same situation faced by people and animals when other conditions like eclampsia (milk fever) cause a drop in the blood calcium levels. Milk fever happens shortly after a mother has given birth and she diverts a lot of her own calcium to her milk for her baby. If her own blood levels drop too low then her nerve cells become unstable and may fire impulses spontaneously, especially to the muscles.

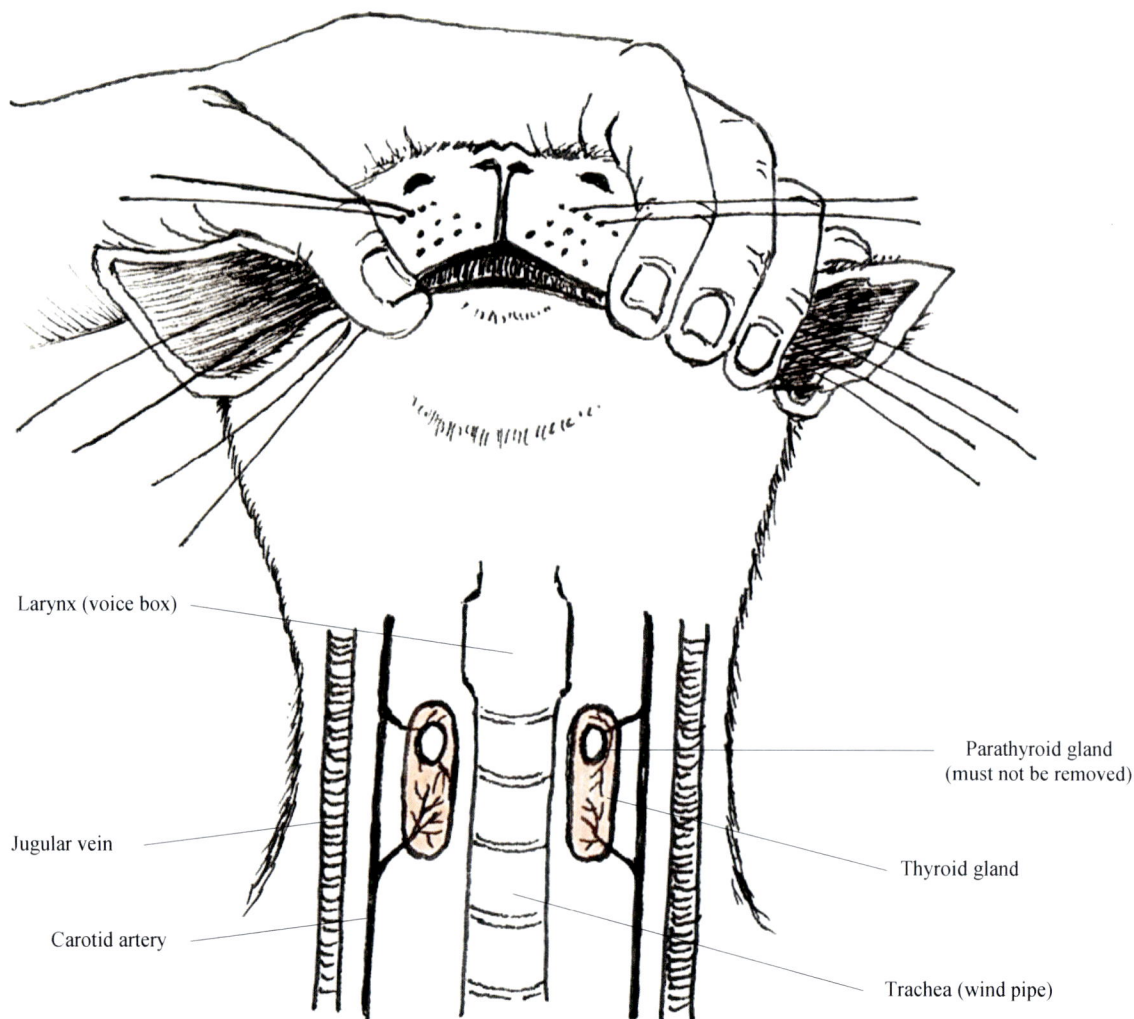

Fig 37 – Anatomy of the neck for thyroid surgery

Thus the clinical symptoms of low blood calcium levels, irrespective of the cause, are initially twitching and muscle tremors, which may progress to full seizures, convulsions and possible death if treatment is not started in good time.

Treatment of low blood calcium is simple and highly effective. The treatment is a simply a matter of injecting calcium into the veins and the patient recovers within minutes. The need for ongoing calcium treatment/supplementation depends on the cause of the low blood calcium in the first place. If the cause is damage to the parathyroid glands during surgery, the period of calcium supplementation with tablets (after the initial treatment has been administered intravenously) depends on the extent of the damage to the parathyroid blood supply. The blood supply may recover within a few weeks after surgery as discussed above and in these patients the supplementation of calcium is a temporary arrangement. If both parathyroids have been permanently destroyed then the cat will require permanent calcium supplementation but, with it, can lead a full, active and healthy life.

Two important points are, first, that calcium supplementation will only be necessary if both parathyroid glands are damaged or destroyed. The second point is that although this is not a common final outcome for patients undergoing thyroid surgery, in some cases it may be unavoidable if the capsules of both glands are so tightly adhered to them that the surgeon is unable to free the thyroid glands without stripping the capsule containing the parathyroid glands. The process of stripping the adhered capsule involves tearing it from the surface of the thyroid and, as tearing is less predictable and controllable than dissection, it is often not a reflection on the surgeon if the parathyroid blood supply is inadvertently damaged. In reality this is a situation I have only encountered once in the course of performing a few hundred of these operations and the cat in question required oral calcium supplementation for 12 weeks before the parathyroid blood supply recovered and calcium treatment could be withdrawn. The important point is that if both thyroid glands are to be removed this is an important possible complication to discuss with your vet prior to surgery. I find that within a month of surgery most cats are eating normally, gaining weight and are much happier and more content.

Conclusion of the consultation about weight loss in the older cat:

The above conditions are, in my experience, the more common causes of weight loss in the older cat. The vet's thinking will be directed towards the most likely diagnosis by their examination of your cat and your answers to their questions. Most of these conditions, once suspected, need to be confirmed by performing appropriate blood tests. One of the strong arguments for testing for all of the conditions even though one of them seems the most likely is that two or more of them may be present at the same time, causing the same symptoms, or one may be overshadowing the other. There will always be controversy regarding the scientific approach as opposed to a possibly more pragmatic one to the process of diagnosis and treatment in both the human and veterinary contexts. I am largely guided by my client's wishes, which are often dictated to some extent by their budget. I will often be prepared to accept that if a condition is very apparent, such as an overactive thyroid function, then I am prepared to address that problem without confirming it on blood tests first. If after treatment the cat's condition fails to improve then we may re-discuss the wisdom of casting a wider net in our search for a diagnosis. This approach is based on the principle that "if it walks like a duck, talks like a duck and looks like a duck, then it's probably a duck". I accept that strictly speaking this is neither scientific nor thorough. If cost is a factor in resolving the cat's condition, if I am very confident of my diagnosis, if I have discussed the options with the owner of the cat and they want to proceed with treatment on the strength of my presumptive diagnosis, without confirming it or investigating other possible diagnoses, then I will proceed with the indicated treatment. The fear from the vet's perspective is that they may have been wrong and thereby may have subjected a cat to an unnecessary treatment protocol. If this point has been discussed with you, the owner of the cat, and both you and the vet are prepared to accept that their diagnosis may have been incorrect and the cats condition may not be resolved by the prescribed treatment, so the condition may have to be further investigated thereby incurring the additional costs that we may have been trying to avoid, then I would proceed. My preferred approach to this situation is to be thorough and perform all the appropriate testing to confirm my diagnosis and exclude all other possibilities prior to treatment but I accept that not everyone has the financial resources to go this route.

The above discussion is by no means all-encompassing but in my experience represents the most common explanations for, and approaches to, the older cat losing weight. Many other conditions may produce this presenting symptom and a thorough examination by your vet may elicit other diagnoses. The vet will have their own opinions regarding the most appropriate treatment for your cat and the final decision regarding the approach to the problem should be the culmination of a meeting of minds. I feel strongly that we should all be as well informed as possible on any subject before making a decision. The final decision will be made by our minds and hearts and should pivot on the quality of life of the cat.

INDEX

Eye problems, page 92

FIP, page 90
Flea allergy, page 39
FLUTD, page 4
Food allergy, page 37
Forls, page 117
Fungal skin infection, page 48

Garbage disease, page 48
Gastritis, page 60
Gingivitis, page 111
Glossitis, pages 76, 119, 191
Gum disease – see Gingivitis

Hair loss – see Alopecia
Hallitosis, page 110
Hayfever, page 96
Heart failure, page 84
Herpes virus, pages 76, 97, 101, 120, 191
Hip problems, page 162
Hock problems, page 155
Hormones, pages 27, 45
Hyperthyroidism, page 211

Idiopathic cystitis, page 13
Inhaled allergy – see Atopy
Insulin, pages 186, 206
Interstitial cystitis, page 13
Intestinal obstructions, page 56
Intussusception, page 58
Irritable bowel syndrome, page 59

Keratoconjunctivitis sicca, page 103
Kidney problems – see Renal failure
Knee problems, page 156

Leukaemia, page 199
Liver problems, page 185
Lung problems, page 79

Megacolon, page 19
Metaldehyde poisoning, page 184
Miliary dermatitis, page 32
Mites, ears, page 171

Mites, skin, page 49

Nares, stenotic, page 74
Nose problems, page 74
Nostrils, narrowed, stenotic, page 74

Obsessive compulsive syndrome, page 48
Osteoarthritis – see Arthritis
Othaematoma, page 170
Otitis externa, page 171
Overgrooming, page 48

Pancreatitis, page 67
Parathyroid glands, page 214
Paronychia, pages 136, 153
Paw problems, pages 135, 153
Pelvis, page 162
Pinna, page 168
Pleural effusions, page 82
Pneumonia, page 81
Polyarthritis, pages 134, 152
Pyothorax, page 89

Renal failure, acute, page 197
Renal failure, chronic, page 194
Rhinitis, allergic, page 96
Rhinitis, infectious, page 97
Ringworm, page 48

Scabs, page 32
Seizures, page 176
Shoulder problems, page 140
Sneezing, page 92
Snuffles, page 97
Steroids – see Cortisone
Stifle problems, page 156
Stomatitis, page 121
Stranguria, page 3
Stress, page 23
Stroke, page 183
Sugar diabetes – see Diabetes mellitus

Tarsus problems – see Hock Problems
Teeth problems, page 110
Thyroid gland , overactive – see Hyperthyroidism

Tumours – see Cancer

Ulcers, cornea, eye, page 104
Ulcers, lips and gums, page 192
Ulcers, mouth, page 190
Ulcers, tongue, page 191
Uroliths – See Bladder stones
Uveitis, page 108

Vomiting, page 50

Warfarin poisoning, page 185
Wrist problems – see Carpus Problems